CAN AMERICA SURVIVE?

Can America
SURVIVE?

10 PROPHETIC SIGNS
THAT WE ARE THE
TERMINAL GENERATION

JOHN HAGEE

HOWARD BOOKS
A DIVISION OF SIMON & SCHUSTER, INC.
New York • Nashville • London • Toronto • Sydney

Howard Books
A Division of Simon & Schuster, Inc.
1230 Avenue of the Americas
New York, NY 10020

Can America Survive? © 2010 by Pastor John Hagee

First Howard Books hardcover edition June 2010

HOWARD and colophon are trademarks of Simon & Schuster, Inc.

For information about special discounts for bulk purchases,
please contact Simon & Schuster Special Sales at 1-866-506-1949
or business@simonandschuster.com

The Simon & Schuster Speakers Bureau can bring authors to your live event.
For more information or to book an event, contact the Simon & Schuster Speakers
Bureau at 1-866-248-3049 or visit our website at www.simonspeakers.com.

Designed by Joseph Rutt

Manufactured in the United States of America

10   9   8   7   6   5   4

Library of Congress Cataloging-in-Publication Data
Hagee, John.
  Can America survive? 10 prophetic signs that we are the terminal generation / John Hagee.
    p.   cm.
  Includes bibliographical references.
    1. United States—Foreign relations—2009–   2. United States—Foreign relations—
Middle East.   3. Middle East—Foreign relations—United States.   4. Bible—
Prophecies.   5. Christianity—United States.   6. Jerusalem in the Bible.   7. End of the
world—Biblical teaching.   8. Israel (Christian theology)—Biblical teaching.   I. Title.
  E907.H34   2010
  261.70973—dc22   2010012409

ISBN 978-1-4391-8985-6
ISBN 978-1-4391-8993-1 (ebook)

Dedicated to the brave and heroic men and women in the United States military who have fought and died to birth and preserve freedom from 1776 until today. May God help us not to throw their valiant sacrifice to the wind by a federal government out of control!

Contents

PART ONE
A NUCLEAR IRAN

ONE	Anatomy of Disaster!	3
TWO	Iran Is Ready for War!	21
THREE	Iran's Plan of Attack	49

PART TWO
THE FALL OF AMERICA

FOUR	The Day After the Bomb	63
FIVE	Death of the Dollar	75
SIX	The Rejection of Israel	105
SEVEN	The Criminalization of Christianity	151

PART THREE
THE BEGINNING OF THE END

EIGHT	Can You Trust Biblical Prophecy?	165
NINE	We Are the Terminal Generation	181
TEN	What's Going to Happen Next?	201

PART FOUR
THE FINAL DAYS

ELEVEN   The Fourth Reich: The Coming Antichrist   217

TWELVE   Armageddon: The Final Battle for Planet Earth   237

THIRTEEN   The Year 2012: The Beginning of the End?   249

            Notes   261

PART ONE

A Nuclear Iran

ONE

Anatomy of Disaster!

Where were you the day John F. Kennedy was shot in Dallas, Texas? If you were alive on planet Earth, you know exactly where you were and what you were doing when Walter Cronkite took off his thick black glasses and announced to America, "John F. Kennedy, president of the United States, died at 1:00 p.m. Central Standard Time."

He paused and looked again at the studio clock. "Some thirty-eight minutes ago." The seasoned newscaster momentarily lost his composure, winced, and cleared his throat before resuming with the observation that Vice President Lyndon Johnson would take the oath of office to become the thirty-sixth president of the United States.

The heart of America was broken!

We had been swept up in the dream that was Camelot. We wept as a nation when Jackie walked into the Capitol Rotunda with Caroline and kissed the flag-draped coffin of JFK. His cortege of matched, prancing black horses pulled the caisson past the White House and the Capitol for the final time while John-John saluted his father and our president with a final farewell. It was a tragic and heartbreaking moment in history America will never forget! There is no greater agony of the soul than to live in the wonder of what might have been.

Where were you on 9/11?

What did you feel when you watched radical Islamic terrorists fly hijacked commercial airlines as missiles of death into the Twin Towers in New York City?

What did you feel when you saw fellow Americans jumping to their horrific and gruesome deaths from hundreds of feet in the air in a futile attempt to escape the blazing inferno?

Every living soul was someone's beloved father or mother, someone's loving husband or wife, someone's cherished son or daughter that would never come home again. Their families would forever after gather on special days of celebration—Thanksgiving, Christmas, birthdays, and anniversaries—and look with pain and heartache at their pictures with tearful eyes knowing that the nightmare of 9/11 would never end in their lifetime.

What did you feel as you watched the Twin Towers implode, floor after floor, and in a handful of thundering seconds see concrete, steel, and the lives of three thousand fellow Americans crushed together into an eternal monument of pain and suffering.

Brave New York City firefighters dashed into the blazing inferno and gave their lives trying to save the lives of others. "Greater love has no one than this, than to lay down one's life for his friends" (John 15:13 NKJV).

They gave their all without hesitation. They died and will forever remain American heroes. We make a living by what we get out of life, but we make a life by what we give. No man was ever honored by what he received. Honor is the reward for what he gave. The New York City firefighters gave their all!

Do you remember American citizens running in terror down the streets of New York City, screaming as a massive mushroom cloud of dust from the Twin Towers filled the air and turned a golden day into darkest night? For the first time since the British burned the White House in 1813, we had been attacked in the continental United States—the land of the free and the home of the brave.

The American illusion of being untouchable by foreign military powers was shattered in a day by the agents of radical Islam. America would never be the same!

It couldn't happen . . . but it did happen!

THE PERFECT STORM

On April 12, 1912, the *Titanic* raced through the icy waters of the Atlantic trying to set a new transatlantic speed record. This mountain of steel and mechanical genius had been pronounced "the unsinkable ship!"

Minutes before the *Titanic* struck the iceberg, some of the richest and most powerful people in the world danced the night away, unaware that disaster was imminent and that the Angel of Death was aboard. They would have gladly traded their power and their fortunes for a crude lifeboat, but none was available for the more than 1,500 souls who drowned in the frigid waters of the Atlantic on this night of unspeakable disaster.

The demons of denial pushed the agony and horror off the celebrated ship. Even after striking the iceberg and with the ship sinking by the head and taking on tons of water, Mr. J. Bruce Ismay, president of the company that owned the *Titanic,* pledged to his powerful passengers: "Not to worry, all is well. This ship is unsinkable and it's clear as far as the eye can see."

That message was so desired by the masses that twenty-four hours after the *Titanic* was at the bottom of the ocean, twenty-four hours after 1,522 souls had slipped into eternity the headlines in the New York paper screamed: "All Saved from Titanic After Collision."

Telegrams were received reading, "All Titanic Passengers Are Safe!" Another telegram read, "The Virginian Is Towing Titanic into Halifax." There was a total and complete denial of reality.

It couldn't happen . . . but it did happen!

The unthinkable horror became reality.

The unbelievable nightmare was a fact!

How did it happen?

Why did it happen?

It happened because a perfect storm of human error driven by the winds of complacency and overconfidence birthed an unspeakable disaster.

First, the well-known fact that there were not enough lifeboats—because the *Titanic* was said to be "unsinkable," which proved to be absolutely false—led to the deaths of many souls.

Second, there was no one to receive the distress signal from the *Titanic* as it was sinking because all ships closed their telegraph systems at midnight. This maritime law was promptly changed after the *Titanic* disaster so that all ships at sea would have an operator on duty twenty-four hours a day.

Third, had there been a ship nearby, the *Titanic* had no red flares that were the international maritime signal for "emergency" or "need help."

The *Titanic* had only white phosphorus flares used for many things, but never danger.

Think of it!

If they had had but one red flare, the ship *California,* which was less than ten miles away, might have seen it. It could have come quickly to the rescue and not one life would have been lost. One red flare could have saved 1,522 lives!

Fourth, there were no binoculars available to the watchmen in the crow's nest staring into the frigid and clear night looking for any sign of danger. When the watchmen spotted the massive iceberg by natural sight, it was too late.

With one pair of binoculars, they could have seen the iceberg in plenty of time to turn the ship away from danger and the certain death lurking beneath the icy water. One set of binoculars could have saved 1,522 lives.

Last, it was customary for all ships to measure the water temperature when in this part of the ocean. Water in the 30-degree range meant icebergs were near. They read water temperature by dropping a canvas bag overboard by rope and reading the seawater with a thermometer. The temperature of the seawater was then entered into the logbook for the captain of the ship to read.

In Senate hearings, it was discovered that the rope that let the canvas bag overboard was too short to reach the water in the ocean. It was too short because this was the largest ship in the world. The crew made a small but deadly miscalculation.

The seaman in charge of taking the temperature of the seawater filled the canvas bag with drinking water taken from the ship. When the captain read the temperature report in the log, there was absolutely no concern of danger.

Think of it!

Fifteen hundred and twenty-two of the most powerful people on the earth could have been saved if the rope had been long enough.

Why do I belabor this point?

Because America, believed to be the most powerful and "unsinkable" nation on the face of the earth, is now racing across the stage of history in a similar perfect storm—this one driven by the winds of political correctness, economic meltdowns leading to the death of the dollar, the rejection of Israel, the maniacal nuclear ambitions of the theocratic dictatorship in Iran, the ten prophetic signs that we are the terminal generation now being fulfilled in Bible prophecy for the first time in world history, and the very real fact that in the near future planet Earth is going to experience, on a specific day, global ecological disaster in which one-third of humanity will die.

Could this specific day be 12/12/12? Before you throw this book into the fire, read the final chapter. The concepts are not mine, but those of St. John on the Isle of Patmos in the book of Revelation.

So the four angels, who had been prepared for the hour and day and month and year, were released to kill a third of mankind.
—Revelation 9:15 NKJV

Think it can't happen?
Think again!
St. John the Revelator confirms to his readers in all generations that follow him until the end of days . . .

These words are *faithful and true . . . Blessed is he who keeps the words of the prophecy of this book.*
—Revelation 22:6–7 NKJV

America and Western civilization have made and are making a series of serious blunders that are now pushing America in the twenty-first century toward the edge of the abyss. It is far more than a banking crisis!

It is far more than just a credit crunch!

It is a perfect storm that has been brewing for centuries that is about to explode in all its fury affecting the lives of every person on planet Earth.

IN THE THROES OF DEATH AND BIRTH

In America, we are watching the *death* of capitalism and the *birth* of European socialism; because of our titanic debt, we are watching the *death* of the dollar. The *birth* of nuclear warfare in the Middle East with a nuclear Iran will change the world forever!

We are watching the *birth* of a shadow government of Czars that are not answerable to Congress and therefore escape the protections of the

Constitution of the United States. This is not a government of "We the People." We are watching the *birth* of a New World Order where nations surrender their sovereignty and follow a Global Czar that will be the world's new Caesar. The Bible calls him the Antichrist.

With geopolitical and financial danger signals in abundance the word of absolute denial we get from Washington is "All is well, America is the unsinkable nation, entertain yourselves by shuffling deck chairs on the *Titanic* while the band plays on."

Think it can't happen?

Think again!

Consider the following facts: Our recent credit crisis has revealed that the Federal Reserve, which no one in America controls, has loaned $2 trillion in the span of two months but will not tell us to whom they loaned the money. Who asked for it? Who authorized the loan? *You,* the taxpayers of America, will most certainly pay for it.

America has ceased to be a producer nation and has become a consumer nation. Think what that could mean in a time of war for our national defense when we have to get what we need to defend ourselves from a nation or nations hostile to the United States.

We have intentionally dumbed down our schools, ignored our history, and no longer teach our students the founding principles of America. Students graduate who cannot read, write, or speak intelligently. A significant percentage do not graduate from high school, thus forever joining the legions of the unemployed and poverty-stricken who will be slaves of the state for life!

America lives under the iron fist of judicial tyranny. Federal judges who are not elected by the people rule over the will of the people after they go to the polls and vote. We do not have a government "of the people, by the people, and for the people." Why can't we have the right to vote federal judges off the bench?

The prophet Isaiah writes:

> Woe to those who decree unrighteous decrees, Who write misfortune,
> Which *they have prescribed.*
>
> —*Isaiah 10:1 NKJV*

Abortion is an unrighteous decree!

Roe v. Wade has made it possible for 40 million babies to be murdered in the wombs of their mothers. Mother Teresa said, "The nation that kills its unborn has lost its soul." I agree!

Think about it!

Forty million souls is a river of blood that cries out to God for justice.

> *Then the LORD said to Cain . . . "What have you done? The voice of your brother's blood cries out to Me from the ground."*
> —*Genesis 4:9–10 NKJV*

A new CNN poll finds that 61 percent of Americans oppose taxpayer funding of abortion. But we know from comments of top White House officials that the president himself will intervene behind the scenes to make sure that ObamaCare subsidizes abortion on demand. (The poll also found that 63 percent of Americans think that abortion should be illegal in most cases.)[1] Let me tell you why Social Security is broken and will remain broken. *Abortion!*

The Baby Boomers are retiring and there is no "next generation" to pay the tab for Social Security. They have been killed under the banner of the "right to choose."

This infamous law that celebrates *death* over life will be one of the principal causes for the *death of the dollar*! Why? Because capitalism thrives on supply and demand! If there is no demand for a product, the economic engines of America stop!

Fact! There will be no demand from 40 million Americans for new homes, new cars, or college educations. Why? They have been murdered through abortion!

Our universities and colleges are now filled with students recruited from foreign countries. They have no love or loyalty to America. They come from the global community with the "One World" view. They could not care less if America surrenders its sovereignty to the United Nations, and they are here by the millions. Is the big picture coming together?

We have mainstreamed Marxist organizations, like ACORN, which are corrupting the political process of fair and open elections. Even after being caught on film educating prostitutes and their pimps on how to dodge taxation from the IRS and how to run a brothel with underage children, some U.S. congressmen defend this toxic and corrupt organization. Why do they have such a vested interest in the preservation of Acorn?

Why doesn't someone in Congress call for a full investigation by the FBI?

If there is no confidence in the political process through which we elect our leaders, there can be no confidence in government.

A NATION OF CONSUMERS

Long before America was founded, the Greeks decided that a democracy could never work. Their logic was that once the citizens discovered they could vote themselves money from the public treasury, their numbers and demands would grow until they outnumbered the financial producers in any democracy, bringing bankruptcy to the state. We are at that point in America! The welfare state has far more voters than those who pay taxes to pay for the demands of the welfare legions.

Washington's present solution is to tax those who are working day and night and to give it to people who are sometimes social parasites, who are able to work but refuse to do so. It's a numbers con game where the producers cannot reverse the burden of extreme taxation because the consumers are demanding more . . . more . . . more, and Congress, desiring to be reelected, gives them more. What happens when the producers stop producing? What happens when Washington runs out of other people's money to spend?

Consider the fact that there are about 8 million people in New York City, more or less. The vast majority of all taxes for New York City are paid by fewer than 45,000 people. The New York *Post* reports that almost two million New Yorkers fled the state over the past decade. They're leaving for new jobs, lower taxes, and better opportunities. Simply put, the state is in a self-inflicted economic death spiral that won't be solved by resorting to Albany's usual tricks.

Anyone who can read a newspaper knows that California is swimming in an ocean of debt.

We have reached a point in our national economy where the consumers outvote the producers and a change from the socialistic concept will not be possible. Remember: the government that's big enough to give you everything is big enough to take everything from you. You cannot tax your way to wealth. Socialism has failed in Europe and will fail miserably in the United States.

We are facing a nuclear war in the Middle East as Iran threatens to "wipe Israel off the map" and then release a sophisticated series of terrorist attacks against America via sleeper cells which are already here.

Our president has been much tougher on Israel than he has been on either Iran or North Korea, which is launching missiles at will, or Russia, which has bluffed America into backing away from the European missile shield, and Venezuela, whose leader Hugo Chavez never misses an opportunity to demonize America.

A CLEAR AND INCONVENIENT TRUTH

Why are we so tough toward our "only friend in the Middle East," while apologizing for America's strength before nations sworn to our destruction?

On November 18, 2009, America read this glaring headline: "Obama Calls Israeli Settlement Building in East Jerusalem 'Dangerous.' "

President Obama called it "dangerous" that Israel plans to add nine hundred new apartments to an existing Jewish settlement in East Jerusalem, an area Palestinians hoped to claim as their capital absent a peace agreement with Israel.

Prime Minister Benjamin Netanyahu said that building permits were permitted for construction in Gilo for what would be upscale dwellings in the lower-middle-class neighborhood.

The U.S. administration has roundly criticized the decision to expand the neighborhood, a point of bitter contention for Palestinians who wish to make East Jerusalem, as well as other sites holy to Jews, Muslims, and Christians, part of its capital in the future.[2]

There is a clear and inconvenient truth about Israel that America and Europe need to remember. That truth is: Israel is a sovereign nation and not a vassal state of the United States. It does not need the approval of the White House or the U.S. State Department to build in its capital city. This land was given to Israel by covenant from God Almighty to Abraham 3,500 years ago and that covenant stands *today*!

The president of the United States does not have the authority to tell the Jewish people they cannot live in East Jerusalem, their own capital, and/or in Judea and Samaria, where Jews have lived for millennia.

GOVERNMENT-CONTROLLED HEALTH CARE—IMPENDING DISASTER

Our health care system is broken, and the government wants complete control over your medical future. Just for good order, let's review the U.S. government track record for managing mega-corporations. Remember that health care is going to control 20 percent of America's income. This is HUGE!

- Medicare . . . BROKE!

- Medicaid . . . BROKE!

- Social Security . . . BROKE!

- Amtrak . . . BROKE!

- Health care . . . you guess!

Dr. Jeffery Flier's op-ed article in the *Wall Street Journal* diagnosed the Democrats' health care "reform" legislation. Here are some key excerpts:

> As the controversy heads toward a conclusion in Washington, it appears that the people who favor the legislation are engaged in collective denial . . . In discussions with dozens of health-care leaders and economists, I find near unanimity of opinion that . . . the final legislation . . . will markedly accelerate national health-care spending rather than restrain it. Likewise, nearly all agree that the legislation would do little or nothing to improve quality . . . Worse, the legislation would undermine any potential for real innovation . . . by overregulating the health-care system . . . there are important lessons to be learned from recent experience with reform in Massachusetts. Here, insurance mandates similar to those proposed in the Federal legislation increased total spending.[3]

In case you're wondering, Dr. Flier is not on the payroll of some right-wing think tank; he's the dean of Harvard Medical School.

If the government gets control of the health care system, you can expect long delays for medical treatment. I get calls on a regular basis from friends in Canada, where socialized medicine reigns, asking for my help to get them into American medical facilities.

When you have a deadly cancer attacking your body and you can't get into a hospital for months, it's a death sentence.

In recent days, the *Wall Street Journal*'s website has posted two columns that have exposed the glaring contradictions of the health care policy now being proposed before Congress.

In the first column, Peter Suderman notes that in our federalist system of government the states have been called "laboratories of democracy" free to try "novel social and economic experiments without risk to the rest of the country." Several states have already experimented with key elements of the proposed health care policy, and the results are not good.

The second column by Peter Suderman, entitled "Obama's War on Specialists," was an analysis of how the proposed health care plan will impact any American suffering from heart disease, cancer, or any ailment requiring a specialist. Here is what it said:

> Democrats are systematically attacking specific medical fields like cardiology and oncology . . . trying to engineer a "cheaper" system so that government can afford to buy health care for all . . . even if the price is fewer and less innovative ways of extending and improving lives . . . the increase in specialists has tracked advances over 50 years in medical science and technology. Democrats look at these advancements and see only the cost, not the benefits.
>
> Markets are supposed to determine the composition of the workforce, not a command medical economy run out of Washington . . . Americans might take a different view of health care "reform" if they understood that it means snuffing out the best medicine.

This is a very important point that cannot be ignored. Last year, the director of the Congressional Budget Office told Congress, "In explaining why health costs rose over the past several decades, most analysts agree that *the most important factor* has been the emergence, adoption and widespread diffusion of new medical technologies and services"[4] (emphasis added). Do we want to save money by going back to 1970s technology, by denying MRIs, mammograms for women until they are fifty, and life-saving drugs like the socialized "command medical economies" in Europe?

The *Washington Times* recently pointed out a new study by the University of Pennsylvania which shows that for the eight most common types of cancer, Americans have dramatically higher survival rates than Europeans. The study indicated, "For all malignancies, the five-year survival rate for men is 66.3 percent in America. In Europe, it is only 47.3 percent. The rate is 63 percent for women in America, but only 55 percent for European women." The lives these statistics represent are yours and mine!

It's *your life* that's on the line in the health care "reform" being presently considered in Washington, DC.

OUR MILITARY IS BREAKING DOWN!

Our military is breaking down! We are fighting two wars, Iraq and Afghanistan, and our economic engines are sputtering. General Stanley McChrystal has asked the president for 40,000 more troops in Afghanistan and as of this date, none has been sent.

U.S. Army Major Nidal Hasan has just murdered thirteen soldiers in cold blood at Fort Hood while shouting "Allahu Akbar" and firing his semi-automatic weapon, injuring thirty more. Military suicides and stress disorders are running off the chart.

Was Major Nidal Hasan a psycho under too much stress or was he a radical Islamo-fascist who was only practicing his faith? In chapter 2, I'll give you fourteen facts concerning this situation and let you decide.

What is the solution?

Could it be that too few are being required to do too much for too long?

The rights and privileges of veterans are being revoked, and the care of our military personnel is being conducted in rat-infested facilities that are substandard in third world countries. This is not the way to treat our heroes. This is not the mark of greatness.

General McChrystal, who was appointed by President Obama, is credited with capturing Saddam Hussein and killing the leader of al-Qaeda in Iraq, Abu Musab al-Zarqawi. The general told CBS reporter David Martin that he had talked to the president one time in seventy days.

This revelation comes amid the explosive publication of a classified report written by the general that said the war in Afghanistan *"will likely result in failure"* if more troops are not added next year.

Former U.S. ambassador to the United Nations John R. Bolton said the lack of communication with the general was indicative of Mr. Obama's misplaced priorities.[5]

THOUSANDS OF AMERICAN FARMERS ARE OUT OF WORK

A portrait of our food supply can be seen on national television with Sean Hannity of Fox News talking to thousands of American farmers who are out of work and cannot produce on their farms because the federal government has turned off the water to save a two-inch minnow that feeds the salmon in Washington State.

Think about it!

Farms in California that are usually lush and green with vegetables now look like a dry and barren desert. Farmers who want to work can't work because environmental extremists see a two-inch minnow as having more value than human life.

Everyone who eats has an interest in agriculture! Reduced farming will lead to food shortages, food shortages will lead to food fights, rioting, and martial law.

WAKE UP, AMERICA!

Wake up, America! This is not going to happen . . . it is happening right now.

Through tax-and-cap and a plethora of other methods to increase your taxation, people will stop working, work less, or lie to the IRS about their taxes to survive. You can't spend your way to wealth, and taxation shuts down the economic engines of any family or nation.

Simply stated, America's present economic crisis was caused by widespread greed in government and on Wall Street. That corruption has not been corrected and cannot be legislated out of existence. Our economic future is very uncertain!

Could the reason why America's financial masterminds are announcing that the financial crisis is over be because they are standing on the crow's nest staring into the future without binoculars? Lurking just ahead of America and the world, a radical Islamic terrorist attack that could make 9/11 pale by comparison or an attack on several American cities simultaneously that will shake the economic foundations of the nation.

THE NIGHTMARE OF RADICAL ISLAMIC TERROR

Within the past few days of this writing, the FBI has arrested radical Islamic terrorists making bombs for Denver, Dallas, and New York. Congratulations to the FBI for its fantastic efforts to keep us safe.

The worst nightmare for the intelligence community has become reality: American Muslims going abroad to be trained in the art of terror to return home and kill us as a tribute to their theology of death. Or homegrown radical Muslims like Major Hasan.

Think the unthinkable!

In the near future a nuclear Iran, whose passion is to utterly destroy America and Israel, will have the power to do the "unthinkable."

The *New York Times* reports:

The Israelis have argued that there will be little or no warning time before Iran completes building an actual weapon, especially if Iran has hidden facilities. Israeli officials cite two secret programs in Iran, Project 110 and Project 111, the code names for what are believed to be the warhead design programs run by Mohsen Fakrizadeh.

Israeli officials say privately that the Obama administration is deluding itself in thinking that diplomacy will persuade Iran to give up its nuclear program. Even inside the White House, some officials think Mr. Obama's diplomatic effort will prove fruitless.[6]

The only thing that can prevent the imminent nuclear attack on America, Europe, and Israel is to prevent Iran from becoming a nuclear nation. The best way to win a nuclear war is to make sure it never starts.

America's government does not presently have the will to face down Iran with the military option. Can it be that Europe and America will stand down and let one of the smallest nations on Earth, Israel, attempt mission impossible to save themselves from a nuclear holocaust and give Western civilization a very brief time to solve the problem?

Think the unthinkable! Think about a day in the near future when you may see a screaming headline on your newspaper: "Nuclear Bombs Crush Seven American Cities!"

Millions dead . . . chaos reigns.

Think it can't happen? Think again!

Paul L. Williams, a former consultant to the FBI on terrorism, claims these seven cities as being New York, Miami, Houston, Las Vegas, Los Angeles, Chicago, and Washington, DC. He warns that the attacks are planned to occur simultaneously at the seven cities.

Paul Williams indicates "that there is empirical proof that al-Qaeda possesses nukes. British agents posing as recruits infiltrated al-Qaeda training camps in Afghanistan in 2000. In another instance, an al-Qaeda operative was arrested at Ramallah with a tactical nuke strapped to his back."[7]

If you are having trouble believing that teams of terrorists maintaining a nuclear weapon in the United States wouldn't be detected, think about this. Williams reports that there isn't just one team, but at least seven. They are working with mosques and Islamic centers. In the United States, a federal judge will not provide any FBI or law enforcement agent with a warrant to search a mosque or an Islamic center for any reason since such places are listed as "houses of worship."[8]

Intelligence experts believe Iran has developed the technology to unleash an electromagnetic pulse (EMP) designed to be used against America in a time of war.

Here's what the EMP does. This electromagnetic blanket does not kill people . . . it kills electrons. In short, it stops every form of electricity instantly and for months, maybe years. Here's how it could be used against America in warfare.

A fake satellite crossing over America at the height of 280 miles suddenly explodes over the Great Plains of the United States, releasing several pounds of enriched plutonium, blanketing the United States of America with gamma rays. Instantly, in a fraction of a second, all electrical power is cut off, and cut off for months.

No lights or refrigerators will work in your home. Every ounce of food you have will rot in your freezer. Your car won't work because it starts with electricity. Trucks won't work, meaning transportation bringing you everything you use will stop. All machinery will stop. The radio and television stations will go off the air. Planes that are in flight will crash because their electronic systems will fail. The missile systems will fail to function. We will cease to be a superpower in a fraction of a second.

The president will not be able to communicate with his military people in the field because the phones will not work. America's refineries will shut down. There will be no gas and no oil. The gas at the service station won't be available because those pumps get the gas out of the ground with electricity. Computers won't work, which means city, state, and government offices will be shut down. There will be a nationwide food and gas shortage within a few days.

You say this can't happen?

The enemies of democracy are planning it right now! It's not new. It's been talked about for decades. Only now, rogue states have the ability to put this weapon to use, and it will happen unless they are stopped by force.

Can Iran do it?

Our government says yes. Iran is presently ruled by a theocratic dictatorship under Ahmadinejad who would be more than willing to use those weapons to destroy America and Israel.

The *Congressional Report* reads: "Even primitive scud missiles could be used for this purpose (electronic blankets). And top U.S. intelligence officials reminded members of Congress that there is a glut of these missiles on the world market. They are currently being bought and sold for about $100,000 apiece."[9]

Think about that!

This great, magnificent, "unsinkable" nation so technically oriented has created an obvious Achilles' heel: electricity. With one $100,000 missile fired from a used submarine two hundred miles offshore and a few pounds of enriched plutonium exploding over the United States, every form of electricity would stop instantly and for months. In one second, we would be living in the nineteenth century. Military experts believe that Iran would launch this electronic blanket as the opening shot of a nuclear war.

9/11 proved that radical Islam has the will to kill us. When Iran gets nuclear weapons they will have the power to kill us. Headlines that you could read in the near future will be a global game changer: IRAN HAS NUCLEAR WEAPONS.

Think it can't happen?

It probably already has!

In the following chapter some very creditable people believe it has . . . everyone except America.

Iran Is Ready for War!

The intelligence coverage of Iran's nuclear readiness varies greatly. One reason for the extreme variation is that if American intelligence admits there is a problem, they must take positive action to solve the problem.

Punting the "nuclear crisis" down field is comforting to the general population who are absorbed by *Desperate Housewives* and *Dancing with the Stars,* comforting to politicians running for office who have mastered the art of almost saying something while standing boldly on both sides of every issue on the evening news.

It's very much like the owner of the *Titanic* cheerfully admonishing his deluded silk-stocking millionaires with "all is well" as the nose of the ship was sinking into the frigid waters of the Atlantic, the eternal resting place of more than fifteen hundred souls.

This "see no evil" political skill was demonstrated recently by the U.S. intelligence community in the Senate Foreign Relations Committee hearings as reported by the *Washington Times.*

Nicholas Burns, former Undersecretary of State for Political Affairs said: "There is no question [Iran is] seeking a nuclear weapons capability. No one doubts that."

No one?

Actually, America's spy agencies belittle the Iranian threat. On March 12, 2009, the CIA released a report to Congress that concluded: "We do not know whether Iran currently intends to develop nuclear weapons."

Their report was a rework of the controversial conclusions made in the December 2007 National Intelligence Estimate to wit that Iran had stopped its nuclear weapons program in 2003 and kept it frozen. The U.S. spy agencies reached this dubious conclusion while apparently knowing about the secret nuclear site near Qom. Why the discrepancy?

New York District Attorney Robert Morgenthau, who testified at the same Senate Foreign Relations Committee hearing, stated that the message from Iran was "loud and clear."

His investigations of the multibillion-dollar criminal financial schemes Iran is using to finance its programs indicated "it is late in this game, and we don't have a lot of time to stop Iran" from developing nuclear weapons and the missiles to deliver them.

"The Iranians are deadly serious about proceeding with this program," he said. "It's later than a lot of people think." [1]

Experts at the University of Wisconsin investigated the nuclear capability of Iran and they agree with New York attorney Robert Morgenthau. They report the following:

Combining the data advanced by Iranian authorities and the estimates made by the IAEA, University of Wisconsin experts who have long monitored the Iranian nuclear program think that Iran appears to be producing about 2.77 kg of low-enriched uranium (LEU) a day. As of September 10, 2009, Iran had already stockpiled 1,602.31 kg of this nuclear material.

In order to produce military uranium for a bomb, one would need 800 kg of LEU, which means Iran might already have enough material to make its first two nuclear bombs *whenever it sees fit*.

Converting LEU into military uranium would only take Tehran approximately three months. [2]

UN SECRET REPORT SAYS IRAN HAS THE ABILITY TO MAKE A NUCLEAR BOMB NOW!

Senior staff members of the UN nuclear agency have concluded in a confidential analysis that Iran has acquired "sufficient information to be able to design and produce a workable" atomic bomb. The report's conclusions, described by senior European officials, go well beyond the public positions taken by several governments, including the United States.

According to the information gathered from rogue nuclear experts around the world, Iran has done extensive research and testing on how to fashion the components of a weapon.

The report, titled "Possible Military Dimensions of Iran's Nuclear

Program," draws a picture of a program begun in 2002, run by Iran's Ministry of Defense, "Aimed at the development of a nuclear payload to be delivered by using the Shahab 3 missile system," which can strike the Middle East and parts of Europe."[3]

HOW MANY SECRET NUCLEAR FACILITIES DOES IRAN HAVE?

Recently, the chief of Iran's Atomic Energy Organization, Ali Akbar Selehi, told Iranian State Television that he was working out a timetable for the inspection of the just revealed secret nuclear site outside of Qom.

Then Selehi said he was preparing a letter for international inspectors "about the location of the facility *and others.*" That got everyone's attention.[4]

Some intelligence officials and inspectors have suspected that Tehran maintained a network of secret nuclear sites, projects, and personnel that paralleled the nuclear program that Iran declared. Said in another way, they have as many *secret* facilities as they have facilities that are *known*.

BRITISH INTELLIGENCE

Britain's Secret Intelligence Service (SIS) says that Iran has been secretly designing a nuclear warhead "since late 2004 or early 2005," an assessment that suggests Tehran has embarked on the final steps toward acquiring nuclear weapons capability.

Britain has always privately expressed skepticism about the U.S. assessment on Iran but is only now firmly asserting that the weapons program started in 2004–2005.[5]

Here is the "$64,000 question" that no one is asking: If Iran is producing this nuclear energy for peaceful purposes, as they claim, why do they have to do it in secret? Clearly, their purpose is to fulfill the promise of President Ahmadinejad of Iran to the Islamic world: "to wipe Israel off the map." Iran is ready for war!

It is important to remember that the Iranians are a very intelligent and persistent people. They are Persians and are insulted if you refer to them as Arabs. The Persians invented the game of chess that requires contestants to always conceptualize future moves—not to be fascinated by where you are at the moment on the chessboard, but how to cleverly maneuver your forces to entrap your opponent into submission. Iran has been manipulating Washington, DC, and Europe on their political chessboard with great finesse. Stated bluntly, Iran has been playing the West like a harp.

Rather than face the wrath of the UN Security Council that claims it is determined to call a halt to Iran's illicit nuclear program, Ahmadinejad has bought Iran more time without making any serious nuclear concessions. During the six years that Iran has been negotiating with the West over its nuclear program, it has taken the politics of delay and procrastination to an entirely new level.

Keep the talks going, keep those centrifuges spinning, and stay on schedule with their nuclear weapons program. From the outset of the West's attempts to negotiate a nuclear deal with Iran, the Iranians have promised much and delivered little. They have repeatedly promised to freeze their enrichment activities at Natanz, only to resume enrichment once they realized there was nothing the West could do to stop them.[6]

IRAN: A BRUTAL THEOCRATIC DICTATORSHIP

The Iranian people now find themselves under the iron fist of a theocratic dictatorship. This is a corrupt, fanatical, ruthless, and unprincipled regime which is detested by the masses as seen in the riots following the last presidential election.

Tens of thousands of Iranians took to the streets to cry out for freedom and democracy. Some were beaten, others were shot dead while the world watched on global television without a word of encouragement coming from America.

It is urgent that Americans understand the brutality and cunning of this theocratic dictatorship. How brutal are they?

During the Iran-Iraq War, the Ayatollah Khomeini imported 500,000 small plastic keys from Taiwan. The trinkets were meant to be inspirational. After Iraq invaded in September 1980, it had quickly become clear that Iran's forces were no match for Saddam Hussein's professional, well-armed military. To compensate for their disadvantage, Khomeini sent Iranian children, some as young as twelve years old, to the front lines. There, they marched in formation across mine fields towards the enemy, clearing a path with their bodies. Before every mission, one of the Taiwanese keys would be hung around each child's neck. It was supposed to open the gates to paradise for them.

At one point, however, the earthly gore became a matter of concern. "In the past," wrote the semi-official Iranian daily *Ettela'at* as the war raged on, "we had child-volunteers: 14-, 15-, and 16-year-olds. They went out into the mine fields. Their eyes saw nothing. Their ears heard nothing. And then, a few moments later, one saw clouds of dust. When the dust had settled again, there was nothing more to be seen of them. Somewhere, widely scattered in the landscape, there lay scraps of burnt flesh and pieces of bone." Such scenes would henceforth be avoided, *Ettela'at* assured its readers. "Before entering the mine fields, the children [now] wrapped themselves in blankets and they roll on the ground, so that their body parts stay together after the explosion of the mines and one can carry them to the graves."[7]

At the height of the Iran-Iraq War, the child volunteers of Iran were part of a Revolutionary Guards' mobilization force, known as the Basij. They reached a total strength of 400,000 children.[8]

The willingness of the Iranians to fight and die when the cause is hopeless is demonstrated in this Iran-Iraq War. The war could have been over after its first two years, when Iran recovered the territories it lost from the initial assault that had been launched by the armies of Saddam Hussein in 1980.

However, Iran kept the war going for another six long years, despite losing hundreds of thousands of its people and facing repeated chemical attacks upon its troops. Iran's absolute fanaticism could not be deterred. The Islamic Republic continued to fight on even as Tehran itself absorbed hundreds of Iraqi missile attacks toward the war's end.

At the time of the Islamic Revolution, Dr. Hadi Modaressi provided some insight into this military behavior that would become a trademark of Tehran's policies in the coming years: "We welcome military aggression against us because it strengthens the Revolution and rallies the masses around it."[9]

The Western mind cannot grasp the fanaticism of this radical Islamic culture of death. Consider the following comparison between Hitler's Nazis and the Islamo-fascists lead by Ahmadinejad of Iran.

COMPARISON OF HITLER AND AHMADINEJAD

Few people connect Adolf Hitler and his Nazis with the Islamo-fascists of the Middle East and terrorist cells operating in America. But there is a very clear and direct connection between the two.

First, consider that Adolf Hitler wrote the book titled *Mein Kampf,* which means in German, "my struggle." The question must be asked: struggle with whom? Hitler's struggle was with Jews and Christians. Hitler systematically slaughtered 6 million Jews in the Holocaust and killed 5 million Christians. He also killed 7,000 Polish priests who rejected his theology of hate.

The Arabic word *jihad* means "my inner struggle." Again the question must be asked, with whom do Islamo-fascists struggle? The answer is: their struggle is with Christians and Jews, just like Adolf Hitler's. Their struggle is exactly the same and against the same people.

Second, consider the fact that Adolf Hitler's youth camps taught German youth to hate in elementary school. They were given pets (dogs and cats) to kill to turn the hearts of the innocent into stone. Those young hearts became hard enough to throw live Jewish children into the blazing ovens in the death camps without pain of conscience. Their conscience was seared with a hot iron of hate. They had hearts of stone. They were educated barbarians.

In like manner, Islamo-fascists teach elementary school children to hate America and to hate Israel. School administrators dress young children in military apparel and give them toy guns as they all shout in unison, "Death to America . . . Death to Israel."

Hitler's book *Mein Kampf* is a number-one bestseller to this day in Islamic nations.

Third, consider that in 1935, Hitler said, "Kill the Jews!" No one listened, and his rhetoric became a hellish reality. Today the president of Iran, Mahmoud Ahmadinejad, is saying, "Kill the Jews." Ahmadinejad is trying to put nuclear weapons together to bring a nuclear holocaust in Israel.

A shocking historic reality is in the process of developing. Hitler systematically murdered 6 million Jews in Europe. There are approximately 6 million Jews in Israel today. There's another Hitler promising to exterminate the Jewish people in our generation: Ahmadinejad.

The Jewish people often say "Never again." The phrase means that they intend for there never to be another holocaust. But it is closer to happening again than we can dare imagine. Iran must be stopped from obtaining nuclear weapons. Iran with nuclear weapons will transform the Road Map for Peace into a race track to Armageddon.

Fourth, consider that England was in denial in 1935 about Hitler, just as America is in denial today about radical Islamo-fascism and President Ahmadinejad.

Why do people in America want to ignore the threat Iran presents to America and Western civilization? Because if you admit there is the threat, you have to do something about it. America's liberal politicians, lost in a politically correct fog, deny there is a threat, insisting that no action is required. And the security of our nation is greatly threatened.

Fifth, how did England try to appease Hitler? They offered him land for peace. England sent Prime Minister Neville Chamberlain to appease Adolf Hitler by offering him a portion of Czechoslovakia.[10] Hitler accepted joyously. He smelled the weakness and fear in the Europeans.

Chamberlain returned to England as the crowds cheered, and the press praised him and printed bold headlines that screamed, "Peace for Our Time!"[11]

Hitler laughed at the weakness of his enemies. Their appeasement proved they were afraid of him. He then attacked England with the fury of a ravenous lion and killed 40,000 of its citizens with the Nazi bombing raids.[12]

How is America trying to obtain peace in the Middle East? We are trying what the British and Chamberlain tried in the 1930s: land for peace. America is trying appeasement . . . trying to pressure Israel to surrender more land to Palestinians, who will not stop acts of terrorism against Israel. Israel has a Bible mandate to the Holy Land. God promises that all nations that use their influence to divide the land of Israel will be brought to a swift and severe judgment (see Joel 3:2).

WHY DO THEY HATE US?

1. They hate us because it's their religious duty to hate us.

Radical Islam is a doctrine of death. Any religion that could slaughter its innocent children running through the mine fields has a love for death the Western mind can't possibly comprehend. It is their desire, their hope, and their absolute ambition to die in a war against Christians and Jews to please Allah. This is their absolute ticket to heaven and to the seventy-two virgins who await them there. Radical Islam not only *condones* violence; it *commands* it.

> *What are militant Muslims taught to do to those who resist Islam? The Qur'an teaches: Fight and slay the Pagans wherever you find them, and seize them, beleaguer them, and lie and wait for them in every stratagem of war.*
>
>   *—Surah 9:5*

> *The punishment of those who wage war against Allah and his Messenger, and strive with might and main for mischief through the land is: execution, or crucifixion, or the cutting off of hands and feet from opposite sides, or exile from the land: that is their disgrace in this world, and a heavy punishment is theirs in the Hereafter.*
>
>   *—Surah 5:33*

In America, cutting off someone's hand or feet because they would not accept your religion is unthinkable—but many believe that the Qur'an commands it. Iran's Ayatollah Khomeini declared: "The purest joy in Islam is to kill or to be killed for Allah."[13] Is this teaching fanaticism or simply being faithful to the radical interpretation of the Qur'an?

Muhammad, the founder of Islam, slaughtered thousands of people in establishing and spreading Islam. He told his followers: "Who relinquishes his faith, kill him. I have been ordered by Allah to fight with people till they testify there is no god but Allah, and Muhammad is his messenger."

Islamic fundamentalists believe the Qur'an teaches them not to befriend Jews and Christians.

O you who believe! Take not the Jews and the Christians for your friends and protectors; they are but friends and protectors to each other. And he amongst you that turns to them [for friendship] is of them.

—*Surah 5:51*

The Jews call Uziar a son of Allah, and the Christians call Christ, the son of Allah . . . Allah's curse be on them: How they are deluded away from the truth.

—*Surah 9:30*

Not only does the Qur'an deny Christ's deity, but also, in the verse from the Qur'an above, it puts a curse on all who confess Jesus Christ as the Son of God.

Why do they hate us?

Their interpretation of their faith demands that they hate us.

They believe it is the will of their god to kill us, both Christians and Jews, if we do not convert to their faith.

Islamic anti-Semitism in Europe is shockingly similar to the terrors of Nazi Germany. In 1938, only two weeks after "Kristallnacht," the S.S. journal *Das Schwarze Korps* chillingly prophesied the final end of German Jewry through "fire and sword" and its imminent complete annihilation. Today, the specter of such apocalyptic anti-Semitism has returned to haunt Europe and other continents. In the Middle East, it has taken on a particularly dangerous, toxic, and potentially genocidal aura of hatred, closely linked to the "mission" of holy war or *jihad* against the West and the Jews.

Islamist anti-Semitism is thoroughly soaked in many of the most inflammatory themes that initially made possible the atrocities of Kristallnacht and its horrific aftermath during the Holocaust.

The scale and extremism of the literature and commentary available in Arab or Muslim newspapers, journals, magazines, caricatures, on radical Islamist websites, on the Middle Eastern radio and television news is comparable only to that of Nazi Germany at its very worst. Yet the Western world largely turns a blind eye to the likely genocidal consequences of such a cultural hatred, much as it did seventy years ago.[14]

2. They hate us for allowing women's rights!

In one of the most informative and dramatic interviews in the thirty plus years of John Hagee Television Ministries, it was my pleasure to interview Brigitte Gabriel, author of the bestselling book, *Because They Hate*.

Brigitte is a beautiful, intelligent, and articulate Arab Christian and a victim of radical Islam during the Lebanese Civil War. Gabriel's departure from the anti-Israel mind-set of her Arab culture followed her 1982 visit to Israel in search of medical assistance for her seriously wounded mother.

Faced with the compassion, the respect, and the kindness of the Israelis, Gabriel denounced her government's propaganda about the Jews and the people of Israel. Gabriel returned to Israel two years later and began her career as a journalist. She quickly rose to the position of news anchor for *World News*. She married an American war correspondent in Jerusalem and relocated in America, where she became a U.S. citizen.

I asked Brigitte to address the issue of women's rights in Islam, an issue about which America's liberal and politically correct press is in full retreat. Listen to Gabriel's response:

"Women have no rights even in a regular Islamic society. Let's not talk about radical Islam. Let's take Jordan, for example, and look at the honor killings there.

"An honor killing is when a father, a brother, or any male member in the family can kill the female member of the family for supposedly soiling the honor of the family. And that is by either being seen with a man in an inappropriate way, by not marrying the person that the father wanted her to marry, or simply even marrying the love of her life just because her family does not approve of him.

"Sometimes a husband can come up with lies against his wife just to divorce her or to hurt her. He can come up with the lie that she cheated on him. A woman doesn't need a witness; she needs *four witnesses* just to compare with one male to back her story. If she is raped, the woman is killed for soiling the honor of her family.

"A thirteen-year-old child is slaughtered by her father or her brother simply because she has been raped by a family member. Her family honor is soiled because she is supposed to be a virgin. It's horrible! And then the male family members kill the female member out in public . . . and there's no punishment for the men. The greatest punishment is when a man goes to jail maybe for four months. It's a slap on the hands. He is looked at like a local hero. And the woman is completely forgotten.

"So we are seeing the rates of suicide in the Arabic world skyrocket now, and the human rights organizations are looking into it. The rate of suicides in the Arab world is huge for a woman. They can't even keep tabs on how many honor killings have really happened because usually it's swept under the carpet. No one wants to talk about it. Usually it's done in public, and the family is proud that they did something like that. It's a crime.

"We are seeing more female suicide bombers because they believe they are going to die anyway. They're going to be killed by their family members. And now radical Islamics are approaching them. There are actually organized terrorist gangs in the Palestinian territories under the leadership of the government that rapes these young ladies. They pick up a young woman who is insecure or doesn't come from a large family and they rape her. Then they recruit these young ladies to be terrorist bombers, telling them, 'You're going to be killed in an honor killing, so you might as well join us and become a suicide bomber.'

"One of the suicide bombers that we saw, a mother with two children, was driven by her husband to the place where she was to blow herself up. And it was her boyfriend, with whom she had supposedly committed adultery, who made her suicide belt. This mother was twenty-three years old. She blew herself up at a crossing in Israel, offered her two children, and became a suicide bomber simply because they [her family] wanted to kill her. She became an instant hero.

"As a Muslim woman in the Middle East, you look at your options. Death with shame and humility or death with honor. You become an instant hero as a suicide bomber. Which are you going to choose? The obvious answer is death." I asked Brigitte, "When you lived in Lebanon as the only child of your mom and dad, why and when were you and your family attacked by radical Muslims?"

Brigitte responded, "My 9/11 wake-up call happened when I was ten years old. I was the only child of a retired Christian businessman. We lived in a Christian town in South Lebanon called Marjayoun. We had already heard about war breaking out in different parts of Lebanon, with Christians being killed and massacred.

"My parents had tucked me in bed one night and were sitting down to eat their dinner in the family room. All of a sudden, we heard a big explosion close to the house. The Muslims targeted our area because we were Christians living in a Christian town.

"They targeted our town, trying to take over to create a base from which to fight Israel. The Muslims and the Palestinians had come together as two Muslim forces fighting the Christians. They bombed my home, bringing it down and burying me in the rubble.

"I was wounded. I was ten years old, and I ended up living in a hospital for two and a half months. When I was in the hospital, I would ask my parents, 'Why did they do this to us?' And my father would tell me, 'Because we are infidels. Because we are Christians. Because the Muslims consider us infidels and they want to kill us.' So I knew ever since I was ten years old that I am wanted dead simply because I was born into the Christian faith.

"The militant Muslim commitment to kill infidels does not change even when they come to America and become citizens. It does not change even if the convert is a member of their family."

AMERICA'S DECEPTION CONCERNING MILITANT ISLAM

When I interviewed Brigette Gabriel, who lived as a Christian in Lebanon, an Islamic nation, I asked her the question: "What mistakes do you see America making that the Lebanese government also made concerning radical Islam?"

Brigette responded: "We were a country that was multicultural. We respected everybody. We were fair minded. We were tolerant and respected other religions and made sure they had freedom in our country to worship as they please.

"Lebanon, more than any other country in the Middle East, allowed Muslims to pray in their mosque. You can hear imams praising their god in Arabic and saying Islamic prayers from the mosques. At the same time, you could hear the church bells ringing and see devout Jews going to the synagogue to pray.

"What we underestimated was the hatred and the teaching of hatred in the Qur'an against Christians and Jews. We saw the writing on the wall, but we refused to accept what we were reading. We thought that we were reading too much into it. We cannot judge others, because we as

Christians are raised not to judge others, lest we be judged. So we always thought the best of other people. And we always gave people the benefit of the doubt.

"We did not have a point of reference to acts of barbarism, such as beheading people or killing people, or understand the act of killing and the teaching of hatred and raising children on hatred like mother's milk. We as Christians raise our children to respect everybody, to love everybody. We always tell them, 'What would Jesus do?'

"You live your life like God is watching you all the time. But our God condemns people that kill other people. Our God condemns people that behead others. We did not realize the hatred that the Islamics had for us. They had no respect for us, they had only hatred for us.

"I see America making the same mistakes because in America we believe in freedom of religion. But we have Islamic schools, who are taking advantage of our freedom in the United States, which are funded by Saudi Arabia and/or teaching American Muslim students to hate America.

"They are teaching American Muslim students that Jews and Christians are apes and pigs because we are cursed by Allah for adopting polytheism. We welcome people in our country to practice any religion they desire. We do not welcome people who believe it is the will of God to kill us.

"As we respect others, we expect others to respect us. And how can we allow Muslim students in this country to be taught that Christians and Jews are apes and pigs and expect them to grow up and be productive and respectful members of society who are going to look at you and me and respect who we are as Christians and Jews or whatever religion we choose to practice.

"Look at the Palestinian authorities since 1993, teaching the hatred of Christians and Jews in public schools from a common textbook. Saudi Arabia distributes these textbooks throughout the Arabic world and globe. We see the results in the lives of the students who are taught this hate education in public schools. We see the suicide bombings where people place no value on themselves or on humanity and are willing to kill so they can go to heaven, because they believe a good deed for Allah is killing Christians and Jews.

"We see this happening in America. How can we allow it? We allowed it in Lebanon. We didn't pay attention to it. We're letting the same thing happen in America because Americans are refusing to pay attention to what's happening before their very eyes."

Muslim TV Mogul Is Accused of Beheading His Wife

This shocking story was carried by the *Buffalo News* stating that the founder of American-Islamic TV station is accused of beheading his wife.

> The gruesome death of Orchard Park resident Aasiya Zubair Hassan, who was found decapitated, and the arrest of her estranged husband are drawing widespread attention, as speculation roils about the role that the couple's religion may have played.
>
> Muzzammil Hassan, 44, was arrested . . . and charged with second-degree murder after telling police his wife was dead at the office of their television station in the Village of Orchard Park. . . .
>
> "This was apparently a terroristic version of honor killing, a murder rooted in cultural notions about women's subordination to men," said Marcia Pappas, New York State president of the National Organization for Women. . . .
>
> While domestic violence affects all cultures, Muslim women find it harder to break the silence about it because of the stigma, she said.
>
> "Too many Muslim men are using their religious beliefs to justify violence against women," she said. . . .
>
> A teacher of family law and Islam at the University at Buffalo Law School, [Nadia] Shahram said that "fanatical" Muslims believe "honor killing" is justified for bringing dishonor on a family.[15]

Honor Killing in a Parking Lot

A young Iraqi woman—Noor Faleh Almaleki—whose father, by his own admission, hit her with his car because she became too Westernized, died from her injuries after lying in a coma for nearly two weeks. Police say her father ran down her and her boyfriend's mother with his Jeep as the women were walking across the parking lot in the west Phoenix suburb of Peoria.

The father fled the scene for the United Kingdom, which denied him entrance and sent him back to Atlanta, where he was arrested. County Prosecutor Stephanie Low told a judge that Almaleki admitted to committing the crime.

"By his own admission, this was an intentional act and the reason was that his daughter had brought shame on him and his family," Low said. "This was an attempt at honor killing." [16]

Police said the Almalekis moved to Peoria from Iraq in the mid-1990s. Evidently, after living in America for more than a decade, the theology of death did not surrender to the love of life.

JIHAD: A CLEAR AND PRESENT DANGER TO THE WEST

While sitting on the platform waiting for my time to deliver the keynote address at the Night to Honor Israel event, I heard this astonishing testimony from David, a person I have known for years as a man of truth, honor, and integrity.

David and his wife were on a vacation in an Arab country when they heard the call to prayer echoing across the city from the Islamic mosque nearby. Their guide was a young Arab man who was the portrait of poise and sophistication. He was immaculately dressed, he spoke the English language flawlessly, and was totally confident as a consummate professional.

With the echoes of the call to prayer reverberating between the buildings, David asked his young Arab guide, "Are you Muslim?"

"Absolutely," was the immediate and polite response.

"My wife and I are Christians. If the spiritual leader now making the call to prayer were to ask you to kill Christians, would you?" David asked.

Without hesitation the educated, poised, and sophisticated young Arab guide said, "Yes!" Why? Because his interpretation of his faith demands that he hate Christians, Jews, and anyone else who will not proclaim, "There is no God but Allah."

THE DANGER WITHIN—MILITANT ISLAM

Historian Daniel Pipes, writing for *Commentary* magazine's November 2001 issue, recorded the following shocking evidence concerning the loyalty of some Muslims to America:

In June 1991, a convert to Islam, Siraj Wahaj, a recipient of the American Muslim community's highest honors, had the privilege of becoming the first Muslim to deliver the daily prayers in the U.S. House of Representatives. On that occasion he recited from the Qur'an and appealed to the Almighty to guide American leaders and to grant them righteousness and wisdom.

But the story about Siraj Wahaj did not end there. A little over a year later this same Muslim, addressing an audience of New Jersey Muslims, "articulated a completely different message from his mild and moderate prayer given before the U.S. House of Representatives." He said, "If only Muslims were more clever politically, they could take over the United States and replace its constitutional government with a caliphate (Islamic leadership body)." He concluded his remarks with these words: "If we were united and strong, we would elect our own leader and give allegiance to him . . . Take my word, if the six or eight million Muslims in America unite, the country will come to us."[17]

This is not loyalty . . . this is sedition!

Calling for the overthrow of the United States government is resistance to or insurrection against lawful authority. In 1995, Siraj Wahaj served as a character witness for Omar Abdel Rahman at the blind radical Islamic terrorist's trial that found him guilty of conspiracy to overthrow the government of the United States. More alarming still, the United States attorney in New York listed Wahaj as one of the "unindicted persons who may be alleged as coconspirator to blow up the Twin Towers in New York City in 1993."

This is the point!

This radical Islamic leader, selected by the U.S. House of Representatives as the award-winning model of the Islamic faith in America, is on record calling for the overthrow of the United States government. Think about that when you hear a politician or talk show host on television jabbering about radical Islam's loyalty to America.

Another case in point is Abdurahman Alamoudi, once a prominent figure in the American Muslim community, who had been invited to the White House on numerous occasions, who was also an admitted supporter of Hamas and Hezbollah. Speaking before the Islamic Association for Palestine's 1996 convention in Illinois, Alamoudi predicted that Muslims would one day take over America, saying:

> I have no doubt in my mind, Muslims sooner or later will be the moral leadership of America. It depends on me and you, either we do it now or we do it after a hundred years, but this country will become a Muslim country. And I [think] if we are outside this country we can say, "Oh, Allah destroy America," but once we are here, our mission in this country is to change it.[18]

ISLAMIC POPULATION BOMB

Few Americans consider the power and influence Muslims demand as a result of the Islamic population bomb. A Muslim man is permitted to marry up to four wives at a time and birth control is not typically on his mind.

The most famous Muslim in the world today is Osama bin Laden, who is one of fifty-three children.[19] He himself has twenty-seven children.[20] Look at those numbers. If you look at Osama bin Laden and his father, they have produced eighty children. How many parents do you know in America, Christians or Jews, who have produced that many children in such a brief period of time?

The Islamic population bomb is what is tipping the scales in Europe. Once the Muslims become the majority, they will start demanding more rights in government. They will demand more representation.

The Civil War in Lebanon happened when the Muslims became the majority with the influx of Palestinians out of Jordan when King Hussein kicked Yasser Arafat out of Jordan in the Black September conflict. Yasser Arafat and the PLO joined forces with the Muslims in Lebanon and declared war on the Christians. The strategy of militant Muslims in conquering a new country is to concentrate their numbers in a specific region and take it over via population explosion. That's why they view their war with America as a fifty-year war that they fully intend to win.

A BRIEF HISTORY OF RADICAL ISLAM—NOT PEACEFUL

The truth of history is this: When Muhammad died in A.D. 632, much of Arabia having being forced to embrace this new faith by the sword, tried to defect, thinking they had the freedom to quit Islam.

They had forgotten the words of Muhammad, passed on from Allah: "Who relinquishes his faith, kill him." [21]

During two years (A.D. 630–632), in obedience to Allah's command to behead apostates, Muhammad's successor and father-in-law, Abu Bakr, with loyal Muslim warriors, killed about 70,000 former Muslims because they had left the faith. This is not peaceful.

Abu Bakr sent forth his troops, saying, "Call them [those who tried to quit Islam, known as apostates] to re-embrace Islam; if they refuse do not spare any of them. Burn them with fire and kill them with force and take the woman and children as prisoners of war." [22]

This is a fact of history!

In Saudi Arabia, the practice of any religion besides Islam is strictly prohibited now, just as it was in Muhammad's lifetime.

Saudi Arabia is building mosques in America from coast to coast with riches from America's gas tanks. But if you go to Saudi Arabia and try to worship any other God than Allah, you can be killed.

In July 1977, an Englishman with a miniature camera was able to take photographs that shocked the world . . . the public execution in Jeddah of Princess Mishael bint Fahd Bin Mohammed, a young married but separated mother, and her lover, Khalid Muhallah. She was shot six times in the head and he was beheaded. [23] Is this peaceful?

The photographs became a part of the documentary *Death of a Princess,* and Western governments hurried to suppress the showing of the film.

Saudi Arabia is the only country that officially practices beheadings for apostasy. By decree from Muhammad, still honored as Islamic law, no Jew may enter Saudi Arabia. Saudi Arabia has accomplished what Adolf Hitler dreamed of—a Jew-free society.

Saudi officials promised they will continue to support Palestinian terrorism against Israel. In April 2002, Sheikh Saad al-Buraik, a prominent Saudi government cleric, said in a government mosque in Riyadh, "I am against America until this life ends . . . she is the root of all evil and wickedness on earth . . . Muslim brothers in Palestine, do not have any mercy, neither compassion on the Jews . . . their women are yours to take . . . God made them yours . . . why don't you wage jihad? Why don't you pillage them?"[24]

Fifteen of the nineteen Muslims who murdered three thousand people on 9/11 were from Saudi Arabia. This was an act of mass murder. This is not peaceful.

On 9/11 Islamic terrorists flew hijacked commercial airliners into the Twin Towers of New York City killing three thousand wonderful American people. They went to work that day not knowing it would be their last day on the earth. They went to work to provide for their wives, children, husbands, and families. They died horribly—some jumping to their deaths to escape the flames.

I guarantee that Khalid Sheikh Mohammad and the four thugs who helped plan this murderous deed will have high-profile criminal attorneys lining up for the "honor" of defending these murderers against the United States. This trial will give global terrorism a platform to praise and deify the crimes of these mass killers, inspiring millions of young Muslims to match or surpass their acts of murder.

It sends the signal to all terrorists to stop fighting in Iraq or Afghanistan and come to America where you will be given a high-profile ACLU lawyer at no cost to defend you. You will be covered on national and global television for months and become a hero to all terrorists. Bring the fight to the streets of America. be charged in America, tried in America and, who knows, you might be acquitted in a jury trial. Remember: they turned O. J. Simpson loose.

Holding these trials in civilian courts for war criminals is an act of massive irresponsibility in government. Why? Because our CIA, under oath, is going to have to testify and give classified information and secret data in an open court that will be a treasure trove for radical Islam.

America will be put on trial, and the practices that kept us safe after 9/11 will be exposed, condemned, exploited by radical Islam, and Americans will die in the future because those protections for our citizens will be removed. How positively stupid!

Here are some bipartisan reactions to the news:

- Senator John Cornyn (R-TX): "These terrorists planned and executed the mass murder of thousands of innocent Americans. Treating them like common criminals is unconscionable."[25]

- Rep. Peter King (R-NY): "This, I think, will go down as one of the worst decisions any president has ever made." [26]

- Tim Brown, a former New York City firefighter: "The only thing they're going to do is give them a stage to mock us . . . and this makes me sick to my stomach." [27]

- Senator Joseph Lieberman (ID-CT): "The terrorists who planned, participated in, and aided the September 11, 2001, attacks are war criminals, not common criminals. Not only are these individuals not common criminals but war criminals, they are also not American citizens entitled to all the Constitutional rights American citizens have in our federal courts. The individuals accused of committing these heinous, cowardly acts . . . should therefore be tried by military commission rather than in civilian courts in the United States." [28]

MUSLIM'S WEBSITE CALLS FOR GOD TO "KILL THE JEWS!"

A New York bicycle cabbie, who last year used his website to mock the beheading of journalist Daniel Pearl, posted a prayer calling for the murder of Jews and exhorting Muslims to "throw liquid drain cleaner in their faces." And there's nothing authorities can do about it.

Yousef al-Khattab, who runs RevolutionMuslim.com and pedals a pedicab in New York City, insists the words he has posted on his website are a prayer and not a threat and that his hatred is protected by the First Amendment.

"If it was a threat, I'd be in jail," the forty-one-year-old al-Khattab said on his website from his home in Queens. "I'm asking my God, that's what it is. Every supporter of Israel is an enemy combatant, and the immune system is not anti-Semitic for resisting disease." Al-Khattab called on Allah to carry out "wrath on the Jewish occupiers of Palestine and their supporters."

"Please throw liquid drain cleaner in their faces," he wrote, "burn their flammable sukkos while they sleep . . . Oh God, answer my prayer." ("Sukkos" refers to the Jewish holiday during which the Jews build and eat their meals in outdoor huts known as "sukkahs," which represents the huts the Jews lived in during their exodus from Egypt.)

Judge Andrew Napolitano, senior legal analyst for Fox News, said the posting is "absolutely protected by the First Amendment." [29]

The posting reflects the "prayer of every true Muslim," al-Khattab said. Every true Muslim would say the same thing. The pedicab operator for the past three years is married with four children and said he has driven plenty of Jewish passengers without incident.

"I've never killed one . . . I suffer from mental Tourette's [syndrome]. I say what's on my mind. We have freedom of speech." [30]

Al-Khattab stated that his mission is "preserving Islamic culture" and seeking support of the "beloved Sheik Abdullah Faisal, whose preaching the religion of Islam and serving as a spiritual guide." [31]

Sheik Faisal was convicted in the United Kingdom in 2003 for spreading messages of racial hatred and urging his followers to kill Jews and Westerners. In sermon recordings played at his trial, Sheik Faisal called on young, impressionable Muslims to use chemical weapons to "exterminate unbelievers" and to "cut the throat of the Kaffars [nonbelievers] with a machete." [32]

JIHAD AT FORT HOOD

Every American should be outraged about the murderous rampage against U.S. soldiers in Fort Hood, Texas, by jihadist Major Nidal M. Hasan, who killed fourteen and wounded thirty. I am aware that presently only thirteen counts of murder are being charged against Major Hasan, but one of his victims was pregnant and that baby, in the eyes of God, is a living soul. He killed fourteen people!

Can you believe it?

America has been fighting radical Islamist around the world for eight years, and one of the greatest tragedies in U.S. military history happened on a U.S. military base at the hands of an Islamic terrorist who was a U.S. Army officer.

Major Hasan's attack was the third incident this year in which U.S. military installations were targeted by radicals. The sleeper cells buried in the U.S. military are watching how the government handles Hasan's case with kid gloves. It's an invitation for future deaths of America's military personnel.

In September, two North Carolina men were charged for conspiring to kill U.S. personnel at Quantico, home of the Marine officer training school and the FBI Academy.

In June of 2009, Abdul Hakim Mujahid Muhammad, an American Muslim convert fired at two soldiers outside a recruiting center in Little Rock, Arkansas, killing one and injuring the other.

Here are the facts concerning Major Hasan. You decide if he was an Islamic radical carrying out the principles of his faith.

1. Several months before the tragedy, Major Hasan defended Muslim suicide bombers on his webpage and compared such acts to the sacrifice a U.S. soldier makes when he falls on a grenade to save his fellow soldiers.[33]

2. Colonel Terry Lee, who worked with the killer, said Major Hasan said, "Muslims shouldn't be fighting Muslims." In June 2009, when a Muslim convert assassinated a U.S. soldier at a recruiting station in Little Rock, Arkansas, Colonel Lee said that Major Hasan seemed happy about the event and that he was confronted by other officers.[34]

3. No one seemed to notice the significance of the attire Major Hasan was wearing the morning of his premeditated murders. It was captured on a store surveillance video where he bought coffee and put on national television. Hasan was wearing the *shalwar-kameez,* the traditional attire worn by Pashtuns on both sides of the Pakistan-Afghan border. Hasan was dressed for war the day he died.[35]

4. Major Hasan passed out Qur'ans on the morning of the shooting.[36]

5. Survivors in the facility where Hasan went on his murderous attack reported that he yelled, "Allahu Akbar [Allah is great]" before he opened fire. This is the same phrase the jihadist used on 9/11 and which has been repeated by our enemy in every Islamic attack on America.[37]

6. Lieutenant Colonel Val Finnell, Hasan's classmate at the Uniformed Services University of Health Sciences in Bethesda, Maryland, told Fox News: "There were definitely clear indications that Hasan's loyalties were not with America. Hasan told his classmates and professors, 'I'm a Muslim first and I hold the Sharia, the Islamic law, before the United States Constitution.' "

Major Hasan is an officer in the U.S. military who took an oath to defend the Constitution of the United States against all enemies both foreign and domestic.

His remarks are words of outright sedition. Why didn't the professors and officers in Bethesda confront him? Lieutenant Colonel Val Finnell states: "They were too concerned about being politically correct."

7. Lieutenant Colonel Finnell recalled one time when his classmates were giving presentations in an environmental health care class on topics like soil and water contamination and the effects of mold. When it was Major Hasan's turn, he got up in front of the class and began to speak about his topic: "Is the war on terror a war on Islam?" Hasan's anti-American vitriol continued for two years as he worked toward his degree in public health funded by the taxpayers of America.

8. Senator Joe Lieberman has announced his intention to lead a congressional investigation into the Fort Hood murders, saying there were "strong warning signs" that Hasan was an "Islamic extremist. The U.S. army has to have zero tolerance. He should have been gone," said Lieberman, who is chairman of the Senate Committee on Homeland Security and Governmental Affairs.

9. Hasan attended a mosque in northern Virginia that two 9/11 hijackers also attended.

10. The thirteen men and women who died and the dozens who were wounded at Fort Hood richly deserve to receive the honor of the Purple Heart. Again, political correctness may prevent that from happening. Here's why: Congressman Frank Wolf (R-VA) is calling on President Obama to award the heroes at Fort Hood with the Purple Heart. There's just one problem: in order to award the Purple Heart, the Secretary of the Army must acknowledge that what occurred at Fort Hood was not a random attack, but an act of terrorism.

In 1973 the army modified the requirements to present an individual with the Purple Heart. It may be awarded "as a result of an international terrorist attack against the United States or a foreign nation friendly to the United States, recognized as such an attack by the Secretary of the Army."

I am hopeful that our president will not allow political correctness to get in the way of awarding these men and women the proper recognition for their service to the United States. What happened at Fort Hood *was* a terrorist attack. There is overwhelming evidence that Major Hasan was a radical Islamist who carried out the attacks because of his ideological beliefs. The families of the victims at Fort Hood deserve better than political correctness. They deserve the truth![38]

11. We now know that Major Hasan sent between ten and twenty messages to Amwar al-Awlaki, an Islamo-fascist cleric known for his exhortations for Muslims to rise up and kill infidels. Counterterrorism officials intercepted the communications but concluded—are you ready for this?—that the emails were probably part of a research project on posttraumatic stress disorder that the psychiatrist had been conducting at the Walter Reed Medical Center.

Amazing!

Amwar al-Awlaki is an expert on jihadist methodologies in cutting the throat of a nonbeliever and what an appropriate ritual beheading requires. He's not a normal resource for posttraumatic stress disorder.

No matter how "innocent" the emails seemed, our "intelligence" community alarm bells should have gone off when an army major sent messages to a murderous monster.

After the Fort Hood rampage, al-Awlaki praised Major Hasan on his webpage. He wrote, "Nidal Hasan is a hero. He is a man of conscience who could not bear living the contradiction of being a Muslim and serving in an army that is fighting against his own people. Any decent Muslim cannot live, understanding properly his duties towards his Creator and his fellow Muslims, and yet serve as a U.S. soldier."[39]

Think about this!

Perhaps our homeland security people are so traumatized by the constant left-wing attack accusing them of violating Constitutional rights that they have been rendered ineffective. CIA officers have been threatened with prosecutions, and phone companies may be sued out of business for cooperating with the Bush administration on wiretaps in the aftermath of the 9/11 attacks. Some of our counterterrorism officials may be so worried about ending up in jail if they are too aggressive that they have become paralyzed by political correctness.

This is exactly why there is serious concern across the nation as millions of Americans are now thinking the unthinkable: Can America survive?

12. Major Hasan once gave a lecture to other doctors at Walter Reed Army Medical Center in Washington in which he said nonbelievers should be beheaded and have boiling oil poured down their throats.

Colleagues had expected a discussion on a medical issue but were instead given an extremist interpretation of the Qur'an, which Hasan appeared to believe.

One army doctor who knew him said a fear of appearing discriminatory against a Muslim soldier had stopped fellow officers from filing formal complaints.[40]

When military officers who lead our army are completely intimidated by political correctness to do nothing, can America survive?

13. *The Washington Post* reports that Major Hasan delivered a one-hour, fifty-picture PowerPoint presentation titled "The Koranic World View as It Relates to Muslims in the U.S. Military."

The last bullet point simply read: "We love death more then [sic] you love life."

This is the hard-core doctrine of radical Islam. The death of a martyr is the only absolute guarantee you gain entrance into heaven with virgins waiting your arrival.

If the radical Muslims are willing to die by the millions for what they believe without hesitation, can an American nation paralyzed by political correctness possibly hope to defeat them? Can America survive?[41]

14. A photograph taken November 6, 2009, in Killeen, Texas, shows a business card that Major Nidal Hasan gave his neighbors a day

before going on a shooting spree at the Fort Hood Army Base. The business card had the initials SoA, the abbreviation for "Soldier of Allah," ABC News reported.

15. After hearing the shocking story of Major Nidal Hasan, Fox News contributor Monica Crowley stated, "Political correctness is turning out to be the death of this country." Amen, Monica!

These are the facts. You decide! Was Major Nidal Hasan an Islamic terrorist practicing his faith chapter and verse? Or was he a traumatized psychiatrist?

WHO ARE THE MUSLIMS?

The global Muslim population stands at 1.57 billion, meaning that nearly 1 in 4 people in the world practice Islam, according to a Pew Forum on Religion and Public Life.

Islam is the world's second largest religion behind Christianity, which has an estimated 2.2 billion followers. The idea that all Muslims live in the Middle East is a false impression.

Germany has more Muslims than Lebanon, China has more Muslims than Syria, and Russia has more Muslims than Jordan and Libya combined.

"This whole idea that Muslims are Arabs and Arabs are Muslims is just obliterated by this report," said Amaney Jamal, an assistant professor of politics at Princeton University.[42]

This AP report estimates that Shiites represent 10 percent to 13 percent of the Muslim population, with 80 percent of the world's Shiittes living in Iran, Pakistan, India, and Iraq.[43]

Below is a list of descriptions of what Muslims believe and how they differ from Christians and sometimes from Christians and Jews.

- Muslims say Allah made a covenant with Abraham to give the Promised Land to Ishmael's descendants, but Christians and Jews say Jehovah made a covenant with Abraham to give the Promised Land to Isaac and his descendants forever.

- Muslims say Jesus was created just like Adam, but Christians say Jesus was born of a virgin whose name is Mary.

- Muslims say Jesus was a messenger of God, but Christians say Jesus is the Son of God.

- Muslims say Judas Iscariot died on the cross, but Christians say Jesus died on the cross.

- Muslims believe in a messiah called the Mahdi, but Christians say the Messiah is Jesus.

- Muslims say the Messiah will be a descendant of Muhammad, but Christians and Jews say the Messiah will be a descendant of King David.

- Muslims say the Messiah will reign on earth for seven years and die, but Christians say He will reign on Earth for one thousand years called the Millennial Reign of Peace and never die.

- Muslims say the Messiah will conquer Israel, but Christians and Jews say the Messiah will rescue Israel.

- Muslims believe in a great war at the end of the age called the Mother of All Battles, but Christians call it the Battle of Armageddon and Jews call it the Battle of All Battles.[44]

WHAT DO RADICAL MUSLIMS BELIEVE?

The three main goals of militant Islam is to:

1. Drive all Westerners out of the Middle East.

2. Exterminate Christians and Jews who refuse to convert to Islam.

3. Establish a one-world Islamic government and religion.

In general, radical Muslims believe:

- All Muslims are soldiers in Allah's army, and they must either fight or give financial support to those who do.

- All non-Muslims are their enemy.

- All non-Muslims must be forced to submit to Islam.

- All territory that has ever been under Islamic rule must be brought back under Islamic rule forever.

- When Muslims become the majority in any country, they must control the government.

- The Jews are only temporary residents of Jerusalem and Israel.

- There can be a temporary peace of up to ten years between Islam and others but no permanent peace.

- There can be no concessions to non-Muslims; all concessions by non-Muslims are signs of weakness and an indication that Muslims are winning.

- Muslims can sign a temporary peace treaty and break it if doing so advances the cause of Islam.

- Muslims are in a Holy War (jihad) until Judgment Day.

Those who say that Christianity and radical Islam are sister faiths are completely mistaken. President W. George Bush gave moral clarity to this clash of civilizations, saying, "This nation is at war with Islamic fanatics."[45]

Cal Thomas said, "It is life or death. We want to live and they want us dead. Any questions? . . . We had better overthrow them before they overthrow us. Who can doubt their ultimate objective?"[46] Can America survive a fifty-year war with radical Islam?

Israel is the front lines in the war between a democracy and the Islamic theocratic dictatorship. Unless the world community acts immediately and aggressively to deter Iran through sanctions and diplomacy, Israel will have only two options remaining. The first is a vigorous military preemptive strike against Iran, setting their nuclear ambitions back for several years, or living every day of their lives under the very real threat of a nuclear holocaust.

A confidential source from Israel came to my office and gave me in detail what he believes to be Iran's plan of attack on Israel and America!

It's *bold!*

It's *believable* . . . and it's in the following chapter; "Iran's Plan of Attack!" Can America survive?

THREE

Iran's Plan of Attack

Insider information has shaped the destiny of nations and the financial fortunes of empires. Noah built the Ark based on insider information that a great flood was coming that would destroy all living flesh on the earth.

The three wise men came all the way from the east to visit Jesus at the time of his birth when people next door didn't know who he was much less his global spiritual significance.

Mayer Rothschild bought the wealth of Europe for a fraction of its value in a matter of hours because the carrier pigeons coming to him from the battle front where Wellington and Napoleon were battling for the control of Europe produced insider information that was much faster and more accurate than messages by horseback that the stock traders in London were using. Rothschild knew that Wellington had won at Waterloo hours before other stock traders in London heard the truth. In that handful of hours, he became the richest man in Europe. The Rothschild family ruled Europe financially for centuries because on one particular day one man had insider information no one else had.

Each nation's intelligence agencies are created and designed to give that nation inside information that no one else has, information that may mean the difference between a smashing victory and disastrous defeat. Any nation without an aggressive and sophisticated intelligence agency will soon become an historical footnote.

For several years I have had a special source in Israel whose confidential insider information over the years has proven extremely accurate. Months ago, this source flew from Jerusalem to San Antonio to give me what he believes to be Iran's plan of attack against Jerusalem, Saudi Arabia, and America. The source never tells me in advance that he's coming; he just appears without notice, gives the message, and leaves.

He entered my office, we warmly greeted each other, then he sat across the desk from me. There is never a waste of time or words. The message is given and he leaves.

"What can you tell me about the present crisis in the Middle East?" I asked.

He responded without hesitation: "I believe that it's the absolute intention of President Ahmadinejad to attack Jerusalem with a nuclear missile, to attack Saudi Arabia's oil fields with conventional missiles, thereby crushing the American economy in a day. This attack will all be done in one day at the same hour!"

As he spoke, I thought about America's addiction to foreign oil. Thanks to radical environmentalists, we have not built an oil refinery in this nation since 1976, and although we have plenty of oil, we refuse to drill for it. OPEC must be laughing its head off at the stupidity of our national energy policy.

If Iran attacked the Saudi oil fields or blocked the Strait of Hormuz, America's delicate economy would shatter.

"How soon do you think Iran will have the ability to make and deliver a nuclear warhead?" I quizzed him.

"I can only tell you what everyone knows . . . we are running out of time . . . and the time factor is now critical as Iran has become the master of diplomacy, which is deception by design with the West."

"Why would Ahmadinejad attack fellow followers of Islam in Saudi Arabia?"

"Because he believes they are an apostate branch of Islam, and there are strong doctrinal differences about who the true descendants of Muhammad happen to be."

"When do you think this might happen?"

"Only God knows the day and hour, but we are down to two options: The first is a military preemptive strike against Iran's nuclear facilities before they get the Russian missiles to protect those sites. The second option is for the world to get ready to live with a nuclear Iran because dialogue and sanctions will not stop Ahmadinejad. If he gets his hands on nuclear weapons, he will use them to initiate a nuclear holocaust, and he will use them against America. Remember, he believes that if he can create a global chaos, his messiah will suddenly and mysteriously appear to lead the world into global Sharia."

"What will Israel do if the missiles start falling on Israel?" I probed.

"We will do exactly what we have done for centuries. As Jews, we will do everything in our power to protect ourselves, and then we will get ready to defend our actions against the world press that will accuse us of overreacting." He smiled, rose from his seat, and thanked me for my friendship as we embraced, then he left the office.

DECEPTION BY DESIGN

All war is based on deception.
                                        —*Sun Tzu*

Iran's chief nuclear negotiator was Hassan Rowhani from 2003 to 2005. He represented Iran in the key negotiations that resulted in a temporary suspension of its uranium enrichment activities in 2003.

This did not prevent Rowhani from making a staggering disclosure in a speech delivered in a closed-door meeting in Tehran when he bragged that he had cleverly outmaneuvered—and essentially deceived—the Western powers, led by the European Union, with whom he had negotiated. Rowhani stated bluntly: "When we were negotiating with the Europeans in Tehran, we were installing [nuclear] equipment in parts of the facility in Isfahan."[1]

Isfahan is known by Western intelligence agencies to be exactly where the Iranians had erected a facility for completing the second important stage in the production of fuel for their clandestine nuclear weapons program.[2]

Rowhani was proud of Iran's technological success in completing this second critical stage of uranium fuel production. He boasted that as a result of what his deceptive diplomacy had accomplished, "the world would face a fait accompli" [an accomplished fact] which "would change the entire equation."[3]

In another interview Rowhani detailed the real magnitude of Iran's success by relying on the diplomatic process with Europe: "The day we started the process, there was no such thing as the Isfahan project."[4]

In fact, during the period of Rowhani's talk with the Europeans, Iran began actually converting thirty-seven tons of yellowcake into UF_6 which was enough by Western assessment to build five atomic bombs.[5]

Iran was so completely successful in deceiving the West despite Western diplomatic efforts that Britain's *Daily Telegraph* reporting on Rowhani's speech on April 3, 2006, ran a headline that tersely captured the significance of what Rowhani had said: "How We Duped the West, by Iran's Nuclear Negotiator."[6]

Rowhani also boasted of successfully driving a wedge between the United States and the Europeans. "From the outset, the Americans kept telling the Europeans, 'The Iranians are lying and deceiving you and they have not told you everything.' " Rowhani then sarcastically noted: "The Europeans used to respond, 'We trust them.' "[7]

Then there was the admission of Abdollah Ramezanadeh, government's spokesman under President Khatami, who looked back on this entire period of time and summarized Iranian negotiating strategy in very blunt terms: "We had an overt policy, which was one of negotiation and confidence building, and a covert policy, which was a continuation of the [nuclear building] activities."[8]

Iran's use of diplomacy that was deception by design was bluntly admitted before dozens of network television camera by former deputy foreign minister Mohammad-Javad Larijani, who stated: "Diplomacy must be used to lessen pressure on Iran for its nuclear program."[9]

Foreign Minister Larijani added that diplomacy, for him, was a "tool for allowing us to reach our goals."[10]

For Iran, nuclear talks were a "contest of the wills" for Tehran and not an opportunity to reach some kind of "common ground" that American politicians constantly try to achieve. Iran's diplomatic duplicity—saying one thing at the negotiating table while doing the exact opposite—was not something of which to be ashamed, but was rather considered a source of national pride.

What the admission of Iran's chief nuclear negotiator, Hassan Rowhani, clearly demonstrated was that Europe's efforts at diplomatic engagement with Iran concerning its nuclear program were a complete failure. America's present diplomatic engagement with the Islamic Republic is going nowhere. It's more of what we have seen for the past thirty years: diplomatic deception designed to give Iran time to achieve its maniacal dream of nuclear power to dominate the Middle East and the world.

The clock is running out!

The ship is sailing toward the iceberg full speed ahead. The perfect storm in the Middle East has arrived.

Just after the Islamic Revolution in Iran in 1979, Aytollah Khomeini came to power and made the following statement, which is a shocking revelation of the mind-set of radical Islam:

> *We do not worship Iran, we worship Allah. For patriotism is another name for paganism. I say let this land burn. I say let this land go up in smoke, provided Islam emerges triumphant in the rest of the world.*[11]

Iran's radical Islamic leadership does not fear war; they welcome it as evidenced by the statement of Dr. Hadi Modaressi, a leading religious leader who was close to Khomeini:

> *We welcome military aggression against us because it strengthens the revolution and rallies the masses around it.*[12]

President Ahmadinejad believes that creating a global chaos with nuclear weapons would only hasten the reappearance of the Hidden Imam from the ninth century, a Messianic figure known in the Shiite religious tradition as the Mahdi. War will accelerate the arrival of this Shiite version of the "end of days."[13]

Ahmadinejad himself linked the spread of chaos to the arrival of a new era of divine revelation. In a meeting with foreign diplomats in New York City on September 15, 2005, Ahmadinejad asked the diplomats: "Do you know why we should wish for chaos at any price?" He then answered his own rhetorical question: "Because after chaos, we can see the greatness of Allah."[14]

Even more dramatic, Ahmadinejad pressed the issue that the return of the Hidden Imam was not an event in the distant future. He stated: "Those who are not versed [in the doctrine of Mahdism] believe the return of the Hidden Imam will only occur in a very long time, but according to the divine promise [his return] is imminent."[15]

Most Americans feel that to announce a massive attack against Iran for using nuclear weapons would prevent a rational people from pursuing nuclear weapons.

Not so!

The prospect of thousands of Iranian civilians lying dead in the street would fulfill the radical Islamic obsession with martyrdom and death. Remember the last PowerPoint slide on Major Hasan's presentation was "We love death more than you love life."

The cold, naked truth is this: Iran has thumbed its nose at Europe and America through a diplomacy of planned deception designed to give Iran time to do the unthinkable.

There will be a nuclear war in the Middle East unless prevented by military force. Does Israel have a partner for peace in the Middle East? Unless the world community acts aggressively and immediately through sanctions and diplomacy, Israel will be down to two options: a military preemptive strike or life under the constant threat of a theocratic dictator with nuclear power.

The world is watching and waiting!

Time is running out!

The iceberg is just ahead!

Iran has begun war games to practice the defense of its nuclear sites. There is the sound of diplomats shuffling deck chairs in the background as the music plays on.

HOW IRANIAN NUKES WOULD
RESHAPE THE MIDDLE EAST

An Iranian nuclear program would rearrange the political, economic, and cultural furniture in the Middle East. When Iran gets the bomb, other regional powers will be forced to pursue nuclear programs or bow to the demands of Iran, which will become the bully of the Middle East.

Inevitably, in a region as volatile as this, there could be a few small-scale nuclear catastrophes. History proves that the radical Islamists are not shy about killing their own people. Remember that Saddam Hussein gassed the Kurds and slaughtered the Shiites, Hafez Assad massacred the Sunnis of Hama, and mass graves throughout the region testify to the willingness of Arab leaders to kill their own people. Nuclear weaponry under their control is merely an upgrade in repressive technology to force their will on anyone who opposes them.

An Iranian bomb is concrete evidence that Iran's strategy of "resistance" to America is a winning one. This will change the region's political culture from radical to many times more radical. An Iranian bomb sends a message to the rest of the terrorists in the Middle East that they should feel free to make a run at open terrorism in America. There is no military solution to terrorism!

If the Americans are folding by giving known war criminals like 9/11 mastermind Khalid Sheikh Mohammed an ACLU lawyer and prime-time television coverage for years without the threat of nuclear retaliation, how much more quickly and completely will America fold when Iran has the bomb.

How much more daring will they be in controlling the oil in the Persian Gulf while yanking the chain around America's neck forged by our addiction to foreign oil? Be certain Russia is in the corner clapping in thunderous applause for Iran.

WHY RUSSIA IS NOT AFRAID OF AN IRANIAN BOMB

Years ago after Prime Minister Benjamin Netanyahu had completed his first term in office as Israel's bold and aggressive leader, we sat together in my office chatting moments before we were to go out and have the "Night to Honor Israel" at Cornerstone Church, which was telecast to the nations of the world.

The prime minister and I were discussing how reluctant American intelligence was to admit that years ago, in the 1990s, Russian scientists were helping Iran build its nuclear facilities and medium-range missiles that had the ability to reach Jerusalem, London, and the East Coast of America.

I asked the prime minister: "How did you convince our government that Russia was in fact helping Iran?"

"I took the time and effort to get photographic proof and hand delivered the photos to Washington, DC, so there could be no denying that Russia was and remains an ally with Iran."

The conversation ended and we left the office for the auditorium packed with five thousand dedicated pro-Israel Christians who believe that Israel has the right to exist, the right to defend itself against all enemies, the right to control and to build anywhere within the city of Jerusalem.

Why is Russia so committed to Iran?

Russia's tactical and strategic interests cannot be ignored. Iran is an existential threat to Israel and Saudi Arabia. Iran traditionally opposes radical Sunni Islamic movements such as the Taliban and Wahabiyya, which have become a serious threat to the Russians in their Northern Caucasus area, especially Dagestan. These common enemies unite Russia and Iran.

Russia and Iran will be committed partners until the end of time. According to the prophet Ezekiel, they will unite their forces and invade Israel at some time in the future.

The end result is that God, according to the prophet Ezekiel, will crush the Russian-Islamic army in much the same manner as He destroyed Pharaoh and for the same reason—they attacked the Jewish people! Russia and Iran will be annihilated by the hand of God as He defends the "apple of his eye"—Israel.

At the present time, Iran's most powerful military force, the Revolutionary Guard, says Tehran will "blow up the heart of Israel" if the Jewish state or the United States attacked Iran." [16]

THE ATTACK ON AMERICA HAS BEGUN!

Do you remember 9/11? Every terrorist who hijacked American commercial airliners and used them as missiles of death were radical Muslims. You can be sure they were quoting the Qur'an, anticipating the appearance of seventy virgins as they crashed into the Twin Towers and killed some three thousand Americans. The 9/11 terrorist attack proved that radical Islam has the will to kill us en masse, they just lack the power. When Iran has the nuclear power, America's security will be in constant and deadly peril.

Paul L. Williams, a former consultant to the FBI on terrorism, indicates that seven cities in America have been targeted by radical Islamic terrorist organizations who are here and who are highly organized and sophisticated enough to execute an attack on seven cities simultaneously. Those cities are New York, Miami, Houston, Las Vegas, Los Angeles, Chicago, and Washington, DC.

A recent headline in *USA Today* was a wake-up call for all Americans. It proved the radical Islamic passion to kill us has not passed nor abated.

The *USA Today* headlines scream "Alleged Terror Threat Seen as 'Most Serious' Since 9/11." [17]

This breaking story was the worst nightmare for the American intelligence community. Najibullah Zazi, an American homegrown terrorist living in the United States, flew from Newark, New Jersey, to Pakistan for terrorist training.

Zazi attracted the FBI's attention with his August 28, 2008, visit to Peshawar, a global crossroads for terrorist groups. After five months of training in the al-Qaeda terrorist camp in Pakistan, Zazi returned to America and morphed from an anonymous Denver airport shuttle driver to the central figure in a national terrorism probe "committed" to attacking the United States by detonating bombs against targets here.

Federal officials warned that sports stadiums, entertainment venues, and other places could be targets of terrorist strikes.

"This is the most serious threat . . . I've seen since 9/11," says Tom Fuentes, a former FBI official who once directed the bureau's operations in Baghdad. "You had a person here who received explosives and weapons training, and he was apparently trying to assemble a team to carry out the operation." [18]

Georgetown University professor Bruce Hoffman, who has examined terrorism issues for three decades said, "For anyone who doubted whether al-Qaeda was still in the picture, this should answer that question." [19]

In addition to the Zazi case, federal prosecutors are charging Jordanian immigrant Hosam Smadi with plotting to blow up a Dallas skyscraper. Zazi may have been in the country legally, but Smadi was not. He was here on an expired visitor's visa. His case highlights the troubling fact that, as the *New York Times* put it, "Eight years after the September 11 terrorist attacks . . . the United States still has no reliable system for verifying that foreign visitors have left the country."

Once again, the outrageous deficiencies of our immigration system are proving to present tremendous national security risks.

PRESIDENT REASSURES MUSLIM WORLD

When President Obama gave his first TV interview as the President of the United States, he chose to do so on an Arab-language satellite network. In his remarks, the President made two assertions that give us an insight to his worldview.

First, the President said he felt his "job" was to communicate "to the Muslim world . . . that the Americans are not your enemy." Why does the President feel he must reassure Muslims that "Americans" are not their enemies?

It was the United States that was attacked on 9/11 by jihadists acting in the name of Islam. America's response to that cowardly act was to send our military not to subjugate Muslims but to liberate millions of them in Iraq and Afghanistan from the rule of tyrants and thugs.

People of both countries were able to vote for the first time in their lives. In Afghanistan today, in those areas where the United States is in control, Muslim girls are permitted to go to school. Where radical Islamists are in control, acid is thrown in the faces of girls who try to go to school, and their classrooms are blown up.

After the 9/11 attack, America went out of its way to ensure that mosques in the United States were safe from any kind of backlash. Throughout the Muslim world, Christians and Jews continue to be persecuted. Jews are not permitted to enter Saudi Arabia lest the soil be contaminated by the soles of their feet. Saudi Arabia has what Hitler was trying to achieve: a Jew-free country. In spite of all the good America has done, the President feels a need to tell the Muslims that we are not their enemy.

The President told his Muslim audience that he had another task. Here is how he put it: "And my job is to communicate to the American people that the Muslim world is filled with extraordinary people who simply want to live their lives and see their children live better lives."

Here's the problem!

Those Muslims who simply want to enjoy peace and quiet are not the problem. It is the Muslims who nurture groups like al-Qaeda, the Taliban, Hamas, Hezbollah, Islamic Jihad, and countless other religious fanatics who matter most. From London to Madrid, Manhattan to Mumbai, Beslan to Buenos Aires, it is those Islamists who have intentionally inflicted death and destruction on helpless civilians in the name of Allah. If only 10 percent of the "Muslim world" supports these murderers, then our enemies number 150 million.

Unfortunately, there is ample evidence that the number is much, much larger. Add to that the vicious Jew-hatred that appears to infect the populations of "moderate" Muslim countries, like Indonesia and Jordan, and the magnitude of our problem becomes obvious.

If I had the opportunity to speak personally to our president, I would make the following statement:

Mr. President, you are our duly elected leader and the leader of the free world. As the spiritual leader of a congregation of some twenty thousand people and many thousands of people across the nation and around the world on global television daily, I have asked my national and international congregation to pray for you, to pray for the members of your family, and to pray for the members of Congress on a daily basis.

Mr. President, your read on Israel is pushing Israel toward a military preemptive strike on Iran's nuclear facilities. That strike could be successful or it could fail. Whatever the result, the price of oil will skyrocket, there will be another war in the Middle East, perhaps nuclear, and American troops will be caught in the middle in Afghanistan. The fragile American economy would crash, and the world as we know it will end.

Mr. President, Iran is beyond the reach of eloquence. We have been talking to Iran thirty years and have absolutely nothing to show for it. The truth is, our "negotiations" have advanced Iran's goals above all else. With each day that passes, Ahmadinejad's regime gets closer to the day when it will be able to transform the Middle East and the world by proudly declaring itself a nuclear power.

We know Iran has lied to us about its "secret" nuclear facilities.

We know it is willing to murder its own citizens in the streets on global television who cry out for freedom when a presidential election has been stolen.

We know Iran is directly responsible for the murder of U.S. troops in Iraq and Afghanistan.

We know Iran's leaders are Shiite radicals who believe an Islamic messiah is coming soon to destroy the infidels (anyone who does not accept Islam) and Iran has a special role to play in forcing their messiah to appear by creating great global chaos.

We know that Ahmadinejad denies the holocaust, while promising his followers that the day is coming when Israel will be "wiped off the map" and America will no longer exist.

Most importantly, we know it is an abdication of a superpower's responsibility to outsource matters of war and peace to another state: Israel.

We know you have given the driver's seat to Prime Minister Benjamin Netanyahu, whom I know personally. He has been in my home and my office on several occasions and I have been in his. He is a man of boundless courage and will defend Israel with every weapon at his disposal. His words are recorded for the world to read, as captured in the headlines of the Atlantic . . .

"STOP IRAN—OR I WILL!"

Mr. President, would it be possible for the two democracies, America and Israel, to join forces to defeat the radical theocratic dictatorship that threatens world peace?

Will we wait until global terrorists, encouraged and emboldened by the trial of KSM in New York City, pour into this country to make bombs or deliver nuclear suitcase bombs via Iran that could kill millions of Americans per blast?

What would it be like if a suitcase nuclear bomb exploded in your city? Discover the truth in the following chapter: "The Day After the Bomb."

Think it can't happen?

Think again!

PART TWO

The Fall of America

FOUR

The Day After the Bomb

I stood on the shores of Normandy Beach where almost ten thousand hopeful, handsome young American soldiers stormed those beaches on June 6, 1944, and sacrificed their all for life, liberty, and the pursuit of happiness.

Those who perished died a horrific death! Standing there, I saw them in the theater of my mind climbing out of more than five thousand ships that covered the English Channel as far as the eye could see. This battle theater stretched for seventy miles, the largest amphibious military operation in the history of warfare. It was the Longest Day and the last day for thousands of America's finest heroes.

They scrambled over the sides of their respective ships on cargo nets into the flat-bottom Higgins boats bound for the shore and the deadly fire of the demons of the Third Reich.

As the small boats plowed their way through the churning tide of the English Channel, thousands of those youthful troops were looking into their last sunrise. Those who had spiritual roots were praying the Lord's Prayer aloud; others were kissing the cross that had been given to them by some praying mother thousands of miles away.

The boats struck the sands of the shore, the front ramp lowered, and many stepped into eternity as German machine gun fire killed them to the last man before they got out of the boat. Survivors leaped over the sides of the boat in full battle gear, while others had a few more moments of precious life as they ran up the beach only to face the unspeakable terror of a beach covered with machine gun crossfire, mortar blasts, and barbed wire strung through long rows of steel crossbars to prevent their progress. The steel crossbars were designed to sink any boat whose captain was foolish enough to attempt a landing at high tide.

The first waves of Americans to reach Omaha Beach were slaughtered. They stained the beaches and shoreline of Normandy with the most precious gift one human being can give another—their life's blood. "Greater love has no one than this, than to lay down one's life for his friends" (John 15:13 NKJV).

They died on those beaches screaming in agony, calling out to God, pleading for a medic to come. Finally, when no one came and death was tugging at their sleeves, they turned to the ultimate source of love and comfort all men know—they cried out in their agony for their mothers.

With a gifted guide giving me every gory and heartbreaking detail of the vicious and historic battle between America's freedom-loving sons and Hitler's Nazis, we climbed the bluffs to the cliffs where Hitler's massive artillery, shrouded in thick concrete walls, blasted their rain of terror and death upon America's sons on that historic day.

Between the monster cannons—which could shoot for miles into the ocean, sinking approaching ships—were concrete fortifications for Nazi machine guns that could fire 1,200 rounds per minute, creating a lethal crossfire with three machine guns in each "nest" of weapons.

I stood in one of those machine gun concrete bunkers staring out at Normandy Beach and marveled that any living soul could make it from the boats, through the barbed wired barriers with crossed steel beams, to climb the bluffs, to fight against impossible odds for the sacred cause of life, liberty, and freedom.

Finally, I left the scene of battle for the cemetery and saw the endless rows of marble white crosses and Stars of David planted in the rich green grass, row upon row upon row as far as the eye could see.

Every cross was some mother's precious son, some child's daddy that would never come home, some wife's husband, someone's brother, some father's son. These people would forever sit at the dinner table looking at a photo of their missing loved one and at his empty chair.

I walked between the rows of fallen heroes, reading their names and observing their dates of birth. Most were between the ages of eighteen and twenty years. They had everything to live for, and they willingly laid down their lives on the altar of sacrifice that the next generation might live in freedom. Freedom isn't free!

I sat down on a marble bench and stared at the ocean of human sacrifice before me in Normandy, and in the theater of my mind, I was transported to another battlefield. It was not on foreign soil!

It was a battlefield in the streets of America between the trained terrorists of radical Islam and America. It was a battle for survival and, unlike WWII and Normandy, America was stumbling in a politically correct fog, not even aware that the do-or-die battle had begun.

People in our government refuse to use the word *terrorist,* and our national leadership is bowing to the leaders of foreign countries who are funding the war to destroy us. War criminals are being tried under civilian law in New York City, giving the radical Islamic terrorists a global platform to preach their "kill for Allah" theology and vomit their anti-American and anti-Israeli venom to the four winds of the earth.

There are now about seven thousand headstones in the cemetery in this battle for America with radical Islam. Four thousand in Iraq and Afghanistan and three thousand in New York, victims of 9/11, murdered by radical Muslims quoting the Qur'an as they flew their missiles of death into the Twin Towers.

Now, tragically and unbelievably, thirteen more brave warriors have fallen at Fort Hood at the hand of a radical Muslim, and our leaders are saying we shouldn't race to judgment on the U.S. Army Major Hasan, who slaughtered and wounded our troops.

How many thousands more will fall before our leaders snap out of this politically correct fog and admit we are at war? Will they wait until a series of nuclear dirty bombs set off at one time in seven cities send millions of Americans to their deaths?

Think it can't happen?

Think again!

Radical terrorists have been slipping across our open borders for years to form sleeper cells across the nation. They have been recruited from our colleges and universities to be trained in the terrorist boot camps of Pakistan in the art of making bombs, shooting automatic weapons, becoming masters of murder and mayhem, all to return home and kill innocent Americans at some appointed date in the future to please their Islamo-fascist masters.

History in the future may call it "The Fifty-Year War" between America and radical Islam, but its final battles will be fought in the streets and cities of this nation. The jihad against America began on 9/11 . . . and it will not end until America defeats radical Islam or the flag of Islam flies over the White House.

HOW IRAN'S ATTACK ON AMERICA COULD BEGIN!

I have on my desk an intelligence report stating that Iran has very probably developed something that is called an electromagnetic pulse (EMP) designed to be used against America in time of war. The threat has been considered so viable that the Senate Judiciary Subcommittee on Terrorism Technology and Homeland Security, chaired by Senator Jon Kyl of Arizona, held a hearing on the electromagnetic pulse threat against America.

Here is what the EMP does!

This electromagnetic blanket does not kill people; it kills electrons. In short, it stops every form of electricity instantly and for months, maybe years.[1]

Here's how it could be used against America in warfare with terrorists on the ground setting off a series of nuclear bombs after the EMP is exploded in the atmosphere over America.

This is how it works! A fake satellite crossing over America 280 miles above the earth suddenly explodes over the Great Plains of the United States, releasing several pounds of enriched plutonium, blanketing the United States of America with gamma rays. Instantly, in one-billionth of a second, all electrical power is cut off and cut off for months.

No lights, no refrigeration will work in your home; every ounce of food you have in your freezer will rot. Your car won't start because it needs electricity. Trucks won't start, meaning transportation bringing you everything you use will stop. All machinery stops. The radio and television stations will go off the air. Planes that are in flight will crash because their electronic systems will fail. The missile systems will fail to function. We will cease to be a superpower in a fraction of a second.

The President cannot communicate with his military people in the field because the phones do not work. America's refineries will shut down. There will be no gas or oil. The gas at the service station can't be used because those pumps get the gas out of the ground with electricity. Computers won't work, meaning city, state, and government offices will be shut down. There will be a nationwide food and gas shortage within a few days.

You think that can't happen?

Think again!

There are enemies of the United States who have been planning this for years. It's not new. Only now, rogue states have the ability to put this weapon to use, and it will happen unless Iran is stopped from its maniacal dreams of global domination via nuclear power.

The *Congressional Report* reads: "Even primitive Scud missiles could be used for this purpose (electronic blankets). And top U.S. intelligence officials reminded members of Congress that there is a glut of these missiles on the world market.

"They are currently being bought and sold for about $100,000 apiece."[2]

Think about it!

This great, magnificent nation that is so technically oriented has created an Achilles' heel—electricity. With one $100,000 missile fired from the deck of a ship two hundred miles offshore and a few pounds of enriched plutonium exploding over the United States . . . in a fraction of a second, we will be living in the nineteenth century.

THE DAY OF THE BOMB

What will it be like for *you* in your city the day terrorists set off a nuclear 10-kiloton uranium fission nuclear bomb without warning at or about ground level? What difference will it make?

A ground-burst nuclear weapon would spread blast damage and fire over a smaller area than an airburst nuclear bomb released from a highrise office building. A nuclear bomb released from a high-rise office building would have far greater radioactive fallout and would kill more people than the initial blast. On the day of the bomb, the way the wind is blowing would determine who lives and who dies!

The nuclear express is coming!

President Ahmadinejad of Iran has faithfully promised all Islamic terrorist groups that he will share his nuclear power with them to conquer the infidels.

Ahmadinejad's friendship with fellow dictator Hugo Chavez of Venezuela would make it a piece of cake to send dirty bombs via ship to Venezuela, then to cross them into America by walking them across the Rio Grande with the legions who cross on a regular basis without detection.

The Islamic terrorist cells that have the ability to make and set off nuclear dirty bombs are not coming—they are already here. They are trained! They are ready! They are willing! *You* and your family are the targets!

A former consultant to the FBI on terrorism, Paul L. Williams, indicates that there is empirical proof that al-Qaeda possesses nukes. British agents posing as recruits infiltrated al-Qaeda training camps. In another instance, an al-Qaeda operative was arrested at Ramallah with a tactical nuke strapped to his back.

If you are having trouble believing that teams of terrorists maintaining a nuclear weapon in the United States wouldn't be detected, think the unthinkable!

Williams reports that there isn't just one team, but at least seven.[3] They are working within mosques and Islamic centers, and in the United States a federal judge will not provide the FBI or law enforcement agents with a warrant to search a mosque or an Islamic center for any reason since such places are listed as "houses of worship."[4]

Williams also states that seven cities in America have been targeted by terrorist as prime targets. Those cities are identified as New York, Miami, Houston, Las Vegas, Los Angeles, Chicago, and Washington, DC. The attacks are designed to occur simultaneously in these seven cities.

Before you breathe a sigh of relief and say "I don't live in one of those major cities," do you remember Oklahoma City and the Murrah Building? The truth is, jihad came to America on 9/11, and every city in America is a potential target.

Headlines of a recent *USA Today* express the worst nightmare of America's intelligence community. Homegrown Islamists are being recruited by foreign governments hostile to the United States, trained in terrorist boot camps, and returned to America with bomb-making knowledge, automatic weapons skills, and a burning desire to kill Americans. That would be *you* and *your* family!

Recently federal officials unsealed terrorist charges against eight new suspects that say they were key actors in a recruitment effort that led young Americans to join al-Shabaab, a violent insurgent group in Somalia with ties to al-Qaeda. The recruitment operation largely focused on Somali-American men from the Minnesota area. The recruits attended training camps in Somalia run by Somali, Arab, and Western instructors who taught them to use machine guns and rocket-propelled grenades and indoctrinated them with anti-American and anti-Israeli beliefs, according to the court documents.

There is evidence the aggressive recruitment of young American Muslims continues. Recently, the Nevada Highway Patrol stopped a rental car carrying five young Somali men who said they were en route to a wedding in San Diego. A lawyer with knowledge of the case said three of the men soon crossed the border and boarded an airplane for destinations unknown.[5]

The day of the bomb will begin like any other day. You will take your children to school, your spouse will go to his or her job, you will arrive at your office and send an email to your child at the university who is trying to cram six years of education into four, as you begin your daily rat race to pay your ever-escalating taxes to fulfill Washington's never-ending pipe dreams.

Suddenly the lights go out, as does everything electrical! Cars and buses are stopping in the middle of the street. People are standing in groups with puzzled faces, asking each other, "What's going on?" "Why is no one's car working?" They reach for their cells phones; they don't work!

Minutes later, there is a thunderous BLAST! The noise is deafening! You see buildings melting like butter before your eyes, now blazing in what appears to be a spontaneous inferno.

Then you see the mushroom cloud. It's surreal!

This can't be happening in America. The unthinkable has become reality. The unsinkable ship has just hit the iceberg. Jihad has come to *you,* your children, your family; and in seconds, your life is forever changed.

How will you get in touch with your children?

With your spouse? With your child at the university? You can't; all electronic communication is over!

There will be no warning the Day of the Bomb!

First, catching a city by surprise would increase the destruction and chaos. Second, advance warning would put the mission at risk and have the plot foiled by the FBI before it released its reign of terror. Third, there is no reason to believe that terrorists with "loose nukes" would have only one.

They could set off one bomb and claim that many more were coming, spreading national panic and creating an environment for terrified politicians to bow to the demands of radical Islam.

The terrorists have all the advantages. They know when, they know where, and they know how the attack will take place. It will be planned to kill as many as possible. These attacks are meant to break the will of the American people so they won't be able to resist the coming demands that radical Islam will make on the American people to live by the law of Sharia.

Maybe the target will be one of the most prestigious high-rise office buildings in your city, which has proven to be a prime target for radical Muslims in times past. The Twin Towers were selected because they represented American power and wealth.

Maybe the target will be a major shopping center during the holiday season, when it's packed to the walls with unsuspecting Americans who have lived every day of their lives in absolute freedom. It is simply beyond belief that jihad could reach out and destroy their magical lives in an instant.

Just like it was beyond belief that the *Titanic* could ever sink!

Perhaps the seven targets in seven different cities would be seven professional football stadiums across the country, packed with hundreds of thousands of people cheering for their teams to get to the Super Bowl. These cheering fans would never suspect that a very powerful theocratic dictatorship in Iran had the power of nuclear arms and the passion for martyrdom to attempt to crush America in one infamous day.

Think it can't happen?

Think again!

If a bomb in Washington, DC, is successful and the leadership of our country is killed or out of contact, who will lead us? With all electronic systems malfunctioning and without the ability to communicate with the people across the nation, with panic in the streets, with supermarkets filled with screaming, shoving, and shouting Americans who fear extreme hunger or even starvation for their children, who will bring food and water to the cities in devastation? With gun-toting mobs robbing banks, stores, and citizens at will, who will bring law and order? Who will bring medical supplies?

Do you remember Hurricane Katrina? There were people in Louisiana without food, water, shelter, and medical attention for days. Dead people were lying facedown in the street. Dead bodies were floating facedown in the canals.

This chaos and suffering from one hurricane in one city. What happens when America is hit from coast to coast at one time with nuclear disaster that leaves millions dead and millions more dying from radiation?

Who will make the decisions to chart our course from this national disaster? Whom will we attack? Because these nuclear dirty bombs will be set off by individual terrorist cells, there is no nation we can attack. There is no military solution for terrorism!

The grisly effects of a 10-kiloton ground burst are very clear. One mile in all directions of the downtown area with the high-rise office building, the football stadium, or the shopping mall that was the epicenter of the blast would be totally contaminated.

The massive buildings would be piles of rubble ten to fifteen feet high for one mile north, south, east, and west. There will no human survivors in that one-mile circle of death.

Outside that one-mile circle leveled by the blast, people will be wounded by the flying debris, by instantaneous fires that are an unstoppable inferno, and severe radiation. They stand little chance of survival.

It will be days before emergency workers can get to them because any downtown hospitals would be blasted into rubble, lying in ruins. If emergency workers were instantly available, the victims' burns and acute radiation exposure would require intensive and sustained medical treatment to offer any chance of survival.

Downwind from the detonation point, the cloud of radioactive debris will began to spread. It is the cloud of death! Its shape and size would depend on wind and rain conditions, but within one day, people who live within ten square miles who do not find shelter or flee within hours would receive a lethal dose of radiation. In a city like New York or Los Angeles that could represent more than a million people.

Because there is little that can be done for those in and around the blast zone, medical responders will probably divide the city into zones and concentrate on the population downwind from the epicenter, where the radiation cloud was reduced, thus giving them a greater chance to save some. Those in the one-mile epicenter zone will be written off as hopeless, as will most of the people located on the edge of the one-mile blast zone.

In the months and years following the attack, civic leaders would face this dilemma. If they allowed the residents to return early, those residents would experience a higher cancer rate than the rest of the population. Those unwilling to accept the higher cancer rate would have to abandon their homes. The center of the city would remain too radioactive to build on for a year or more.[6]

As this book goes to print, the United States government has no such plan to protect the citizens of this nation from the impact and effects of a nuclear attack!

I'm confident that if a nuclear attack happens with this administration, and if there are enough people left in Congress to vote on a given bill, someone will quickly craft a bill calling for "the rich" to pay for the damages created by the nuclear attack and someone else will craft a bill blaming George W. Bush because the attack happened!

And I am confident that, after the nuclear attack, Congress will have some committee to write a long and politically correct masterpiece titled "What We Wish We Had Done Before the Bomb!"

For the time being the USS *Titanic* sails into the dark night without binoculars, without the proper flares, without enough lifeboats to prevent disaster, getting intelligence reports from a rope too short to get accurate information, while the band plays on and the iceberg gets closer—all while our leadership continues telling all Americans: "All is well!"

If the headline in your newspaper reads "Iran Has the Bomb!" you should do these things to prepare yourself and your family to live in a world where a nuclear attack is a very real possibility.

1. Have the ability with your own transportation to evacuate the city. Be sure to evacuate immediately, traveling perpendicular to the plume of the blast. Said another way, when you see the mushroom cloud forming in the sky, leave your city in the opposite direction.

   Remember: More people will die from the radiation in that cloud than from the nuclear blast. The radiation can kill you through either radiation burns that will not heal and/or by placing you at much higher risk for cancer for the rest of your life. The radiation is *deadly!*

2. If you are trapped in the city and can't evacuate, get below ground level and stay there for at least three days. If your house has a basement, you are blessed.

   If your house has no basement, be prepared to seal your house or apartment around the windows and doors with duct tape. This will greatly reduce the radiation exposure factor for you and your family.

3. You should have enough food and water stored to supply your family for that three-day period at the very least. Storing enough food for longer periods is advisable because if there are multiple attacks or threats of multiple attacks on America, gas and oil may well be rationed by the government, making it impossible for trucks to bring food and supplies to your local supermarket for days.

4. Get a supply of alternative energy, such as batteries for flashlights and generators for electricity; lighting candles is better than sitting endless hours in the dark.

5. Get a battery-powered radio that will pick up civil defense messages when civilization gets back on its feet.

6. I have been asked this question many times and it's an intelligent question: "Why should we be concerned about Iran getting the bomb? What's the difference between Iran having a nuclear bomb and Russia having a nuclear bomb? Russia has had it for years, and there has not been a problem."

   The answer: "During the years of the Cold War, America and Russia had a mutual understanding that if there was a nuclear attack by either side, the other side would execute the MAD Policy! MAD is the acronym for Mutually Assured Destruction.

   Basically, the Russians and Americans had reached a common ground of understanding that any attack by the other would guarantee that the one who launched the attack would be exterminated.

   The simple truth is that when two rational groups of people come to a common understanding, coexistence can happen.

   That's exactly the problem with the leadership of Iran; they are not rational. They are religious fanatics who believe that if they start a global war and their nation and millions of their own people are killed in a nuclear war, they die as martyrs and go immediately to heaven.

Remember: by their own confession, they love death more than life.

They are not afraid to die; they're looking forward to the day. Remember the words of Major Hasan to his fellow radical Islamic terrorist friend just before he murdered thirteen American soldiers at Fort Hood: "I can't wait to join you in the afterlife."

The president of Iran has promised to "wipe Israel off the map" and has threatened a nuclear holocaust. He has also stated that he can see the day when there will no longer be a United States of America. He is a clear and present danger to our national security.

He has promised radical Islamic terrorist groups that he will share with them the nuclear power Iran is developing. It is happening as this book goes to press.

The greatest challenge for our government is not health care: it's stopping Iran from getting nuclear weapons. The only way to win a nuclear war is to make sure it never starts!

The day Iran obtains nuclear weapons, it's a game changer for planet Earth! Life will never be the same!

7. When you pray, pray for America! If we do not use our freedom to defend our freedom, we will lose our freedom.

One of the fundamental truths the Founding Fathers established was the principle that debt made all men slaves. Solomon recorded in his writings: ". . . the borrower *is* servant to the lender" (Proverbs 22:7 NKJV).

America today is swimming in an ocean of debt, and yet we continue to spend money we don't have and bury our children and grandchildren under a mountain of debt making economic slaves of them all.

Soon other nations like China will call for the dumping of the U.S. dollar as the currency for international payment of debt. The nations of the world will respond favorably, and within months, you will see the contents of the next chapter become reality: the *death of the dollar.*

FIVE

Death of the Dollar

The two most powerful symbols of American power in the world are the nation's military might and its economic strength. America's military might has been demonstrated numerous times in the past century, from its rescue of European democracies in World War I, to its defeat of the Axis powers in World War II, to its victory in the long Cold War against Soviet expansionism. In 1991, an American-led coalition defeated one of the largest armies in the world in a six-week air attack capped by a four-day ground assault, ejecting Iraq from Kuwait. Twelve years later, a smaller U.S.-led coalition defeated the Iraqi army again, this time in only three weeks, toppling the government. When it comes to military might, the United States is a hyper-power with no equal.

But a nation's military might is founded on its economic strength, for it is a nation's economy that pays for its military forces, their equipment, and training. Here again, the American economy has been the global leader since World War II, to the point that people casually compare the American currency to a deity, referring to the "almighty dollar." There have been other economic heavyweights in world history. In the ancient world, the Greek drachma was "almighty." In their own large spheres of influence, the Chinese liang and Islamic dinar reigned supreme. Then in the modern world, the British pound sterling was an international power for over two centuries.[1] But the fate of the British pound sterling presents a warning sign to the United States. The dominant global currency until World War II, the pound lost that status by 1945; with that development, the United Kingdom lost its position as a global leader, economically and militarily.[2]

The United States is not immune to a similar fate. The clearest threat to America's ability to remain strong, economically and militarily, is the danger posed by the nation's fiscal policies—or lack thereof. The dollar's decline as the world's reserve currency has been driven by decisions and choices made by political leaders, both in terms of changing the foundation of the nation's currency and in pursuing budgetary policies that have led to skyrocketing budget deficits and out-of-this-world debt. In this chapter, we will explore the *twin problems* of *currency health* and *budget health*. But before we can truly understand these twin problems, we first need a brief history on: How did we get where we are now? Where are we going? And why does it matter? The story told here should be of grave concern to every individual who cares about the future health of the nation.

A BRIEF HISTORY OF THE DOLLAR

To understand the current danger to the dollar, we must first understand its history. The dollar has been the world's reserve currency since the end of World War II. It is part of nearly 90 percent of all foreign exchange transactions. Wherever currencies are traded, they are typically converted to dollars first, testifying to the central place of the dollar in the world. This global currency performs several valuable services for the world economy, including serving as a medium of exchange, a store of value, and a unit of account. In other words, a global currency allows people to agree on prices, preserve savings, and measure the worth of objects or services.[3]

Americans have always been suspicious of central banks. The first Bank of the United States was established by Alexander Hamilton, President George Washington's Secretary of the Treasury, but it died in 1811 when Congress voted not to renew its charter. Congress reversed itself a few years later, chartering a Second Bank of the United States in 1816, but President Andrew Jackson saw it as a tool of elite financial interests and made war against the bank, ultimately destroying it. There followed about eighty years of periodic bank panics and financial crises, with a federal government incapable of dealing effectively with the economic disruptions. Things got bad enough in the Panic of 1907 that political leaders turned to banker J. P. Morgan to bail out the system.[4]

At the same time, Americans were arguing over the existence of central banks, they also argued over the foundation of the dollars that would be placed in those banks. Early Americans constantly debated the question of paper money versus gold and silver coins. The idea behind a "gold standard" for currency is that a nation should fix its currency to a specific amount of gold. In theory, any person could go to a bank and redeem his money in gold. This system restrains inflation, since gold can flow in and out of a country depending on how much money is created, and whether that money is seen as credible. But this system also makes it very difficult to fight major wars, and it is no accident that inflation is associated with warfare, as governments print large amounts of paper currency to fund the war effort. President Abraham Lincoln, for example, suspended the gold guarantee for bank notes and printed large quantities of "greenbacks"—paper money not backed by anything but the government's word—to pay for the Union campaign in the Civil War. Prices rose 74 percent from 1861 to 1864, the sharpest spike in inflation since the Revolutionary War. After the war was over, the greenbacks were gradually retired and the nation returned to the gold standard, and over the next two decades, in a period known as the "great deflation," prices fell to their prewar level.[5]

The gold standard remained the global standard, which benefited Great Britain and its British pound sterling. But in the wake of the Panic of 1907, the United States responded by moving toward the creation of another central bank—the Federal Reserve. The Federal Reserve Act, signed by President Woodrow Wilson in December 1913, created a new central bank, composed of a series of regional banks coordinated by a national board of commercial bankers. As European nations abandoned gold again to finance World War I, the American dollar increasingly became a currency of choice in international trade, and the Federal Reserve became the "lender of last resort." Foreigners knew that when they did business in dollars there was an institution backing up those transactions on behalf of American commercial banks.[6]

The Great Depression and World War II wreaked havoc on the world financial system. In the United States, the run on the banks in the early 1930s led to large-scale business failures and high unemployment. Customers demanded gold for their dollars, prompting President Franklin Roosevelt to take the dollar off the gold standard, declare a bank holiday, and attempt the confiscation of privately held gold. Roosevelt issued an executive order that stated, "All persons are hereby required to deliver on or before May 1, 1933, to a Federal Reserve Bank or a branch or agency thereof or to any member bank of the Federal Reserve System all gold coin, gold bullion and gold certificates now owned by them"—to hand over, in fact, their property. The government paid citizens dollars at the official exchange rate of $20.67 an ounce, then devalued the dollar 69 percent by raising the exchange rate to $35 an ounce in 1934.[7] World War II completed the process of devastating the world economy, but by this time the relative health of the American economy—compared to those in war-torn Europe and Asia—left the dollar the king of the world.

The United States became the dominant economic power in 1944. It was then, at a meeting of delegates from forty-four nations in Bretton Woods, New Hampshire, that the dollar became the world's key reserve currency. Famed British economist John Maynard Keynes proposed a new global financial system in which a global currency called a "bancor" would replace gold. But the United States was the real world power as the war began to draw to a close, and it would control events at Bretton Woods. Rejecting Keynes's proposal, the delegates instead agreed to new plan for the dollar to be fixed to gold at a rate of $35 an ounce, with all other currencies in turn fixed to the dollar, the exchange rate depending on how strong the various countries' economies were. Washington agreed to convert foreign central bank dollar holdings into gold upon request. Thus, the dollar would enforce stability in the world by keeping foreign currencies at fixed values, while the dollar itself would remain stable and legitimate by being anchored to gold. In theory, other countries could not expand their money supply irresponsibly by printing currency, since that would undermine their currency's exchange rate with the dollar. Neither could the United States print more money that it could redeem with gold. The Bretton Woods agreement also created the International Monetary Fund (IMF), which had the power to decide whether a country could change its fixed rate against the dollar. Thus, as World War II ended, the American dollar achieved unprecedented status as the one currency against which all others would be measured.[8]

But the seeds of the dollar's decline were planted even before the dollar achieved its dominant status. While John Maynard Keynes did not win the battle at Bretton Woods, he won the larger war when it came to economic policy. The Great Depression ended the earlier economic paradigm that saw balanced budgets as the appropriate goal for the federal government. This older paradigm was seen by Progressive economists as part of a larger Calvinist vision in which individuals were expected to practice self-denial, sacrifice, and delayed gratification, thinking that one's true reward was in the future—in the long run. Keynes is famous for remarking, "In the long run we are all dead." The important thing, he purported, was to enjoy life *now*. Pleasure should be pursued, and suffering is unnecessary. Instead of delayed gratification, we should embrace self-gratification. Part and parcel with this new philosophy was a government program of more liberal credit. Americans could now pursue the "American Dream" of home ownership, as home mortgages moved from seven- and ten-year limits to an astonishing (for the time) twenty years. Consumption became the popular economic philosophy. The suffering and sacrifice of World War II—not just in battle, but also on the home front—solidified this perspective. High personal savings rates during the war led to pent-up consumer demand and massive consumption once the war was over, resulting in inflation. The combination of Roosevelt's large New Deal entitlement programs and the large defense budgets—required by the new Cold War for postwar demobilization that quickly transitioned to a large-standing military—placed the nation's fiscal health in jeopardy.[9]

In the years following Bretton Woods, the key question was whether the United States could continue to convert dollars to gold on demand, and for nearly two decades, the system worked. Inflation and interest rates were relatively low, and the American economy grew at an average annual rate of 6.6 percent. But the world economy grew faster than the supply of gold. Budget deficits began to rise as the United States helped reconstruct Western Europe under the Marshall Plan, then served as the West's primary military defender by trying to contain the Soviet Union, fighting wars in Korea and Vietnam, all the while supporting large New Deal–inspired social programs. The dominant programmatic liberal governing philosophy culminated in President Lyndon Johnson's Great Society, in which the nation embraced massive new spending in such areas as Medicare and Medicaid, student loans, and low-income housing. As the United States printed or borrowed more money to pay the cost of these programs, leading to greater inflation, it also sent billions of dollars overseas for which it had no gold. Other countries became concerned that America would not be able to exchange all of those dollars for gold. A bank run could devastate the world economy.[10]

If the 1944 Bretton Woods agreement signaled the dollar's rise to dominance, its decline could easily be identified as beginning in August 1971. By then, foreigners held more than $45 billion, even though the United States had only $10 billion in gold reserves. In response to this overvaluing of the dollar, President Richard Nixon took the dollar off the gold standard, suspending the right of foreign central banks to convert their dollars to gold. This move, intended at first to be temporary, ended the Bretton Woods agreement and freed other currencies to trade against the dollar and each other. The Smithsonian Agreement replaced Bretton Woods several months later, devaluing the dollar 7.9 percent to $38 an ounce of gold. Just over a year after that, the government devalued the dollar again—11 percent, to $42 an ounce of gold. In March 1973, officials determined that the system was dead, and they abandoned the gold guarantee completely. From now on all currencies, including the dollar, would "float" against each other, finding their own value in the currency market. The only thing backing the dollar now was the faith of the world that the American government was able and willing to honor all dollars. Unrestrained by limited gold supplies or any other tangible object, the government could now print and borrow more dollars than ever.[11]

With Nixon's move, the value of the dollar would be determined by the foreign exchange market. Currency traders would examine the nation's economic policies, looking at such things as budget and trade deficits, interest rates, and inflation, none of which was healthy in the United States in the 1970s. One aftereffect of Nixon's decision was OPEC's 1973 oil boycott, which quadrupled the price of oil. Inflation erodes the value of the dollar, and people do not want to buy dollars when inflation is higher than the interest paid on bonds. Oil, however, is traded in dollars, so a decline in the dollar's value also leads to less money for oil. Using American support for Israel in the Yom Kippur War as their pretext, Arab oil countries compensated for inflation by raising oil prices. The result was even higher inflation (12 percent) and a recession, with unemployment hitting 9 percent—a combination of factors that led to the "stagflation" of the late 1970s. President Jimmy Carter bemoaned the declining dollar in his infamous "crisis of confidence" speech in 1979. During the era of the gold standard, the annual inflation rate was a mere 0.3 percent. In other words, during this era the dollar declined in value at an annual rate of just 0.3 percent. Since moving off the gold standard, a process that began with Roosevelt, inflation has averaged an annual rate more than ten times its gold standard average.[12]

The Federal Reserve, led by Chairman Paul Volcker, responded to Carter's crisis of confidence by dramatically raising interest rates to crush inflation, which peaked at 13 percent. Interest rates approached an unheard-of 20 percent at this time, and unemployment in the ensuing recession exceeded 10 percent. The combination of President Ronald Reagan's tax cuts and Paul Volcker's interest rate hikes worked. Inflation eventually fell to 4 percent, and the stock market began a quarter-century surge that saw the Dow Industrials rise from below 800 to over 14,000. The end of the Cold War and the collapse of the Soviet bloc opened up new markets, solidifying again the dollar's place in the global economy.[13]

However, the prosperity of the late twentieth century hid lingering and persistent weaknesses in the American economy. The tech-stock bubble that burst in 2000 segued directly into a real estate bubble that collapsed with even greater ferocity in 2006. Following a public philosophy that preached home ownership for all—the American Dream—the Federal Reserve kept interest rates exceptionally low and encouraged the development and use of subprime loans to people who had a weak or troubled credit history—another example of Keynes's belief that consumption is good. Many people believed that the nation had entered a new period of "riskless risk," in which housing prices would stay high permanently and homes could be used as short-term investments.[14] The resulting housing crash and loss of confidence in the credit markets had worldwide consequences, as the nation entered what has come to be known as the Great Recession.

By taking the United States off the gold standard, Nixon allowed the government to print large sums of money. The foreign market for those dollars has enabled the nation to borrow money overseas to increase government spending while also cutting taxes—the ultimate example of eating our cake and having it too. That ability has always depended on overseas markets thinking the United States has a sound economy and has not gone too deeply into debt.[15] The financial crisis that hit in 2008 called these assumptions into question, and the result has been a dramatic decline in the value of the dollar. That decline is not all bad. A lower dollar allows American exports to be less expensive overseas, which could aid American manufacturing, perhaps narrowing the trade deficit.

Of course, this also means that imported goods will be more expensive, as will trips to foreign vacation spots.[16] More important, though, the current decline is tied to the fiscal consequences of the financial crisis, consequences that have their roots in earlier decisions.

We've just seen a brief history of the American dollar. Budget deficits and the national debt have come up several times in this history. Before we can understand the *current* danger America faces, we need to take one more trip down the road of history to focus on *budget politics*.

A BRIEF HISTORY OF THE NATIONAL DEBT

There is nothing new about a national debt. The nation was founded in debt necessary to fight the War of Independence. Debt is a completely constitutional phenomenon, for the Constitution grants Congress the power "to borrow Money on the credit of the United States."[17] America's first and greatest Secretary of the Treasury, Alexander Hamilton, said, "A national debt, if it is not excessive, will be to us a national blessing."[18] The obvious question, of course, is how we define "excessive," but Hamilton skillfully used debt management and the creation of a national bank to place the new nation on a firm fiscal foundation.

Battles Over Debt

Just as early American history saw numerous battles over gold, silver, greenbacks, and national banks, so did those battles include fights over debt. The general pattern in American history has been that the national debt rose in times of war and then declined when the war was over. President Andrew Jackson actually succeeded in retiring the national debt completely in 1835, the only president who has accomplished that feat. Unfortunately, the budget surplus and increased money supply that ensued led to increased inflation and speculation. Jackson fought this early real estate bubble by ordering the government to accept only gold and silver in payment for land. Land prices fell, people defaulted on loans, and Wall Street experienced its first great crash, leading to a depression in 1837. The resulting seventy-two-month economic contraction was the longest one in American history, and it destroyed the reelection chances of Jackson's handpicked successor, Martin Van Buren.[19]

The greatest crisis the country had ever faced led to the highest debt up to that time. The debt rose to unheard of levels as Lincoln used deficit spending to pursue the Union effort in the Civil War. Sitting at $2.76 billion in 1866, the debt was forty-two times what it had been just six years earlier. For the next twenty-eight years, however, the government ran budget surpluses in a largely successful effort to reduce the debt, and by the time the depression of 1893 hit, the debt had been reduced by two thirds, dropping to under $1 billion. Even with that depression and more expansive (and thus expensive) foreign policies under presidents William McKinley and Theodore Roosevelt, the national debt remained stable, even declining as a percentage of gross national product (GNP).[20]

It is important to note that the principal revenue source for the federal budget during this time was not a personal income tax. The income tax had a brief early life for a few years during and after the Civil War, but the Supreme Court eventually declared it unconstitutional. The functions of the federal government were capably funded through tariffs and excise taxes.

The First Income Tax

The cause of the income tax was picked up again first by Populists and then by Progressive-era reformers. The same political faction that established the Federal Reserve also pushed for a constitutional amendment making an income tax legitimate. One month before Woodrow Wilson took office, the Sixteenth Amendment was adopted. The main argument for an income tax was based less on government revenue than it was on social engineering. The primary goal of income tax cheerleaders was to change the distribution of wealth. This was true both for the personal income tax and for the corporate income tax. One reason for the lack of political opposition to the income tax was the fact that the original model affected only 2 percent of the population. As much as 98 percent of families were exempted, either due to the high income level taxed or such features as the marital deduction. Tax rates ranged from a low of 1 percent on incomes above $3,000 to a high of 7 percent on incomes over $500,000 (and keep in mind that these are 1913 dollars—again, 98 percent of Americans were not affected).[21]

Once in place, however, funding streams like an income tax are hard to remove. The core impulse of Progressive reformers at the turn of the century was a suspicion of representative democracy and the constitutional system that governed it. Progressive leaders distrusted the popular will, especially as it was manifested in vigorous political parties and big-city political machines. At the same time, Progressives such as Woodrow Wilson believed that the constitutional doctrine of separation of powers was the central defect of the American political system, since it made rapid change difficult. Thus, Progressive reformers sought to distance the popular will from political power by creating new bureaucratic institutions that would allow public issues to be decided and managed by professional experts—technocrats who knew what was right for the nation and could manage it for the common good. Democratic responsiveness was devalued in favor of management by experts who could institute necessary change without the burden of politics—including people who know what the "appropriate" level of wealth is for everyone and who used the income tax code to pursue that goal. Liberal theory sought to raise revenues by raising marginal rates on the incomes of the rich, even as the rich tended to find ways to shelter that income. With the income tax in place, the revenue structure of the federal budget changed from a bias toward tariffs to one dominated by the income tax. Tariffs and excise taxes have moved from providing more than 90 percent of the federal revenues to less than 10 percent today, while income taxes quickly moved to a dominant role in the tax code as early as 1920, and it has been that way ever since. World War I prompted more borrowing and taxing, as spending and the national debt both skyrocketed, but the new income tax was able to produce revenue very quickly.[22]

It is here that John Maynard Keynes reenters our story. For most of American history up to the Great Depression, the standard practice was to increase the national debt to deal with wars or depressions, but then work to draw down that debt (through balanced budgets or budget surpluses) when those times were over. The Great Depression, however, changed that understanding, and the dominant objective of the federal government since then has been to avoid a repeat of that economic disaster. The pay-as-you-go philosophy was abandoned in favor of managed deficit spending. It is common for contemporary fans of balanced budgets to compare the government and the family. Families are told to spend only what they have, or they will have to borrow from someone else, putting themselves in debt. In the same way, we should expect the federal government to spend only what it takes in. Keynes, however, argued that families and the government are not the same things, for families must borrow from others, but a nation can borrow from itself. Thus, deficits are not necessarily bad, and the national debt does not really matter. The result of this economic philosophy was a change in political practice to use higher taxes and higher spending—not to balance the budget or pay down the debt, but to fund popular social programs and appeal to different segments of the population through fiscal policy. Political leaders use the tax code and government programs to give favors to interest groups, none of whom is terribly interested in cutting anything. Even though the Great Depression ended not through social programs, but through World War II, when the war was over, the government's priority was not debt reduction, but management of its new programs.[23]

John Steele Gordon ably summarizes the weaknesses of this system, all of which revolve around human nature. First, the federal government is incapable of controlling a very complex, dynamic, and unpredictable economic system. The law of unintended consequences often rears its ugly head. For example, in 1947 Congress exempted company-provided health insurance from income taxes, causing a large number of people to stop caring as much about health care costs, since their insurance was provided and often paid by their employer. This seemingly innocent element of public policy, coupled with the addition of Medicare and Medicaid in the 1960s, led to the exploding costs of health care we experience today—prompting a major effort by the federal government to control costs through massive health care reform that are largely an unintended and unforeseen development of public policy. Another example of this inability is the luxury tax on boats and airplanes imposed by Congress in 1990. Designed to bring in $16 million, it actually brought in far less, because wealthy individuals simply stopped buying boats and planes, resulting in layoffs in those industries.[24]

Second, the government lacks timely and reliable data to make decisions. It does not know the nation is in a recession for several months, and economic data is always being updated with new information, making the old data used to make policy decisions outdated. Economic theories often assume perfect information, and such a thing simply does not exist.

Third, it is a fact of political life that no elected politician wants to pursue unpopular policies during bad economic times, even if those policies are wise. Politicians are ambitious individuals who always seek re-election, and it is a rare bird that is willing to take the fall for a tough decision. But spending programs create interest groups that seek to expand and perpetuate those programs at the cost of the nation's fiscal health.[25]

President Ronald Reagan succeeded in lowering income tax rates, making tax cuts one of the signature issues of the last thirty years. But despite a more conservative political philosophy, preaching balanced budgets and cuts in government programs, more and more spending is automatic, geared toward huge untouchable entitlements like Social Security and Medicare that are largely beyond political control. The result is ever-higher deficits as the government spends more money on programs the tax system cannot fund. To put the situation in perspective, the 2009 federal budget *deficit* was larger than the entire federal *budget* in 1993, just sixteen years earlier. And increased deficits lead to spiraling debt. It took the government until 1962 to accumulate $300 billion of debt, most of it to fight wars. In the forty-seven years since then, the debt has grown *thirty-nine times* that amount.[26]

This fiscal train wreck has exacerbated the problems with the dollar that are spelled out in the earlier section of this chapter. With the background for these twin problems now explained—the currency health and the budget health (or lack thereof)—we can turn our attention to the most important questions: Why does it matter, and where are we going? What are the dangers facing contemporary America, and what are the larger consequences of this present crisis?

CURRENT DANGERS: HOW DID WE GET WHERE WE ARE?

First, the mismatch between government revenues and government spending is where many of these problems start, so let's begin there. In addition to the growth in spending described above, the recession that began in 2008 greatly exacerbated the fiscal crisis of the nation. Not only did tax revenues decline, but also government spending spiked in an effort to prevent a worse economic disaster. Examples of this increased government spending include $700 billion for the Troubled Asset Relief

Program (TARP) bank bailout, supported by President George W. Bush in the waning days of his presidency, and $787 billion for the first economic stimulus program under President Barack Obama in 2009. That additional spending led to a record fiscal year 2009 budget deficit of well over $1 trillion, an amount that was triple that of the previous year—the previous record holder.[27]

Figure 1 graphically illustrates the problem, tracing budget surpluses and deficits from the immediate postwar period in 1946 to estimated figures up to 2015. Although there are more deficit years than surplus years even toward the beginning of this series, deficits for the first two decades appear fairly manageable. Only in the 1960s do they become persistent, before exploding in the 1970s and 1980s. The prosperity of the 1990s— now known to be based on a shaky foundation—led to a brief period of budget surpluses late in the decade, but the tech stock collapse and the terrorist attacks of 9/11 brought the nation back to large deficit spending. Even these large numbers pale in comparison, however, to the massive spike in the deficit propelled by the financial crisis of 2008. More optimistic estimates for the following years still see deficits that are significantly higher than pre–financial crisis numbers. They also optimistically assume a growing economy, and do not account for yet-to-be legislated spending projects, such as large-scale health care reform and possible climate change regulations. In fact, the Obama administration projects deficits may total more than $9 trillion over the next decade.

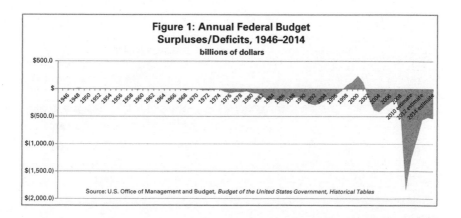

Figure 1: Annual Federal Budget Surpluses/Deficits, 1946–2014
billions of dollars

Source: U.S. Office of Management and Budget, *Budget of the United States Government, Historical Tables*

Another way to understand the deficit problem is to examine budget surpluses and deficits as a percentage of the nation's gross domestic product (GDP). Gross domestic product is the sum of all goods and services produced within the borders of the United States. GDP can be seen as a summary measurement of the overall economic performance of a nation. Growth in the GDP is associated with prosperity; declines are associated with recessions and depressions. The higher a deficit is as a percentage of the GDP, the greater the burden that deficit is on the society. Figure 2 recapitulates the data from Figure 1, this time expressing the surpluses and deficits since World War II as percentages of the nation's GDP. Because of the effects of inflation on the value of the dollar over time, this version of the data is seen as a more accurate and realistic portrayal of the problem. As the figure demonstrates, for most of the postwar era, deficits as a percentage of GDP were lower than they were in World War II. In fact, the deficit in 1943 exceeded 30 percent of GDP— understandable, given that the United States was deeply involved in the greatest war in human history. Until recently, the biggest postwar bulge in the deficit was between the mid-1970s and mid-1990s, when the deficit oscillated between 3 percent and 6 percent of GDP. Again, however, the financial crisis has changed the rules. Deficits as a percentage of GDP tripled from 2008 to 2009, to just under 10 percent. This figure is significantly higher than any other budget since World War II. One analysis suggests that by 2050 federal deficits will comprise 20 percent of GDP.[28] To think of it in another way, the federal government is now beginning to spend money in amounts that are typically necessary to fight world wars.

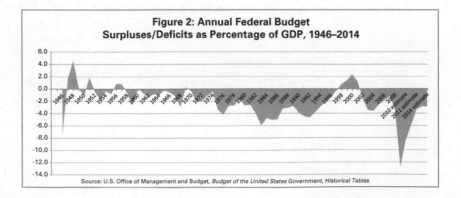

Figure 2: Annual Federal Budget Surpluses/Deficits as Percentage of GDP, 1946–2014

Source: U.S. Office of Management and Budget, *Budget of the United States Government, Historical Tables*

Finally, we can make inflation-adjusted comparisons between sur-
pluses and deficits by comparing the numbers in constant dollars.
When we use a measurement like constant dollars, we are able to compare values based on one specific date. For example, 2010 dollars are
worth significantly less than 1946 dollars, a fact that may serve to exag-
gerate budget performance. Figure 3 recapitulates the data from the first
two figures in constant 2005 dollars—the value of the dollar in 2005.
This gives us a very clear picture of changes across time based on one
constant standard. Thus, we see sharper turns in both surpluses and deficits since 1946, even in earlier years. What does *not* change is the extreme
spike of 2009 and later. Clearly, the financial crisis has rewritten the rules
for what we should consider to be "beyond comprehension."

Of course, all of these deficits create ever-higher debt, in numbers
that are truly astonishing. Figure 4 traces the growth of the national
debt from 1946 to estimated figures for 2015. It is interesting to note
the transformation over time. A national debt of $271 billion in 1946
was only marginally higher a decade later. It took ten years for the debt
to grow by a third from roughly $300 billion in 1962 to $408 billion in
1971. Then the debt more than doubled in the 1970s (from $381 bil-
lion to $909 billion), and tripled in the 1980s (from $909 billion to $3.2
trillion). Growth of the debt slowed down a little in the 1990s, due to
the surge in the stock market. It took a full thirteen years for the 1990
level to double. Unfortunately, it has taken only half that time to nearly
double once again, from $6.2 trillion in 2002 to almost $12 trillion in
2009. The federal Office of Management and Budget (OMB) estimates
that the nation will add over half again to that amount by 2015, a debt

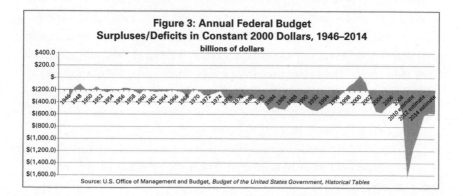

Figure 3: Annual Federal Budget
Surpluses/Deficits in Constant 2000 Dollars, 1946–2014
billions of dollars

Source: U.S. Office of Management and Budget, *Budget of the United States Government, Historical Tables*

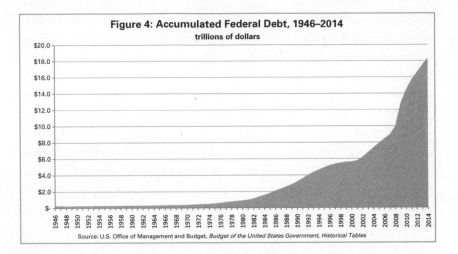

Figure 4: Accumulated Federal Debt, 1946–2014

trillions of dollars

Source: U.S. Office of Management and Budget, *Budget of the United States Government, Historical Tables*

level exceeding $19 trillion. On our scorecard, that represents a tripling from the debt's 2002 level.

A better method of understanding these numbers is to examine the national debt as a percentage of GDP. Comparing the level of the debt to the GDP is somewhat akin to examining a family's debt load and comparing it to their net worth. We tend to be much more concerned at the prospect of a new college graduate entering the workforce $100,000 in debt from student loans, with no prospects for repayment, than we are over someone carrying over a minor amount on his credit card balance. So it is with the national debt. Figure 5 recapitulates the data from Figure 4, this time expressing the accumulation of the national debt since World War II as percentages of the nation's GDP. Again, we find ourselves approaching debt levels that are typically associated with fully mobilized world war. In fact, the national debt during World War II was well above 100 percent of the nation's GDP. The level gradually declined after the war, coming down to its postwar norm somewhere in the mid-30 percent range in the 1970s. Since then the debt has marched steadily upward again, breaking 40 percent of GDP in 1984, 50 percent of GDP in 1987, and 60 percent in 1991. The nation broke the 80 percent barrier in 2009, and OMB projections indicate that the national debt will push through 90 percent in 2010 to over 100 percent by 2012—levels not seen since the end of World War II.

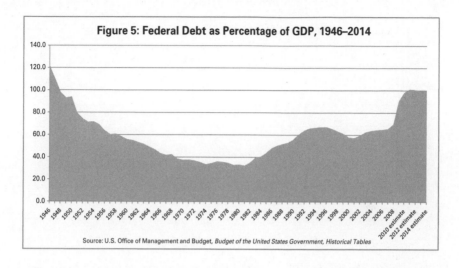

Figure 5: Federal Debt as Percentage of GDP, 1946–2014

Source: U.S. Office of Management and Budget, *Budget of the United States Government, Historical Tables*

Perhaps the most sobering method of understanding the national debt is to examine what it means for each inhabitant of the country. We can think of the debt in per capita terms, which means dividing the entire national debt by the number of people who live in the country— the people ultimately responsible for paying off that debt over time, through taxes or slashed benefit programs. Figure 6 does that, recapitulating the national debt data from 1950 to 2007 (this exercise requires accurate population figures, which come from the U.S. census). For comparison's sake, in 1920 the per capita debt was only $137. By 1940, New Deal spending had raised it to $281 per person. That figure rose sharply in World War II. Nevertheless, we see that the debt per capita was fairly steady until the late 1960s, not rising above $1,700 per person until 1967. Alas, the numbers doubled in the 1970s, moving from $1,858 in 1970 to $3,992 in 1980. In the 1980s, they tripled, to $12,818 in 1990. After leveling out for a few years in the late 1990s, the national debt shot up again to over $29,000 per person in 2007, rising to over $38,000 per person in 2009. That number equates to over $154,000 for a family of four. Budget and population projections from the government estimate a per capita national debt of nearly $59,000 by 2020—a staggering $236,000 for a family of four.[29]

One of the reasons the level of the debt is so damaging is that a significant portion of the federal budget is now dedicated to paying the

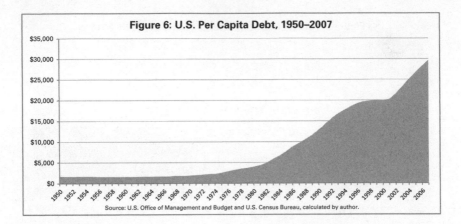

Figure 6: U.S. Per Capita Debt, 1950–2007

Source: U.S. Office of Management and Budget and U.S. Census Bureau, calculated by author.

interest on that debt. This money does not go to any tangible government program. As with credit cards, borrowing is not free, and the higher the debt, the higher the interest payments. Figure 7 traces the growth of the interest paid on the national debt from 1962 to estimated figures for 2015. As long as the interest stays manageable, it is not a large concern, much as small interest payments on credit cards do not adversely affect a family's budget. When the interest starts chewing up more and more of the total budget, however, things are more worrisome, and that is exactly what has happened in the United States. Net interest on the national debt for the 2008 federal budget was over $252 billion, and government projections see that figure doubling in the next few years. We are fast approaching the point where the interest on the debt will consume more than 10 percent of the total federal budget—hundreds of billions of dollars that could be used either for other purposes or for tax cuts. In fact, interest payments on the debt now comprise the fourth largest category in the budget, after Social Security, Medicare/Medicaid, and national defense. Worse still, these numbers do not tell the whole story, for they do not include the interest expense of intragovernmental debt. This is the debt the government owes to the Social Security Trust Fund, because the government borrows money each year from that fund to pay for normal operating expenses. The true interest on the debt for 2008 was in fact closer to $451 billion. By 2015, it may be as high as $888 billion.[30]

It gets worse. The long-term fiscal health of the nation is greatly endangered by the looming financial catastrophes in entitlement

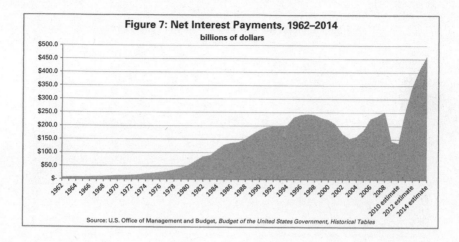

Figure 7: Net Interest Payments, 1962–2014
billions of dollars

Source: U.S. Office of Management and Budget, *Budget of the United States Government, Historical Tables*

programs like Social Security and Medicare. These programs automatically allocate dollars to anyone who qualifies, making them nondiscretionary parts of the federal budget. The number of workers supporting each retiree in America—in other words, the number of people currently paying into these entitlement programs that are supporting current retirees—has dropped from over 5 workers in 1960 to just over 3 in 2008. Projections are that this number will drop even further in the next couple of decades, to 2.2. This means fewer workers supporting more retirees, creating greater stress on the financial health of Social Security and Medicare. Between 2000 and 2030, the sixty-five-and-over set will more than double as the Baby Boomers retire and start to collect their benefits. This cohort will total 20 percent of the population, and entitlement programs that currently comprise 40 percent of the federal budget will jump to 75 percent.[31]

Medicare is in the most dire straits at present. Its insurance benefits have *already* exceeded its tax revenues. Figure 8 displays the growing annual deficits of the Medicare program, with projected deficits of over $50 billion by as early as 2014. The government projects that it will not be able to pay currently scheduled full Medicare benefits as early as 2019—nine years from now. Social Security benefits will begin exceeding its tax revenues as early as 2017, and by the early 2040s will be unable to keep pace with scheduled benefits. The only options to solve this problem—raise taxes, decrease benefits, or change the retirement age—are all unpopular. The three major entitlement programs—Social Security, Medicare, and Medicaid—will consume 100 percent of the federal

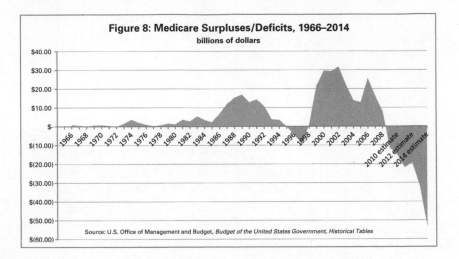

Figure 8: Medicare Surpluses/Deficits, 1966–2014
billions of dollars

Source: U.S. Office of Management and Budget, *Budget of the United States Government, Historical Tables*

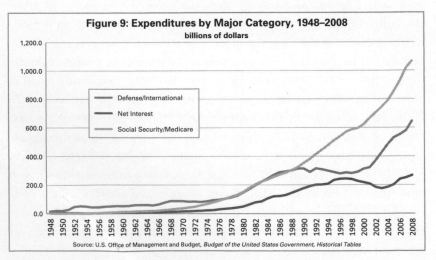

Figure 9: Expenditures by Major Category, 1948–2008
billions of dollars

Source: U.S. Office of Management and Budget, *Budget of the United States Government, Historical Tables*

budget within the next sixty years, crowding out all other budget cat-
egories, including interest payments and national security. Figure 9
illustrates the extent to which Social Security and Medicare have out-
stripped spending on national defense and international programs in recent years. One may expect defense spending to level off, as the Obama
administration draws down the war on terror, but no demographic magic
will prevent entitlements from continuing their upward climb. Indeed,
by 2080 the national debt may increase to over 600 percent of GDP—
almost six times the historical high of 109 percent at the end of World

War II.[32] One analysis suggests that, when one adds unlisted liabilities and long-term unfunded retirement and health care commitments to the national debt, the true level of obligations for the nation is a staggering $56 trillion—a figure that works out to roughly $184,000 per American, or an unimaginable $736,000 for a family of four.[33]

Finally, current and future government policies seem designed to do nothing to alleviate the nation's fiscal train wreck—and in fact, they will likely make things worse. The aforementioned TARP legislation and first stimulus plan added almost $1.5 trillion to the federal budget. There is talk of a second stimulus bill, even though by some measurements, the size of the first doubled that of Franklin Roosevelt's New Deal spending as a percentage of GDP. This is also despite the fact that some scholars argue that government stimulus programs do not really work, and in fact are recipes for inflation. Various plans to fulfill the Obama administration's promise of health care reform all attempt to come in, on, or under $1 trillion, but with full implementation delayed for several years (and thus full spending delayed as well), projections are that actual costs will explode to $2.5 trillion between 2014 and 2023. Any deficit cuts will be marginal at best and will not prevent the already ballooning deficits from continuing their upward path. There will unquestionably be tax increases of various types, totaling, perhaps, half a trillion dollars, many of them targeting employers and small businesses, as well as cuts in Medicare reimbursement rates—assuming Congress actually does that. If not, the costs will be even higher.[34]

All of this, in turn, assumes that government estimates of costs and benefits are accurate. But the federal government has done a miserable job of accurately projecting actual costs of health care reform over time. In 1965, Congress estimated that Medicare Part A would cost about $9 billion annually by 1990; instead, the actual cost was $67 billion. In 1967, the House Ways and Means Committee predicted that the entire Medicare program would cost about $12 billion in 1990; instead, the actual cost was $110 billion. In 1988, Congress estimated the cost of Medicare's home care benefit to be $4 billion in 1993—just five years away; instead, the actual cost was $10 billion, more than twice the projected amount. In 1997, Congress established the State Children's Health Insurance Program (SCHIP), planning on appropriating $40 billion over ten years. Congress had to appropriate an additional $283 million in fiscal year 2006 and $650 million in fiscal year 2007 to prevent mass disenrollments. For a variety of reasons, estimates of health care spending are consistently overly optimistic, at ratios that can exceed 10:1. If that pattern holds, a health care overhaul that is projected to cost in the neighborhood of $3.5 trillion over the next fifteen years could, in fact, run much higher—at significant cost to the nation's fiscal sanity.

In addition to all of this is the possible cap-and-trade legislation to address climate change, which some estimate could bring global expenditures of more than $10 trillion over twenty years in energy infrastructure spending alone—forcing us to paraphrase and revise upward. Former Illinois senator Everett Dirksen said it well in his famous quip: "A trillion here, a trillion there, and pretty soon you're talking about real money." [35]

None of This Bodes Well for the Near Future

The hope of some political leaders is that all of this spending will stimulate the economy and that the resulting prosperity, coupled with various political reforms, will solve our debt problem. It seems more likely, however, that any recovery from the recession will not bring jobs back to their former level. The combination of high unemployment and declining home values has led to a decline in consumer activity. Some analysts believe it may take five years or more to recover all the jobs lost in the recession. A record number of Americans are now working part-time because they have no choice, the average workweek is getting shorter (meaning less money in hourly wages), and youth unemployment is approaching 20 percent. The fact that unemployment in recent recessions peaked long after the recessions ended indicates that there are many more jobs to lose. The uncertainty surrounding current policy proposals further exacerbates the problem, for many companies will not engage in new hiring until they have a better idea what is going to happen with health care reform and climate change legislation. Since those programs will significantly change the economic dynamics in America, companies have every incentive not to hire until they know what those programs will look like in their final form and how they will affect them. Reduced business and consumer activity could mean reduced spending on cheaper imported goods from places like China, in turn slowing down its economy and cutting back on the amount of dollars that flow to the Far East—dollars that finance our debt. If the United States must then resort to printing money to finance its debt, the result will certainly be inflation.[36]

But that brings us back to where we started—the death of the dollar. It is time to conclude our journey through fiscal insanity by briefly examining the consequences of these various choices.

LARGER CONSEQUENCES: WHY DOES IT MATTER?

Recall that it is the foreign market for American dollars that has allowed the nation to borrow money overseas to finance our debt. The United States has been able to increase government spending on all sorts of programs while avoiding European-style taxes. Ever since Nixon closed the gold window, the economic stability of the country has been due not to the dollar being tied to a fixed value of gold, but to faith—faith by overseas markets that the United States has a sound economy and has not gone too deeply into debt. The recent decline in the value of the dollar is tied to the financial crisis that began in 2006 and increased in intensity in 2008. That crisis—and the government's response to the crisis—have greatly exacerbated long-existing fiscal problems. The trend lines in the charts in the previous section provide stark evidence of the train wreck facing the nation if it does not find some way to reverse course.

The decline in the dollar is simply the first manifestation of the consequences that await us. Figure 10 provides one piece of evidence for that decline, based on the value of the metal most often associated with the dollar in history: gold. As discussed earlier, the market price of gold was a constant $35 per ounce after Bretton Woods until the late 1960s. Not coincidentally, it was then that our slow-moving fiscal train wreck began to pick up speed. The market price of gold began to outstrip the official price, prompting Nixon to end the gold standard. Gold immediately surged in value, rising to $159 per ounce in 1974. By 1979, gold broke through the $300-per-ounce barrier and, with the exception of a sharp spike in 1980, it tended to oscillate between a low of $270 per ounce and a high around $450 per ounce for the next twenty-six years. When the housing bubble burst in 2006, gold began its current historic rise in value, matching its previous high of just over $600 per ounce in

Figure 10: Market Price of Gold, Dollars per Ounce, 1946–2009

Source: http://www.measuringworth.org

2006, rising to $768 per ounce two years later, and ending 2009 more than an astonishing $1,100 per ounce.

Of course, one perspective on the *rise* in the value of gold is that it also represents a *decline* in the value of the dollar. By 2003, the dollar had lost 90 percent of its value versus gold since 1971. By 2009, the decline reached 97 percent. Put another way, in 2009 it took thirty-two times as many dollars to buy an ounce of gold as it did in 1971. Gold is often used by investors as a hedge against inflation, which can be triggered by a falling dollar. How far the dollar will fall, one can only guess, but there is clearly room for further movement for gold. Its true peak came in the middle of the stagflation of 1980, when it hit an inflation-adjusted $2,200 per ounce—twice its value in 2009.[37]

In the past thirty years, the United States has moved from being the world's biggest creditor nation to the world's biggest debtor nation. One of the things that made the dollar stable in the 1990s was the willingness of foreign investors to recycle their dollars back into the U.S economy. The nation exports many items overseas, but it imports far more. Cheaper production of goods in places like China allows American companies to close factories in the United States and open new ones overseas, and allows stores like Walmart to sell inexpensive goods brought here from low-wage nations. The result is an annual trade deficit—the difference between the values of what we sell to and buy from other nations.[38] Figure 11 traces trade surpluses and deficits in the United States from 1960 to 2008. Throughout the 1960s, the United States ran slight trade surpluses, averaging over $3 billion per year. The first trade deficit—coincidentally or not—was in 1971. After that, there were only two more surplus years, in 1973 and 1975. Trade deficits in the 1980s averaged $85 billion per year. In the 1990s, they averaged $106 billion per year, with 1999 hitting $265 billion. Since 2000, the trade deficits have continued to soar, averaging over $571 billion per year. The high point was $760 billion in 2006. With the decline of the dollar, the deficits began to draw back, with 2009 seeing a more dramatic fall. As of November 2009, the trade deficit was a "mere" $340 billion.

The trade deficit most famously affects U.S.-China relations, but it exists with Japan and the European Union as well. The advantage of the trade deficit is that Americans enjoy a wide assortment of cheap goods and services from other countries. The disadvantage is that it testifies to the decline in American manufacturing over the past few decades. Also, the trade deficit means that foreign nations like China are stockpiling large amounts of American dollars as reserves to support their own currencies. By 2003, foreign investors owned $9.4 trillion of American assets, while American investors owned just $7.2 trillion of foreign assets.[39] As long as foreign investors recycle their dollars into the U.S. economy, things will remain stable.

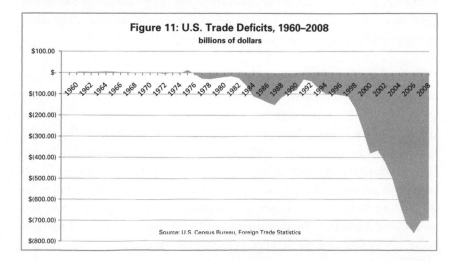

Figure 11: U.S. Trade Deficits, 1960–2008
billions of dollars

Source: U.S. Census Bureau, Foreign Trade Statistics

The fear is that foreign investors may someday take stock of America's shaky fiscal situation and decide that the country is no longer worthy of the faith they have placed in it for so many years. If that occurs, we may find foreign countries dumping their dollars. Dumping would occur if foreign nations lost confidence in the dollar, perhaps due to the frightening trends illustrated in this chapter. A dollar collapse could result from deflation, hyperinflation, or the American government defaulting on its debt payments. These countries might decide to diversify their foreign-exchange reserves, meaning they would dump dollars in favor of the euro or the yen. In fact, in 2005 reports came out that the central bank in South Korea was planning to do precisely that; as a result, the dollar tumbled against all foreign currencies, and the stock market suffered its biggest decline in nearly two years.[40] In addition to cheaper imports, a strong dollar keeps mortgage rates lower and helps fund the budget deficit. All of that changes with a weaker dollar. In many ways, the U.S. economy is as much dependent on foreign cash as it is on foreign oil. One analyst said it best: "Having the reserve currency status is like being able to write check after check and not have anyone cash them. But when you lose the reserve currency status, it's as if all those checks are taken out from under the mattress, and suddenly cashed."[41]

It is not clear what currency could replace the dollar as the world's reserve currency. Many scholars and analysts advocate using the IMF's Special Drawing Rights (SDRs) as the basis for a new world currency. Certainly, the euro is an option, and there has been talk about an "Asian Currency unit" that would serve as another regional currency, but there are significant obstacles to such developments.[42]

Just because there are obstacles to alternative currencies, however, does not mean the threat does not exist. At the G8 summit meeting in July 2009, Russian President Dmitry Medvedev displayed a coin labeled "United Future World Currency" and advocated diversifying the global currency system away from the dollar, a call echoed by France and China. An October 2009 report by *The Independent* suggested that Arab states had joined China, Russia, and France to stop using the dollar for oil trading in favor of a basket of currencies including the Japanese yen and Chinese yuan. The transition would supposedly take about nine years, with gold perhaps serving as the transitional currency until 2018.

Brazil and India are reportedly interested, and the United Nations Conference on Trade and Development also reported on the desirability of shifting away from the dollar to some other system. Such a shift would make it harder for the United States to borrow overseas to finance its budget and trade deficits, leading to much higher interest rates as well as inflation. Gold, in turn, would continue to rise in value. Some analysts even speculate that a dollar collapse could prompt another attempt by the government at 1930s-style confiscation—not gold coins or bullion this time, but assets in 401(k)s and IRAs.[43]

Just as disturbing, it is becoming very clear that these developments are leading to reducing the United States' leverage with other countries. China is the largest foreign lender to the United States. In July 2009, Chinese officials questioned their American counterparts about health care reform and how it would affect the budget deficit. The Chinese wanted to know that the United States would be able to pay them back for financing our debt. The result was a very conciliatory visit by President Obama to China in November 2009—avoiding any earlier meetings with the Dalai Lama and attempting not to antagonize Beijing. China wants to replace the United States as the dominant power in the Pacific region, a move that would have potentially high consequences for the security of Taiwan, freedom for Tibet, and hope for the many sufferers of human rights abuses in the People's Republic of China. Close American ties to China would also have profoundly negative consequences when the China economic bubble bursts. China is attempting to work around some severe internal problems, not the least of which is its attempt to, in the words of David Smick, "Marry a market economy with a Marxist political regime." Such a combination seems unsustainable in the long run, especially considering the demographic implications of China's one-child policy, which has led to a surplus of males over females. Highly accelerated military spending may be one way to absorb the excess males. The result of a Chinese bubble burst would be massive deflation, rising unemployment, stock market collapses, and long-term economic stagnation. One possible response to this prospect sees China withdrawing its reserves from the global system to use them at home. Either way, American dependence on China has profound dangers.[44]

CONCLUSION

We return now to the larger question of the economic strength of the United States. The only reason the dollar has weathered the storm of the financial crisis so far is that the recession hit Europe and Japan worse than the United States. Interest rates will rise eventually, and when they do, the cost of government debt will rise as well. A mere 2 percent rise in interest rates would cause servicing of a $10 trillion debt to cost an extra $100 billion. If current trend lines continue, there is a very real possibility of the nation defaulting on the national debt—or attempting to avoid that prospect by printing new dollars into a hyperinflationary era. So, while there is no single currency that can replace the dollar any time soon, it is clear that the dollar is losing dominance to other currencies. It took decades for the British pound sterling to lose its place to the dollar, and it may take as long for the dollar to do the same. But whether several countries catch up to the United States and compete for dominance—leading perhaps to separate regional currency blocs—or one alternative currency rises to displace the dollar completely, losing its status as the world's reserve currency means the United States loses its status as an economic superpower. If that happens, there will be fewer resources available for the armed forces, compromising the nation's status as a military superpower as well. Historian Niall Ferguson notes that this pattern of imperial decline has been repeated numerous times in world history.[45]

These developments all come back to human choices. By moving off the gold standard, the United States can print large quantities of dollars, which will come at a cost when the market thinks the nation has gone too deeply into debt—which it surely must conclude at some point. By pursuing temporary increases in government spending to deal with the financial crisis, political leaders lay the foundation for new permanent programs and even higher government spending and debt. And when one segment of the population derives benefits from government policies, whether through programs or tax breaks, it is probably a law of human nature that said group will seek to maintain those benefits. Many Americans now think the government is responsible for economic growth and welfare. They have bought into Franklin Roosevelt's argument that government should guarantee not just the traditional natural rights to life, liberty, and the pursuit of happiness, but also "freedom from want" and "freedom from fear"—objectives beyond the ability of any human institution to satisfy. These unreasonable expectations represent a shift in perspective from thinking that we as individuals are responsible for our well-being to a public philosophy of entitlement. We expect the government to do more for us.[46] And because we get the government we deserve, government increases in size to accommodate those expectations. The attempt to ignore human nature has led us to where we are today.

The United States could hardly be in a worse position had its greatest enemy engineered it. But perhaps we have done his work for him. John Maynard Keynes once wrote, "Lenin is said to have declared that the best way to destroy the Capitalist System was to debauch the currency. Lenin was certainly right. There is no subtler, no surer means of overturning the existing basis of society than to debauch the currency."[47] What Keynes—and Lenin—said concerning inflation could easily be applied to the general state of the dollar and the American economy. Decisions, great and small, from philosophers and political leaders rejecting time-honored wisdom to a population too willing to buy what they were selling, embrace conspicuous consumption, and refuse to say no to government overreach, have led us to this point. It will take a new pattern of choices to reverse direction. The question is whether there are any leaders willing to articulate such a vision—and whether the population is willing to follow. If that change in direction is not effected soon, we may very well witness the death of the dollar—killed by our own hands.

SIX

The Rejection of Israel

Israel is unlike any nation on the face of planet Earth: Israel is the only nation created by a sovereign act of God who entered into an eternal blood covenant with Abraham 3,500 years ago.

God told Abraham to leave his land, his birthplace, and his father's house and travel to "a land that I will show you" (Genesis 12:1 NKJV). Seven times God promised the land to Abraham, once to Isaac, and three times to Jacob.

The covenant for this land that God Almighty loves and that radical Islam passionately hates is recorded in Genesis 17:7–8. God speaks to Abraham, saying: "And I will establish My covenant between Me and you and your descendants after you in their generations, for an *everlasting covenant,* to be God to you and your descendants after you. Also I give to you and your descendants after you the land in which you are a stranger, all the land of Canaan, as an *everlasting possession;* and I will be their God."

When Abraham was informed by the Almighty that he would have a son at the age of approximately one hundred years and his wife Sarah, whose womb was dead would come to life and give birth to Isaac at the age of ninety, Abraham pled with God to allow Ishmael (father of the Arabs), to be included in the covenant. God's answer was clear and concise:

> "No, Sarah your wife shall bear you a son, and you shall call his name Isaac; I will establish My covenant with him for an everlasting covenant, and *with his descendants after him.*
> —*Genesis 17:19 NKJV*

The Book of Genesis ends with Joseph telling his brothers, "God will surely come to your aid and take you up out of this land [Egypt] to the *land He promised* [Israel] on oath to Abraham, Isaac and Jacob" (Genesis 50:24 NIV).

The Book of Exodus opens with God commanding Moses to lead the Jewish people to the "land flowing with milk and honey" (Exodus 3:8 NKJV). The night of the first Passover began a forty-year journey for the Jewish people through a barren wilderness. It was a journey of triumph and tragedy, a journey of endless tears and horrific trials.

They were bound for the Promised Land with the cloud by day and the fire by night as a testimonial of God's presence and guidance. They received the Torah of God at Sinai; they received gushing water from a smitten rock from the rod of Moses; they received manna from heaven as the Shekinah glory of God hovered over the Tabernacle, reminding them that their God was Jehovah Shammah: The Lord Is There.

The Jewish connection to the land of Israel did not begin in May 1948 with an emotional declaration at the UN as a result of the Holocaust. It began 3,500 years ago by the will of God to a chosen people who were destined not to live just anywhere on planet Earth but a unique and special place called Israel.

Moses told the children of Israel when they were in sight of the land of Israel that it was a "land flowing with milk and honey."

> *The land you are entering to take over is not like the land of Egypt, from which you have come, where you planted your seed and irrigated it by foot as in a vegetable garden. But the land you are crossing the Jordan to take possession of is a land of mountains and valleys that drinks rain from heaven.* It is a land the LORD your God cares for; *the eyes of the LORD your God are continually on it from the beginning of the year to its end.*
> —Deuteronomy 11:10–12 NIV

Israel is a nation God loves, God created, God defends, and whose eyes are upon it continuously.

In the first battle, the Jewish people had to fight defending themselves against the Amalekites after crossing the Red Sea:

So Joshua fought the Amalekites as Moses had ordered, and Moses,
Aaron, and Hur went to the top of the hill. As long as Moses held up
his hands, the Israelites were winning, but whenever he lowered his
hands, the Amalekites were winning.

—*Exodus 17:10–11 NIV*

The point is this: When Israel looked up to God, their source, they won!
When they looked down, they lost. The secret of Israel's power is not in
horses and chariots; the secret of Israel's power is the God of Abraham,
Isaac, and Jacob.

The spirit of Israel is captured by the words of the prophet Zechariah:

"Not by might nor by power, but by my Spirit," says the LORD
Almighty.

—*Zechariah 4:6 NIV*

God's pledge to curse any nation that attacked Israel is demonstrated in
the attack of the Amalekites upon Israel.

Then the Lord said to Moses, "Write this for *a memorial in the book*
and recount it in the hearing of Joshua, that I will utterly blot out the
remembrance of Amalek from under heaven . . . Because the LORD
has sworn: the LORD will have war *with Amalek from generation to*
generation."

—*Exodus 17:14, 16 NKJV*

The rebirth of Israel on May 14, 1948, was the literal fulfillment of the
promises made by the ancient prophets of Israel. It was the literal fulfillment of the prophet Isaiah who wrote:

Who has heard such a thing? Who has seen such things? Shall the earth
be made to give birth in one day? Or shall a nation be born at once?

—*Isaiah 66:8 NKJV*

My father, an ordained minister of the gospel for fifty-plus years, and I
were sitting at the kitchen table in our home listening to the radio on that
historic day when Israel was reborn. When the radio announcer declared

that the United Nations had recognized the State of Israel, my father, with tears in his eyes, said, "This is the greatest miracle of the twentieth century."

The UN declaration granting statehood to Israel and a homeland for the Jews of the world was recognized by President Harry Truman eleven minutes later. England abstained from the vote, refusing to support the Jews having a homeland to be called Israel. England's long anti-Semitic roots bore bitter fruit on that historic day.

Why is this divine covenant for a specific land to the Jewish people so crucial in the twenty-first century? It's urgent because World War III is about to begin over the failure of humanity to recognize Israel's historic right to the land.

British Prime Minister Benjamin Disraeli, who despite the fact that he had been baptized as a Christian, retained enormous pride in his Jewish ancestry, said in a reply to an insult by the Irish Catholic Daniel O'Connell, "Yes, I am a Jew, and when the ancestors of the right honorable gentleman were brutal savages in an unknown land, mine were priests in the Temple of Solomon."

The point is this: Jerusalem was the capital of Israel long before Berlin, Paris, or New York existed. The city of Jerusalem has been the capital of Israel and the Jewish people since King David defeated the Jebusites there 3,000 years ago.

How strange that ignorant and uninformed leaders in the twenty-first century believe that the ancient biblical city should not be Jewish. The Jewish people have more claim to Jerusalem than the French to Paris or the Germans to Berlin or the British to London.

THE BOUNDARIES OF ISRAEL

The boundaries of this sacred real estate transaction encompass an area far greater than the State of Israel presently controls. Genesis 15:18 states that the land God gave to Abraham, Isaac, and Jacob three thousand five hundred years ago stretches from the Mediterranean Sea on the west to the Euphrates River on the east.

Ezekiel declares the north boundary to be at Hamath, one hundred miles north of Damascus (see Ezekiel 48:1) and the southern boundary at Kadesh, about one hundred miles south of Jerusalem (see Ezekiel

48:28). When Messiah comes, Israel will gain control of every square inch of the promised land given by God to Abraham and the Jewish people for an everlasting possession.

If you look at a map of the Middle East and fix the boundaries recorded in Scripture, the day will come when Israel will own and control all of present-day Israel, including Jerusalem, Lebanon, the West Bank of Jordan, and most of Syria, Iraq, and Saudi Arabia. I believe Messiah will come, and though he delays his coming, he will restore to Israel the promised land given by a sovereign act of God 3,500 years ago as the nations of the world gnash their teeth in anguish.

THE HISTORY OF REJECTION

There is a supernatural curse attached to the land of Israel. It is a divine curse from God himself to men and nations who, with malice aforethought, do harm to the Jewish people or attack the State of Israel.

The prophet Obadiah writes:

"As you have done [to Israel], it shall be done to you; Your reprisal shall return upon your own head."
—Obadiah 1:15 NKJV

The prophet Joel speaks of God's judgment upon nations who divide the land of Israel, which includes the city of Jerusalem, saying:

I will also gather all nations . . . And I will enter into judgment there On account of My people, My heritage Israel, Whom they have scattered among the nations; They have also divided up My land.
—Joel 3:2–3 NKJV

The prophet Jeremiah writes that any nation that attempts to seize Jewish land will lose their land:

The inheritance which I have caused My people Israel to inherit [the promised land]—behold, I will pluck them out of their land.
—Jeremiah 12:14 NKJV

The prophet Zechariah writes:

> For thus says the LORD of hosts: "He sent Me after glory, to the
> nations which plunder you; for he who touches you [the Jewish people]
> touches the apple of His eye. For surely I will shake My hand against
> them, and they shall become spoil for their servants."
> —Zechariah 2:8–9 NKJV

God made this promise to Abraham and his descendants in the Book of
Genesis, and the boneyard of human history is filled with nations who
failed to get the promise that the curse of God Almighty would come to
any people or nation that oppress Israel or the Jewish people.

The Genesis account reads: "I will curse him who curses you" (Genesis 12:3 NKJV).

Let's walk through the pages of world history and discover men and
nations who oppressed the Jewish people and died under the curse of
God. We will discover that what was done to Israel by men and nations,
God did exactly to the oppressors of Israel and the Jewish people.

We will also look into the future at nations seen nightly cursing
Israel and the Jewish people over television and see the judgment of God
crushing those nations and their armies in the future. The prophet Isaiah
writes:

> I am God, and there is none like Me, Declaring the end from the
> beginning, And from ancient times things that are not yet done,
> Saying, "My counsel shall stand, And I will do all My pleasure."
> —Isaiah 46:9–10 NKJV

PHARAOH'S REJECTION: PHARAOH DROWNS
IN HIS SELF-FULFILLING PROPHECY

The Egyptian Pharaoh who held the children of Israel captive had a plan
to kill the Jews by forcing the midwives of Egypt to drown newborn Jewish male babies in the river (see Exodus 1:22).

Why did Pharaoh hate the Jews with such malice that he wanted to
kill their male children? Why were the Jews living in Egypt? To understand how the Hebrew children ended up in a foreign land, from which

they would make an exodus after 430 years of captivity, we must start from the beginning in the book of Genesis.

Jacob, who would later be known as Israel, was the grandson of Abraham; he lived in Canaan and had twelve sons.

Jacob's favorite son was Joseph, who was given a coat of many colors by his father that was suited for royalty. Jacob's favoritism towards Joseph caused his eleven brothers to hate him enough to kill him. In the course of time, they sold Joseph to the Midianites, who took him into Egypt and sold him a second time to Potiphar, a wealthy Egyptian who served in Pharaoh's court.

There was a problem!

Potiphar's desperate housewife lusted after beautiful Joseph and tried repeatedly to seduce him. When Joseph repeatedly refused, Potiphar's wife falsely accused Joseph of rape. He was sent to prison, unknowingly awaiting the day of God's promotion to the palace of Pharaoh—promotion to privilege and power that the mind of a prisoner could never have comprehended.

When Joseph became prime minister in Egypt, an empty stomach drove his brothers into Egypt searching for food. Upon arriving in Egypt, the sons of Israel were forced to appear before the prime minister, their brother Joseph, to receive permission to buy grain. On their third visit into Egypt, Joseph revealed himself to his brothers, who had presumed he was dead.

The reconciled family brought unity, and unity brought the blessing of God. King David writes, "Behold, how good and pleasant *it is* For brethren to dwell together in unity! . . . For there the LORD commanded the blessing" (Psalm 133:1, 3 NKJV).

A family of seventy entered the land of Egypt where they would become a nation of millions in 430 years of slavery.

The Bible says, "But the children of Israel were fruitful and increased abundantly, multiplied and grew exceedingly mighty; and the land was filled with them" (Exodus 1:7 NKJV).

When Joseph died, there arose in Egypt a pharaoh who knew not Joseph. That pharaoh began to dread the children of Israel and feared that Egypt could be taken over by the Israelites should they ever meet in battle. Pharaoh said to his people, "let us deal shrewdly with them, lest they multiply, and it happen, in the event of war, that they also join our enemies and fight against us, and so go up out of the land" (Exodus 1:10 NKJV). So Pharaoh oppressed the children of Israel and forced them to become Egyptian slaves.

Unsatisfied by their bondage alone, Pharaoh planned to decimate the children of Israel, lest they become more powerful than Egypt. In doing so, he commanded the Hebrew midwives to kill any male babies that were born in Egypt.

"But the midwives feared God, and did not do as the king of Egypt commanded them, but saved the male children alive" (Exodus 1:17 NKJV).

As a result, God blessed the midwives and gave them households of their own, and the children of Israel continued to multiply and prosper. Still determined to annihilate the Jewish people, Pharaoh commanded that every Hebrew baby boy be drowned in the river.

About this time, Jacob's great-grandson Moses was born. In an effort to save him from being drowned, Moses was placed in a basket and put at the river's edge where Pharaoh's daughter was known to bathe. All went according to plan. Pharaoh's daughter discovered Moses in the basket, took compassion on him, and raised him as her own son. Moreover, because Pharaoh's daughter hired Moses' biological mother to be his wet nurse, Moses grew up knowing he was a Hebrew and understood his Jewish legacy.

As an adult and living as the prince of Egypt, Moses witnessed the beating of a Hebrew slave. He entered the fight, killed the Egyptian, and buried him in the sand. Having broken the law of Egypt and incurred the wrath of Pharaoh, Moses fled for his life to the depths of the wilderness.

Here he married Zipporah and became a father to Gershom, meaning, "I have been a stranger in a foreign land" (Exodus 2:22 NKJV). As Moses was tending the flock of Jethro, his father-in-law, he saw the burning bush that was not consumed by the fire and heard the voice of God commanding him to return to Egypt to liberate the Jewish people from bondage.

As an eighty-year-old man, Moses returned to Egypt to lead the Jewish people out of Egyptian captivity. Moses begrudgingly accepted this role, and the children of Israel accepted him as their deliverer. Pharaoh, however, did not accept Moses' request to free the Hebrew children.

With every one of Pharaoh's refusals to liberate the children of Israel,

God sent plagues upon the land. Miraculously, the plagues affected only the Egyptians and left the Hebrew children unscathed. Ten plagues befell the Egyptian people. Why ten plagues?

There were ten plagues, because Egypt served ten major gods. With each plague, God Almighty specifically destroyed one of the major gods of Egypt. The Jewish people had lived for 430 years in a land of idolatry with gods you could see and touch. They were about to be introduced to the God no one could see or touch but who had all power in heaven and on earth.

Whether it was frogs, lice, locusts, disease, hail, or darkness, nothing was compelling enough to motivate Pharaoh to release the children of Israel until the tenth plague arrived. The final plague was the death of all of the Egyptians' firstborn. By God's instruction, the Israelites put the blood of a lamb on their doorposts and were spared the Angel of Death. With Pharaoh's own son dead in his bed, he told Moses and the children of Israel to leave the land of Egypt.

Despite Pharaoh allowing the Hebrew children to flee, Pharaoh quickly changed his mind and came after them. Ever faithful as the defender of Israel, the Lord prepared Moses for what was to come. The Lord said to Moses: "I will harden Pharaoh's heart, so that he will pursue them; and I will gain honor over Pharaoh and over all his army, that the Egyptians may know that I *am* the LORD" (Exodus 14:4 NKJV).

As the children of Israel marched out of Egypt with all their animals and carts loaded with the wealth of Egypt, Pharaoh and his army pursued them with a rage fueled by the death of his son and the firstborn of all Egypt.

As Moses and the children of Israel came upon the Red Sea, God prepared to remove Egypt's chief god, Pharaoh himself. The Lord divided the waters so that the children of Israel were able to walk through on dry ground. As the Hebrew children crossed the sea, Pharaoh's enraged army pursued the Jewish people.

Once the children of Israel successfully crossed the Red Sea, the Lord caused the walls of water, which had previously framed a dry pathway, to fall upon the Egyptians. The Word says, "Then the waters returned and covered the chariots, the horsemen, *and* all the army of Pharaoh that came into the sea after them. Not so much as one of them remained" (Exodus 14:28 NKJV).

Little did Pharaoh know that when he plotted to exterminate the children of Israel by drowning their sons in water, that he was merely forecasting the means of his own fate. Exactly what he had done to the Jewish people was done to him by the hand of God.[1] "I will curse those who curse you" could have been chiseled upon his royal headstone.

HAMAN'S AND HITLER'S REJECTION: THE SONS OF HAMAN AND THE TRIAL AT NUREMBERG

"The Sages tell us to study Jewish history carefully— for everything that happened to our forebears, is bound to recur with us—their descendants."[2]

To make the connection between the ancient account of Queen Esther and the part she played in saving the Jewish people from extermination and the Nuremberg Trials requires careful historic examination. An assessment of Hebrew scripture in the book of Esther reveals signs that foreshadow the hanging of Hitler's Nazis at Nuremberg.

Before comparing the hangings of Haman's sons and the Nuremberg war criminals collectively, it is first necessary to consider the accounts separately.

Esther, Haman, and the Feast of Purim

Purim is a Jewish celebration commemorating Queen Esther's salvation of the Jewish people. The book of Queen Esther holds the narrative of Esther's rise to become queen in the kingdom of Ahasuerus and her supernatural intervention on behalf of her people, the Jews, that ultimately saved them from extermination and the first proposed holocaust.

The Story of Esther

An orphan who was raised by her older cousin Mordecai, Esther was a beautiful young Jewish woman. At the time, King Ahasuerus was in search for a new queen, and it was decreed that all young virgins be taken into the king's palace and cared for by the custodian of the women.

Accordingly, Esther was taken with the rest of the young virgins who resided in the kingdom. Before leaving for the king's palace Mordecai urged Esther not to reveal her Jewish roots to the king. Submitting to his paternal authority, she obeyed the command and kept her Jewish heritage a secret. Ultimately, Esther found favor with King Ahasuerus, as he loved her more than he loved all the other young women. Esther, a Jewish woman, was made queen of Persia—today's modern Iran.

Daily, Mordecai sat within the king's gate in an effort to learn of Queen Esther's welfare. While there, Mordecai became aware that two of the King's doorkeepers plotted to harm King Ahasuerus. Mordecai revealed the plot to Queen Esther who, in turn, relayed the message to the king on behalf of Mordecai. As a result, the doorkeepers were hanged and the entire incident was recorded in the king's book of chronicles.

After this, the king promoted one of his men, Haman, to the second highest seat in the kingdom. With this promotion the king commanded his servants to bow and pay homage to Haman. Mordecai, being a Jew, refused to bow to Haman. Haman was "filled with wrath" (Esther 3:5 NKJV).

Once Haman learned Mordecai was a Jew, Haman conspired not only to kill Mordecai, but the entire Jewish population throughout the kingdom of Persia. At this time in world history, the vast majority of Jews lived in Persia. Haman sought an audience with the king and requested a decree be written commanding the destruction of all Jewish men, women, and children and the plunder of their possessions.

The king, still not knowing that his queen was a Jew, consented to Haman's request and allowed to be written the decree that commanded the total destruction of the Jewish people to fall on the thirteenth day of the twelfth month. The decree was sealed with the king's signet ring and dispersed throughout the kingdom. This decree was made according to the law of the Medes and the Persians, which meant the king himself could not rescind his own decree. It appeared the Jews were doomed to death.

Mordecai told Esther of the king's decree and commanded her to go before the king to plead for the lives of the Jewish people to be spared. Mordecai sent the following message to Esther: "Do not think in your heart that you will escape in the king's palace any more than all the other Jews. For if you remain completely silent at this time, relief and deliverance will arise for the Jews from another place, but you and your father's house will perish. Yet who knows whether you have come to the kingdom for *such* a time as this?" (Esther 4:13–14 NKJV).

Although Esther was queen, she was not permitted to appear before the king unless summoned. Anyone who appeared before the king without being summoned by him would be put to death unless the king held out his scepter as a sign he consented to his or her presence.

Considering the possibility of her death for appearing before the king without his royal invitation, Esther requested that Mordecai and the rest of the Jewish people in the kingdom fast and pray on her behalf that she find favor with King Ahasuerus. Determined to protect her people from certain death, Esther resolved to break the king's law, seeking him without invitation, saying, "I will go to the king, which *is* against the law; and if I perish, I perish!" (Esther 4:16 NKJV).

In answer to her prayers, Esther found favor with the king when she entered his court. He asked, "What do you wish, Queen Esther? What *is* your request? It shall be given to you—up to half the kingdom!" (Esther 5:3 NKJV).

Esther asked that Haman and the king attend a banquet that she would prepare; there she would tell the king her request. When Haman learned that he was invited to a private banquet with the king and queen, he was elated that his political star was rising.

Haman saw Mordecai at the king's gate. When Mordecai failed to bow to him, Haman's hatred for him grew. In an effort to conceal his indignation, Haman's family suggested that he make a gallows and ask the king to hang Mordecai for his failure to bow before him. Haman was pleased by this idea and instructed that Mordecai be hanged on that gallows.

The Demise of Haman

That evening, King Ahasuerus could not fall asleep. Consequently, the king requested that the record of chronicles be read to him. As the chronicles were being read, the king heard the account of Mordecai and the role he played in protecting him from the doorkeepers' plot. In light of this, the king sought to reward Mordecai for saving his life. As Haman walked into the king's court to seek Mordecai's execution, King Ahasuerus asked Haman, "What shall be done for the man whom the king delights to honor?" (Esther 6:6 NKJV).

Thinking the king wanted to honor him, Haman suggested that a royal robe the king had worn be put on the man and that he ride a royal horse the king had ridden in a parade that honored him. The king agreed and mandated Haman to honor Mordecai in exactly that manner. In shock, Haman was mortified.

Defeated and deflated, Haman returned to his home to relay all that had happened to his wife. Prophetically, Haman's wife said to him, "If Mordecai, before whom you have begun to fall, is of Jewish descent, you will not prevail against him but will surely fall before him" (Esther 6:13 NKJV).

Not long after that, Haman was ushered to the private banquet hosted by Queen Esther and attended by the king. When King Ahasuerus asked the queen to make her request known, Esther begged that her life and the lives of her people be spared.

Confused by her request, as he had been unaware that she was a Jew, the king asked Esther who had ordered such a vicious decree. Queen Esther lifted her right hand, pointed her slender forefinger in the face of Haman, and said, "The adversary and enemy *is* this wicked Haman!" (Esther 7:6 NKJV).

The king was enraged by Haman's actions. One of the king's servants pointed out the gallows that Haman had constructed for Mordecai, and the king commanded Haman—and eventually his sons as well—be hanged on it. So, Haman died hanging from his neck on the very gallows he built for Mordecai. Mordecai, on the other hand, was given Haman's signet ring by the king and appointed over the house of Haman.

Esther was still determined to save her people. However, because the decree aimed at exterminating the Jews was sealed with the king's signet ring, the king was powerless to revoke it. But, the king allowed Esther to write an alternative decree in an effort to save the lives of the Jewish people.

She did so, and the new decree permitted the Jews to defend themselves from anyone who tried to take their lives. The Jews fought fiercely and, in the end, destroyed all their enemies. Once Queen Esther and her people were saved, King Ahasuerus asked if she had any further requests. Her response was, "let Haman's ten sons be hanged on the gallows" (Esther 9:13 NKJV). The king obliged and like their father before them, Haman's sons were hanged.

On the very day that Haman sought to have the Jews exterminated, the Jewish people assembled and celebrated with a day of feasting and gladness instead. They called the celebration Purim, after the name Pur—which means "the lot," since Haman had cast the lot to destroy the Jewish people (see Esther 9:24–26).

After overcoming their enemies, all of the Jews in the land were determined to commemorate their salvation annually: "The Jews established and imposed it upon themselves and their descendants and all who would join them, that without fail they should celebrate these two days every year . . . that these days should be remembered and kept throughout every generation . . . that these days of Purim should not fail *to be observed* among the Jews, and that the memory of them should not perish among their descendants" (Esther 9:27–28 NKJV).

The Nuremberg Trials

"The wrongs which we seek to condemn and punish have been so calculated, so malignant, and so devastating that civilization cannot tolerate their being ignored because it cannot survive their being repeated . . . that four great nations, flushed with victory and stung with injury, stay the hand of vengeance and voluntarily submit their captive enemies to judgment of the law is one of the most significant tributes that power has ever paid to reason." [3]
—United States Supreme Court Justice Robert Jackson's excerpt
from his opening statement at the first Nuremberg Trial

In 1944, as victory over the Third Reich approached, President Franklin D. Roosevelt sought a strategy from the U.S. War Department to determine how Hitler's Nazi war criminals would be brought to justice.[4] The United Kingdom exercised a comparable approach as the British War Cabinet was brainstorming similar plans as early as December 1942.[5] Ultimately, the result was the International Military Tribunal (IMT), a court created under the Allied powers, as a multinational and multijurisdictional mechanism to bring some of the greatest Nazi offenders to justice.

The IMT would take place in Nuremberg, Germany. The geographic symbolism in choosing Nuremberg is not to be overlooked. Nuremberg was home to major Nazi rallies and conferences.[6] In fact, one of these conferences birthed two laws known as "the Nuremberg Laws." Collectively, these laws were aimed at denying Jews their citizenship rights in addition to criminalizing marriage and "extramarital intercourse between Jews and Germans."[7]

However, with the Nuremberg Trials taking place there, the city whose very name belonged to laws that deprived Jews of their liberties as German citizens, a city once known for its Nazi party rallies would now be made infamous as the city where some of the Nazi party's most atrocious players met their fate at the gallows of justice.

Some decry that the Nuremberg Trials were ex post facto (literally, "after the fact") justice. Naysayers complained that because the Nuremberg defendants were charged with violating laws that did not exist at the time their crimes were committed, but rather laws that were created by the IMT after their capture, the judicial procedure that ultimately condemned them to death was unfair.

Supreme Court Justice Robert Jackson, who would oversee the trial, offered a rebuttal to such a suggestion, undermining any allegation of ex post facto justice in saying, "What we propose is to punish acts which have been regarded as criminal since the time of Cain and have been so written in every civilized code."[8]

Although Nuremberg would eventually host thirteen trials against various war criminals, the first trial would be the most notoriously remembered, as it was against the highest-ranking Nazis, whose deaths all but overshadowed their heinous lives. With twenty-four defendants and the four Allied nations as plaintiffs, the first trial at Nuremberg would last ten months and result in eleven of the defendants being sentenced to death by hanging.[9]

Despite claims that Nuremberg was nothing more than "victors' justice," after copious amounts of incriminating evidence describing the atrocities committed by the defendants was shown at trial, one did not have to possess a great legal mind to concede that the accused deserved a fate worse than death. Some examples of the prosecution's evidence consisted of the following:

USA Exhibit #253: tanned human tattooed skin from concentration camp victims, preserved for Isle Hoch, the wife of the commandant of Buchenwald, who liked to have the flesh fashioned into lampshades and other household objects for her home.

USA Exhibit #254: the fist-shaped shrunken head of an executed Pole, used by Isle Koch as a paperweight.[10]

If the physical evidence left any doubt as to the extent of the grotesque disregard the defendants displayed for human life, such doubts would be eradicated by witness statements. Such witnesses included Marie-Claude Vaillant-Couturier, a young French woman and concentration camp survivor who testified the Nazi orchestra played jovially as those fated for the gas chambers were segregated from those who would be used for labor. Vaillant-Couturier went on to explain that as she slept, she was "awakened by horrible cries. The next day we learned that the Nazis had run out of gas and the children had been hurled into the furnaces alive."[11]

While the eleven death sentences that resulted from the first Nuremberg trial were handed down on October 1, the hangings were not scheduled to take place until October 16, 1946. Additionally, although eleven criminals were scheduled to be hanged, only ten men would swing from the gallows that day. The most prominent defendant, Hermann Wilhelm Goering, an arrogant and unrepentant man who rationalized his actions as simply following orders, escaped the noose only hours before his slated execution. He committed suicide by ingesting a vial of potassium cyanide.[12] An interpreter at the trial described Goering as one who possessed "manipulative behavior" that became "an irritant to the court."[13] The interpreter went on to say: "If one can speak of a dominant personality in the dock, Hermann Goering definitely fits that description as the leading defendant . . . I recall him sitting in the first seat in the front row of the dock, often with supercilious smile, perhaps knowing that he would cheat the hangman."[14]

Goering did indeed cheat the hangman. Late at night on October 15, 1946, Burton C. Andrus, the American commandant of the Nuremburg prison, instead of formally reading Goering his death sentence, discovered him dying in his prison cell. *Newsweek* reported, "Hermann Wilhelm Goering, lying on his small iron cot in Cell No. 5 and wearing black silk pajamas and a blue shirt, crushed between his teeth a glass vial of potassium cyanide, gasped, twitched, and died."[15] With Goering dead, prison guards, "determined that no other victim should escape them," immediately bound the remaining ten defendants and promptly escorted them to the Nuremberg gymnasium, the location where the hangings would take place.[16] At 1:11 a.m. the first of the condemned Nazis walked the thirteen steps to the platform of the gallows; by 2:57 a.m. the last of the Nazi war criminals were pronounced dead.

The mystery surrounding Goering's suicide still lingers today. It is not clear exactly how he came into possession of the poison that ended his life or how his suicide was timed so perfectly, two and a half hours before his execution would have taken place.[17] His person, as well as his prison cell, was routinely inspected, and the prisoners were not made aware of the hour their hangings were scheduled to take place.[18] What is known is that near the start of the trial, Goering bragged to one of the defense lawyers that "they will never hang me."[19] He was right. After Goering's body was discovered, it was photographed as proof of death with "one eye open and the other closed." It is as if he were "winking at the fate he had avoided."[20]

Law school professor Donald E. Wilkes describes the hangings as bearing a "stern, unadorned, Old Testament righteousness." Referring to a witness's impression of the executions, he notes: "It was a grim pitiless scene. But for those who had sat through the horrors of and tortures of the trial, who had learned of men dangled from butcher hooks, of women mutilated and children jammed into gas chambers, of mankind subject to degradation, destruction and terror, the scene conjured a vision of stark, almost biblical justice."[21]

The Connection Between Haman and Hitler

There are many signs in the book of Esther that foreshadow the hanging of the Nazi war criminals at Nuremberg. For instance:

1. 1946 was the year the Nazi war criminals were hanged.

Throughout the Torah, there are various places where letters are written smaller or larger than the surrounding text. Writing certain letters in larger or smaller text is an archaic Hebrew tradition that has been kept since the time of the scribes; the explanation as to why certain letters are written differently is not always ascertainable.[22]

In Esther 9:7–9, the names of Haman's ten sons are listed. Within those verses, the following Hebrew letters are written in a small script, *"tav,"* *"shin,"* and *"zain."* Additionally, the Hebrew letter *"vav"* is written in a larger script than the rest of the text.[23] Since the Jewish calendar year is represented by Hebrew letters, the smaller letters, *"tav,"* *"shin,"* and *"zain"* refer to Jewish calendar year 707. Meanwhile, the large letter *"vav"* equals 6, which is referring to the sixth millennium.[24]

Therefore, when reading all of these letters together, they collectively refer to the 707th year of the sixth millennium, or the year 5707 on the Jewish calendar.[25] Consequently, the year 5707 is the year 1946 on the civil calendar.[26]

2. The Nazi war criminals' death sentences were carried out on October 16, 1946.

> *"On the seventh day of the Sukkot holiday, i.e. Hoshana Raba, the judgment of the nations of the world is finalized. Sentences are issued from the residence of the King. Judgments are aroused and executed on that day."* [27]

Sukkot, also known as the Feast of Tabernacles, is a weeklong holiday memorializing the forty years the children of Israel spent wandering in the desert after their release from Pharaoh's captivity. Sukkot, which translates "booths," refers to the temporary shelters that the Jews lived in during their time in the desert. In the Jewish tradition, the seventh and final day of Sukkot is called Hoshana Raba, which is the day that marks the judgment of the nations of the world.[28] According to the Jews, "God judges the world on Rosh Hashanah and concludes the verdict on Yom Kippur," then, on Hoshana Raba, the verdict receives its final seal.[29]

The significance of Hoshana Roba, as it relates to Nuremberg, is that in the year 1946, Hoshana Raba fell on October 16, the very day the condemned were hung from Nuremberg's gallows. Although the trial for those accused of Nazi war crimes ended in June of that same year, "sentencing was repeatedly postponed due to appeals for amnesty."[30] As a result, the sentencing was not handed down until the beginning of October and then carried out on October 16, the day of the judgment of nations.

3. Esther asked the king to hang the sons of Haman "tomorrow."

While the book of Esther never specifically mentions the name of God in its text, the word *king* is found throughout, and according to Talmudic scholars, has a double meaning. Within the text, the terms "king" and "King Ahasuerus" are used. Whenever it reads "King Ahasuerus," the scriptures are referencing Esther's husband. However, when the word "king" stands alone, without the succession of the proper noun, "Ahasuerus," then the word takes on a double meaning; it can be referring to both King Ahasuerus and to God.[31] In the book of Esther, the queen asked the king to hang Haman's sons tomorrow. She said, "If it pleases the king, let it be granted to the Jews who *are* in Shushan to do again tomorrow according to today's decree, and let Haman's ten sons be hanged on the gallows" (Esther 9:13 NKJV).

In verse thirteen, the word "king" stands alone. Therefore, Queen Esther was not only asking King Ahasuerus to hang Haman's sons, she was also supplicating the same request to God. Furthermore, she asks the king to hang Haman's sons "tomorrow." This is important because in the Talmudic tradition, the word "tomorrow" does not necessarily mean the twenty-four-hour period that follows today. In fact, the word "tomorrow" basically means, "at some point in the future."[32]

Therefore, not only did Queen Esther ask King Ahasuerus to hang Haman's sons tomorrow, she was also praying that God would do the same "at some point in the future." Furthermore, while Haman's biological sons were indeed hanged by King Ahasuerus, it can be said that the Nazi war criminals who were hanged at Nuremberg are surely the spiritual sons of Haman.[33]

Haman is described as "the enemy of all the Jews" who "plotted against the Jews to annihilate them . . . to consume them and destroy them" (Esther 9:24 NKJV). This evil description is one that fits both Haman and his ideological progeny, the Nazis.

4. Ten were hanged.

As previously mentioned, eleven Nazis were sentenced to die on November 16, 1946. However, due to Goering's suicide, only ten were hanged—the exact number of Haman's sons.

5. The number 13.

Every Hebrew number has a meaning correlated with it. For instance, the number 12 is a perfect number that relates perfection of government or perfect rule.[34] A prime example of this number at work is Jesus and his twelve disciples.

However, one added to the perfect number 12 yields 13, which is imperfection. The first time the number 13 appears in scripture, it reads, "Twelve years they served Cherdorlaomer, and the thirteenth year they rebelled."[35] Bible scholar E. W. Bullinger noted that in the Bible, "every occurrence of the number thirteen, and likewise every multiple of it, stands in connection with rebellion, apostasy, defection, corruption, disintegration, revelation or some kindred idea."[36]

Notice that in the book of Esther, Haman demanded that the Jews be annihilated on the thirteenth day of the month: "And the letters were sent by couriers into all the king's provinces, to destroy, to kill, and to annihilate all the Jews, both young and old, little children and women, in one day, on the thirteenth day of the twelfth month, which is the month of Adar, and to plunder their possessions" (Esther 3:13 NKJV).

It is not a coincidence that these words are written in that particular chapter's *thirteenth* verse. With that in mind, see also that Esther asks the king to hang Haman's sons in the *thirteenth* verse of chapter nine. Ironically, the criminals at Nuremberg had to climb 13 steps to the top of their gallows. Additionally, Nuremberg ultimately held 13 trials against Nazi war criminals. Is this a coincidence? I think not.

6. Both the Nuremberg war criminals and Haman were hanged on their own property.

It is worth mentioning that both Haman and the Nazi war criminals met their fates on their own property. Haman was hanged at his own house on the gallows that he had built for Mordecai. Similarly, the Nazi war criminals were hanged in Nuremburg, which was the home of the Reichsparteigelande, the Nazi Party rally grounds. So, both Haman and his ideological offspring met their fate in exactly the same surroundings.

7. The Feast of Purim

Hitler's hatred for the book of Esther has been described the following way: "Hitler harbored a venomous hatred for the Book of Esther, and the holiday of Purim. 'Unless Germany is victorious,' he proclaimed, 'Jewry could then celebrate the destruction of Europe by a second triumphant Purim Festival.' When Hitler invaded Poland in 1939, he banned the reading of the book of Esther and ordered that all synagogues be closed and barred on the holiday of Purim. On Purim in 1942, in one town in Nazi occupied Poland, ten Jews were hanged by Hitler's SS, in a sadistic parody of events in the book of Esther." [37]

This same sentiment resonated on October 16, 1946, when the ten war criminals met their fates. While not all of the condemned spoke last words, the tenth and final criminal that was executed, Julius Streicher, had plenty to say: "Only Julius Streicher went without dignity. He had to be pushed across the floor, wide-eyed and screaming: 'Heil Hitler!' Mounting the steps he cried out: 'And now I go to God.' He stared at the witnesses facing the gallows and shouted: 'Purimfest, 1946.' " [38]

8. The manner in which they killed is the manner in which they died.

Haman built a gallows intending to hang Mordecai on it. Similarly, the Nazis hanged Jews in effigy on Purim in 1942 (as noted above) and routinely executed the Jewish people with hanging throughout the Holocaust. What they had done to the Jewish people, in turn, was exactly done to them.

Without a doubt, the hanging of the Nazi war criminals as foretold by the book of Esther cannot be explained away by irony and coincidence.

> *There is nothing that is not hinted in the Torah.* [39]*: "And I will curse him who curses you . . ."*
>
> —*Genesis 12:3 NKJV*

ENGLAND'S REJECTION UNDER THE REIGN OF "EDWARD THE HAMMER"

Winston Churchill called Edward I one of the greatest kings in European history. It was under Edward's rule in the late 1200s that Wales and Cornwall were merged into the British crown and Scotland and Ireland were invaded and occupied.

Edward I was also the first European monarch to set up an effective administrative bureaucracy, survey and perform a census of his kingdom, and establish laws and political divisions.

Edward I also embraced the financial power of the Jewish people. The

English Jews were not allowed to own land or hold public office, and they could not join most of the trades or professions. They soon discovered that money could be the secret of their survival, and many acquired great wealth.

Ever resourceful, Edward I found a way to separate the Jewish people from their money. First, he borrowed from them to finance his imperial ambitions, and then, rather than repaying the debt, Edward I simply expelled the Jews from England. Edward I was uniquely inventive: he kicked the Jews out of England twice. After a time, he invited the Jews back to their English homeland, borrowed more money, and then expelled them again.

The anti-Semitic roots of England run deep and long. On November 29, 1947, the United Nations Partition Plan for Palestine was adopted by a decision of the general assembly. The resolution was approved by a vote of 33 to 13 with 10 abstentions. England was one of the abstentions refusing to support the birth of a Jewish state.

Recently, Diana and I went to London and, with the assistance of some very gracious and politically well-connected friends, were given an audience with one of the most powerful and influential members of the British government. My intention was to seek his blessing and guidance in having a "Night to Honor Israel" in the Royal Albert Hall for the greater London area.

Diana and I were ushered into his elegant office. We introduced ourselves with Diana pouring on her considerable charm. It was like water off the proverbial duck's back. I was reminded of that old country song: "Is It Cold in Here or Is That Just You?"

We presented the concepts, purposes, and objectives of a "Night to Honor Israel" clearly and concisely. Diana and I waited for his response from a face that reflected no emotion. His statement I will never forget.

With all the frigidity of a massive iceberg, he folded his hands on the desk, raised his eyebrows, and said, "There are times in history when doing nothing is the best thing to do; this is one of those times in history."

Diana and I thanked the politician for his time and left his office with a blast of frigid air following us through the door.

The anti-Semitic climate in England today is covered well by Melanie Phillips in her chilling book, *Londonistan,* graphically describing how radical Islam is rapidly gaining control of Britain.

Britain has become a largely post-Christian society, where traditional morality has been systematically undermined and replaced by an "anything goes" culture in which autonomous decisions about codes of behavior have become unchallenged rights.

"Judaism and Christianity, the creeds that form the bedrock of Western civilization, have been pushed aside and their place filled by a plethora of paranormal activities and cults. So much so that now prisoners are allowed to practice paganism in their cells . . . and a Royal Navy sailor was given the legal right to carry out satanic rituals and worship the devil aboard the frigate HMS *Cumberland*." [40]

"The issues of Iraq, America, and Israel are now conflated in the British public mind in a poisonous stew of irrationality, prejudice, ignorance, and fear. Britons believe that the only reason they are currently threatened by Islamic terror is the UK's support for America in Iraq. They think the main reason for Muslim rage is the behavior of Israel towards the Palestinians, and that America made itself a target simply because of its support for Israel. 'Middle Britain' thinks that America is the fount of all evil and that Israel poses the greatest threat to world peace. The daily invective against Jews, Israelis, and evil Americans upon young Muslims who were already inflamed against the West has turned up the temperature to the boiling point. The relentless demonization of America and Israel by the British media has acted as a powerful recruiting sergeant for the jihad and has entrenched *Londonistan* in Britain's national psyche." [41]

The emergence of "Londonistan" should be of the greatest concern to America, for which it poses acute danger. Clearly, the fact that Britain has become Europe's radical Islamic terror factory presents immediate and obvious risks to America's physical security.

As the Pentagon briefing paper observed, "America's political leaders still think Muslim terrorists, even suicide bombers, are mindless criminals motivated by 'hatred of our freedoms' rather than religious zealots motivated by their faith. And as a result we have no real strategic plan for winning a war against jihadist." [42]

Think about it!

Great Britain began down the road of anti-Semitism by kicking the Jews out of England after taking their money. They kicked out the seed of Abraham, who were loving, peaceful, and law-abiding.

In 1947, they voted against the Jewish people having a homeland in

Palestine. Currently, England is charging members of the Israeli government as war criminals for their role in defending Israel from the rocket attacks of Hamas.

Today, England is flooded by the soldiers of Allah who love war, live by their own law, and threaten to kill anyone who rejects their faith. There comes this haunting refrain that none should ever forget: "I will curse those who curse you."

THE VOYAGE OF THE DAMNED: CUBA'S REJECTION

Herbert Karliner: A Survivor's Story

Herbert Karliner was just twelve years old when he sailed on the SS *St. Louis* with his parents and three siblings. A young boy who lived through Kristallnacht, the voyage of the *St. Louis,* and ultimately his family's demise in the concentration camps, Herbert is a survivor. The son of religious Jews, Herbert attended services at his synagogue every Friday and Saturday.

During Kristallnacht, as his family's synagogue burned, Herbert's father tried to save the Torah, but the Nazi guard stopped him. In addition to their place of worship being destroyed, their family business was also vandalized. Later that evening, Herbert's father Joseph was arrested and taken to Buchenwald. Once a multigenerational member of his community, Herbert was now no longer allowed to attend school and would be "kicked around just walking on the same sidewalk as the Aryan people." [43] After Kristallnacht, Herbert's life would never be the same.

Following these tragic events, Herbert's mother was informed that in order to secure her husband's release from Buchenwald, she had to obtain visas for another country as proof that she and her family would leave Germany. Despite having to sell their home and business at Gestapo-mandated prices, Herbert's mother paid inflated fees to secure landing permits in Cuba for her family. The Karliners planned to stay there until their quota number was called for entrance into the United States. Upon securing the permits to leave Germany, Joseph Karliner returned home after three weeks in Buchenwald. Described by his son Herbert as "unrecognizable," Joseph would not open up about his experiences at the concentration camp until the family was well on their way to Cuba. [44]

Although his father was hesitant to describe what he had gone through, Herbert's uncle had been sent to Dachau a year earlier, never to return. Even at the young age of twelve, Hebert said he "already knew what it meant to go to a camp."[45]

Well on his way to Cuba and hopeful that the worst was behind him, Herbert enjoyed the sense of adventure he felt cruising aboard such a grand ship. Unfortunately, his high spirits would not last long as he and his family quickly realized they would not be able to disembark in Cuba. His sense of adventure had now turned to panic as the passengers sent telegrams looking for a savior. "We sent a plea to Mrs. Roosevelt to allow only the children to enter the U.S., but it came to deaf ears . . . we had to return to Europe knowing full well what it meant."[46] After hanging in limbo on board the *St. Louis,* the Karliners were told that help had been found.

Still uneasy about what the future held, Herbert and his family were taken to France where his older sister and his parents were sent to a tiny village. Meanwhile he, his brother, and his younger sister were taken to a children's home.

He would later celebrate his Bar Mitzvah in that home, as he recalls it: "We were a bunch of boys together, without our parents there, and it was very sad."[47] The following year, in 1940, Herbert's parents came to visit their three children at the home. Upset by the poor accommodations, the Karliners decided to take their youngest daughter back to the village with them; this would ultimately cost the girl her life.

In the end, Herbert's mother, father, and two sisters were killed at Auschwitz; only Herbert and his brother survived. Herbert would not discover this until the American troops arrived in Paris. With nowhere to go, Herbert was sent by a Jewish humanitarian organization to be a counselor in order to receive groups of Jewish children from various liberated concentration camps. Karliner describes the experience: "It was awful . . . children from all nationalities . . . not even speaking the same language, not understanding one another and behaving like cave men; all sick and so pitiful."

After the dust settled in Europe, Herbert and his brother were able to move to America to live with their uncle in 1946.

As a twelve-year-old boy admiring the beaches of Florida from the deck of the *St. Louis* in 1939, Herbert made a promise to himself that he would come back to Miami one day. After moving to America, he kept that promise to himself and went to work in Miami in 1949. However, his new sense of freedom was quickly stripped away since he was drafted into the U.S. Army one year later. A young man who had lived through the worst war the world had ever seen went and proudly served his new country. After deployments to Korea and Japan, Herbert kept the promise he made to himself and finally put down his roots in Miami Beach in 1954. Currently retired and still living in Miami Beach, Herbert is eighty-six years old. He has been married to his wife Vera for forty-eight years and has two daughters.

Herbert remembers his voyage on the *St. Louis,* and with his white hair blowing in the sea breeze, he stares at Florida's crystal waters and says, "I promised myself I would come back to Miami one day . . . it took me a long time . . . but I made it."[48]

Cuba and the Voyage of the SS *St. Louis*

At first, many would not be able to see the likeness between the plight of present-day Cuban political refugees and the Jewish people trapped in the jaws of the Third Reich. However, one need look no further than the 936 Jewish refugees aboard the *St. Louis* to see the striking similarities between the shared fate of those aboard the *St. Louis* and those Cubans who have unsuccessfully fled their nation since Castro's Revolution of 1958.

Indeed, while the circumstances surrounding their stories may be different and although they are separated by cultures and generations, taking to the ocean's waters in overcrowded boats hoping it would carry them to a better life is the tie that binds the two.

In order to understand the voyage of the damned—the *St. Louis* voyage to Cuba—one must start in Paris, France, on November 7, 1938. It was on this day that Ernst von Rath, the third secretary of the German embassy in Paris, was shot and killed by Herschel Grynszpan, a Polish Jew.[49] Grynszpan was "outraged at the brutal expulsion from Germany of 10,000 long-resident Polish Jews with nothing but the clothes on their backs and about four dollars each, who were poorly treated by the Poles when they were dumped at the frontier."[50] As a result of the shooting, one of the most violent pogroms was carried out against Germany's entire Jewish population.

Known as, "Kristallnacht," or the "Night of Broken Glass," from November 9 to 10, 1938, the Jews of Germany were attacked, their synagogues vandalized, and their businesses and homes looted and destroyed. When the dust settled after the two-day attack, ninety-one Jews had been murdered, thousands injured, and over twenty thousand sent to concentration camps.[51]

To add insult to serious injury, the nation's Jews were held liable for the Kristallnacht pogrom and a fine of $400 million was imposed upon Germany's half million Jewish population.[52] Though the world did not realize it then, Kristallnacht marked the beginning of the Holocaust and the systematic extermination of the Jewish people.

After those fateful nights in November, the world was put on notice of the horrors that plagued Hitler's victims. The Jewish people quickly realized their window of opportunity to flee Hitler's Germany was growing smaller by the day. Leaving, however, was not easy. Refugees were not welcome with open arms, as many countries had immigration quotas, most notably the United States.

As a result, visas were hard to come by. Not only was money required to gain entry into a new nation, but Jews also had to pay just to leave Germany. This made travel cost prohibitive, since they had already been experiencing financial oppression under the Nazi regime.[53]

Despite these hurdles, immigration was the only way for German Jews to escape the oppressive regime that plagued them. And, for the 936 who booked passage aboard the SS *St. Louis,* it seemed like their only hope of survival.

Cuba appeared to be a suitable destination for refugees fleeing Germany. Jewish refugees were welcomed in Cuba, and the nation had received 1,500 of them in 1938 alone.[54] With its close proximity to America, Cuba was a choice location for refugees to find temporary solace while waiting to make America's immigration quota.[55] However, unbeknownst to those aboard the *St. Louis,* their arrival in Cuba was doomed before the ship even set sail from its German port in mid-May 1939.

In 1939, there were more than six thousand Jews living in Cuba, mostly in the port city of Havana.[56] Early that same year, immigration levels spiked, and in one twenty-four-hour period some twelve hundred refugees had arrived from various European nations.[57] With local constituents growing more discontent upon the arrival of more refugees, the government passed Decree 55 in the beginning of 1939.[58]

This decree was aimed at curbing immigration to Cuba by requiring refugees to pay a $500 bond to Cuba, ensuring they would not become permanent wards of the island nation.[59] Decree 55 stated tourists were still welcome in Cuba and as such were not required to pay bonds or obtain visas. Manuel Benitez, the corrupt director-general of immigration, saw the new law as an opportunity to generate personal wealth for himself. Accordingly, Benitez began to issue "landing certificates" to all tourists at the cost of $150 each. Benitez used these certificates as a tool to allow refugees to land in Cuba as tourists. The certificates appeared authentic, and even made to look like visas.[60] As a result, those looking to profit off the desperate Jewish immigrants would buy these certificates in bulk and resell them at inflated prices.[61] Benitez's plan to reap personal wealth as a result of the loophole in Decree 55 was successful, much to the chagrin of President Federico Laredo Brú. Additionally, Benitez had the benefit of being protected by Cuba's military leader Colonel Fulgencio Batista, a man whose influence was growing with Cubans. Because Batista had the power of the military behind him, Cuba's President Brú was unable to force Benitez to share his profits.[62]

In an effort to dry up Benitez's steady profit stream, President Brú's government took swift action to end Benitez's power to issue landing certificates.[63] The desired result would be twofold:

1. Closing the immigration loophole would no longer allow Benitez to cash in at Cuba's expense.

2. President Brú would gain favor from the Cubans in not allowing more refugees to enter the nation.

Prior to the *St. Louis*'s arrival in Cuba, Germany sent Nazi "provocateurs" to incite local anti-Semitic sentiment.[64] This was not a difficult task, since Cuba's economy was weak and the native population did not want to see the influx of more Jewish refugees, as many believed Cuba was already being overrun with Jews.[65] Therefore, to stay in good graces with the locals, Brú's government issued Decree 937 in May 1939. Decree 937 made the landing permit of passengers on board the *St. Louis* null and void. They had to find another way to buy their way off the ship, after having already paid an exorbitant amount under the original law.

As a result, the landing certificates, which the *St. Louis* passengers believed would grant them temporary stay in Cuba, were invalidated and would no longer grant refugee access to Cuba. Despite the fact that the Hamburg-America Line was aware of this change in Cuba's immigration policy prior to the *St. Louis* setting sail, it looked the other way and allowed the ship to depart.[66] Truthfully, the Hamburg-America Line did not care whether or not the passengers on the *St. Louis* were ever allowed to disembark in Cuba or any other port for that matter. In fact, the Hamburg-America Line charged its passengers 230 Reichsmarks, on top of the cost for their passage, in the event that the *St. Louis* had to make an "unplanned" trip back to Germany.[67]

Designed as the ultimate propaganda tool by the Nazis, the voyage of the *St. Louis* was intended to serve as a microcosm of the anti-Semitic attitude that spanned from one coast of the Atlantic to the other. Nazi Germany watched the *St. Louis* set sail, hoping that if Cuba refused to admit the Jewish refugees then the increasingly isolationist United States would do the same.[68] They were right.

The true tenor of those aboard the ship may never be fully realized. The captain of the ship, Gustav Schroeder, described by one of the survivors of the *St. Louis* as a compassionate man who ordered decent treatment for his Jewish passengers, noted in his diary at the outset of the trip that, "There is a somewhat nervous disposition among the passengers. Despite this, everyone seems convinced they will never see Germany again."[69]

As the *St. Louis* sailed closer to Cuba, Captain Schroeder was notified that the landing certificates held by most of those on board had been invalidated and would no longer be honored once the ship arrived.[70] Upon hearing that Cuba would not be allowing the passengers to disembark, Moritz Weiler, a man escaping Germany with his wife, succumbed to a deadly heart attack.[71] With no place to store the corpse, Mr. Weiler's body was buried at sea.[72]

This would not be the only fatality aboard during the journey. Less than an hour later, a despondent member of the crew threw himself overboard at the exact spot where Weiler's maritime funeral had taken place.[73] Unfortunately, the morbid mood on the *St. Louis* would only be exacerbated once it reached its destination.

The *St. Louis* arrived in Cuba on May 27. Only twenty-two of its Jewish passengers had the money required to pay the $500 bond in compliance with Cuba's newly refined immigration laws.[74] Therefore, they, along with six other non-Jewish passengers, were the only ones allowed to disembark.[75] While Colonel Batista had the influence to intercede on behalf of those who remained onboard "he dodged the issue, claiming to be ill with the grippe."[76] As the *St. Louis* sat anchored in Cuba's port, the publicity surrounding the ship and the plight of the refugees became a worldwide controversy.

With the ship idled in Cuba's harbor for days, Max Lowe, a Jewish man traveling with his wife and children, went to the location on deck where Mr. Weiler had been buried at sea days before. In an effort to end his life, Lowe slashed his wrists, threw himself overboard, and attempted to pull his own veins out of his arms.[77] Lowe's suicide was interrupted when a Cuban police boat pulled him from the water and sent him to a hospital.[78] Ironically, Lowe, who wanted to die, ended up being saved by the Cubans. Meanwhile, his family was left behind on the ship and prohibited from disembarking in order to accompany Lowe to the hospital.[79]

With seemingly little hope of being admitted into Cuba and increasingly morose events happening on board, Captain Schroeder, concerned about mass suicide attempts, created "suicide patrols" to prevent any additional passengers from taking their own lives.[80] The captain's apprehension was not unfounded. Jules Wallerstein, a young boy traveling with his family, said his father indicated that the passengers would commit suicide should the ship go back to Germany.

Wallerstein stated, "To me that was a shocker, I was twelve years old and realized it was the end of my life. My parents knew that if we went back the trains would be waiting for us."[81] Finally, the *St. Louis* was ordered out of Cuba's waters and Captain Schroeder turned northbound toward Florida.

In what seemed to be an answer to prayer, while the ship was four miles off the Floridian coast, the *St. Louis* was called back to Cuban waters. President Brú did not want to allow the passengers aboard the *St. Louis* into Cuba—doing so would make him appear politically vulnerable. He was struggling to hold on to his power, with Batista's influence and command as it was.[82] Additionally, President Brú felt he had to "maintain the prestige of the Cuban government vis-à-vis the Hamburg American Line."[83] However, the loss of Cuban prestige could evidently be mitigated with money because Brú conceded and agreed the passengers could disembark in Cuba, provided the government was paid $650 per person.[84]

The American Jewish Joint Distribution Committee (JDC), a group dedicated to Jewish aide, agreed to the inflated price—$150 in excess of the required bond—in order to ensure the *St. Louis*'s passengers did not have to return to Germany. The JDC sent Lawrence Berenson, a lawyer who was used to dealing with the Cuban government, with the cash required to close the deal.[85] Berenson felt he was in familiar territory; he had formerly secured one thousand visas for German Jews to land in Cuba and, more importantly, was friendly with Colonel Batista.[86]

However, when he met with President Brú and suggested a price reduction for the $650 bonds in an effort to save the JDC some money, President Brú once again ordered the *St. Louis* out of Cuban waters.[87] Evidently Brú did not want to haggle.

With the possibility of landing in Cuba no longer an option, Captain Gustav Schroeder once again turned the *St. Louis* toward Florida. He gradually sailed the ship up the coast, hoping the public exposure surrounding this humanitarian tragedy would prompt the United States to lend a helping hand. United States Treasury Secretary Henry Morgenthau, along with others, attempted to absorb the passengers into the U.S. Virgin Islands; however, this maneuver could not stand absent an act of Congress.[88]

Moreover, immigration "quotas were jealously guarded by Congress, supported by a strong, broad cross-section of Americans who were against all immigrants, not just Jews."[89] Accordingly, America's elected officials were not overly eager to render aide. Authorities are still mixed as to whether or not President Roosevelt did enough to help those aboard the *St. Louis*. As Conrad Black points out: "734 of the passengers were in quota lines for U.S. entry. Petitions were addressed to [President] Roosevelt from many groups within the United States and from the *St. Louis'* passengers, who pointed out in their plea that over 400 of their number were women and children. There were many editorials asking Roosevelt to be merciful to these unfortunates. He didn't reply to any of it."[90]

However, others suggest that Roosevelt, due to limitations of executive power, was incapable of altering the United States' immigration quota system, and as a result, could not permit those aboard the *St. Louis* to enter the United States.[91] Roosevelt's action or lack thereof, whatever it may have been, does not diminish the tragedy that surrounded the *St. Louis* saga.

With no help coming from the United States, the captain could not allow the ship to linger on the North American coast, as the onboard provisions were running low.[92] Seemingly defeated, the *St. Louis* made the long return trip across the Atlantic. Ironically, the passengers' only advocate was perhaps their most unlikely ally. Schroeder, a German and the captain of a ship sailing under the Nazi flag, promised his passengers that he would run the *St. Louis* aground off the coast of England before he would return his passengers to Germany.[93]

Ultimately, "after extensive diplomatic maneuvering and shameful rejections from many other countries," Schroeder never had to make good on his noble promise, as alternate democratic destinations were arranged for the passengers.[94] In the end, 288 of those aboard were allowed into England while the remaining passengers were absorbed into France, Belgium, and Holland, respectively.[95] Save England, all of the other nations that agreed to accept *St. Louis* refugees were hastily conquered by Hitler, and eventually the Jews living within their borders were systematically slaughtered in the Final Solution. Authorities are mixed as to exactly how many aboard the *St. Louis* met their demise upon returning to Europe; some experts suggest only approximately 450 survived the Holocaust.[96]

In fact, the United States Holocaust Museum continues to search for survivors.[97] What is not disputed, however, is the prominent role Cuba and its corrupt leaders played in the *St. Louis* tragedy. Perhaps the most revolting detail in this disaster is that the *Flander*, another ocean liner, had docked in Cuba shortly after the *St. Louis*.

On board, there were one hundred refugee passengers who held adequate visas, the same visas the JDC was willing to purchase for those on board the *St. Louis*. However, unlike the refugees on the *St. Louis*, the *Flander* passengers were admitted to Cuba without meeting any resistance.[98] This disgusting fact underscores the capricious game of Russian roulette that Cuba willingly played with the innocent lives of the Jewish people—not to mention the complicit role they assumed with the Nazis.

THE CONNECTION

"I will bless those who bless you."

—*Genesis 12:3 NKJV*

Within the shadows of the sad portrait painted by the SS *St. Louis* lie two illustrations regarding the fate of those who persecute the Jewish people and the promise of those who do not. Gustav Schroeder, the captain of the *St. Louis,* did not reject the children of Israel in their time of need. He could have returned his passengers to Germany as soon as they were rejected in Cuba, and arguably rebelled from his obligation to do so. Had he done this, there is little doubt that the majority, if not all of those aboard, would have perished at the hands of the Nazis. Yet, despite his allegiance to Nazi Germany, Captain Schroeder acted bravely and in the best interests of his passengers as opposed to his country. In a twist of fate, by the war's end, Schroeder's ship had sustained heavy damage and was sold for scrap.[99]

After this, the captain had no way to make ends meet, as the *St. Louis* was the last ship in his command.[100] Despite his misfortune, survivors of the *St. Louis* ensured that Schroder, in addition to his family, were taken care of.[101] In addition to this, Yad Vashem, the Holocaust museum in Israel, posthumously recognized the captain as "Righteous Among the Nations."[102] Gustav Schroeder survived because he did not reject Israel.

The Lord said, *"And I will curse him who curses you"* (Genesis 12:3 NKJV).

Unlike the actions of Captain Schroeder in 1939, Cuba blatantly turned its back on the Jewish people in their time of need. Two decades later, Colonel Batista, the military powerhouse who betrayed the Jewish people during the *St. Louis* affair—despite his having the ability to save them—was overthrown by Fidel Castro.

With his rise to power, Castro ushered in a new regime of socialism and dictatorship that isolated the nation and caused its citizens to live in poverty, to live without freedom, and to flee its borders in sinking ships for another country.

We have all seen the images. Makeshift rafts and dilapidated boats overloaded with Cuban political refugees seeking a better life just ninety miles north of their island home. Sometimes the stories end well for those who risk their lives, braving the elements of sun and sea in search of freedom and the American Dream. Yet the nameless and faceless majority who never make that short journey from Cuba to Florida's shore remain captives of communism.

Perhaps they never made it because the vessel carrying them to freedom was not as strong as their will to escape Castro's tyranny at home. Regardless of the outcome, we are all familiar with the story—Cuban political refugees leaving all that they have ever known behind, in search of a life free from the Communist chains that bound them.

In 1939, the Jews sailed to Cuba in a hopeful effort to escape a country that persecuted them, only to be rebuffed by an unwilling host. Is it ironic that less than twenty years later the same country that closed its doors to the children of Israel became a nation that persecuted its own people to such a degree that its citizens are perpetually clamoring aboard vessels set for sea with that same hope in mind? Cuba allowed the children of Israel to sail to their likely deaths. Since then, countless Cubans continue to meet that same fate.

"WHY DID GOD ALLOW THIS?": GERMANY'S REJECTION

I stood in the middle of the Nazi death camp, Dachau, and was stunned at the visible signs of unspeakable horror the Jewish people had suffered at the hands of the Third Reich. They were not here because they had broken the law; they were here because at least one of their grandparents was Jewish. In the Third Reich that was all it took to guarantee your horrific death at any death camp.

Standing in the Quadrangle where the Nazis had forced the Jews to stand for hours during roll call, I looked at the remaining foundations of the sleeping quarters where Jewish people were packed in and stacked on top of each other in a compound of human suffering that defies human imagination. To my left were the ovens where human beings were burned to ash on the altars of Nazi hatred. To the right of the ovens was a blood ditch where thousands, young and old, were mercilessly slaughtered and then carried on carts to the ovens to become ashes flying through the sky.

Standing in the Dachau Quadrangle, I conceived an idea that later brought a degree of comfort and consolation to the Jewish relatives of those who had died such a horrific death there. The idea came from the prophet Ezekiel, who wrote: "I sat where they sat, and remained there astonished among them" (Ezekiel 3:15 NKJV).

It was Elijah's way of saying, "You can't know how people feel about any given tragedy or time of trouble until you feel exactly what they have felt and experienced."

As Diana and I left the death camp, we were bound for West Berlin, where I was to be the speaker for five nights at the U.S. military chapel in a week of spiritual emphasis for our military personnel.

I expressed to Diana my desire to return to Dachau at a later date and have a "lest we forget" memorial service for the Jewish people who died in the Holocaust and were related to our Jewish friends in America. We agreed we would do it.

Months later, we did exactly that. As four hundred Christians stood in formation in the Quadrangle with the Star of David on our arms and the names of the Jewish people who had died in the Holocaust attached to our clothes, we answered a roll call, stepping forward and saying, "I am here!"

Our travel troupe left Dachau for Israel, where we planted those armbands around a tree in a grove of trees with the name of the Jewish people who perished in the Holocaust on the armband. The symbolism was that they had returned to Israel to be a part of the Holy Land for all eternity.

As Diana and I left Dachau on our first visit, I took several minutes studying closely the fence the Nazis had built around the Jews in every death camp of the Third Reich. The concrete posts were square and precisely the same height, adorned with barbed wire from top to bottom.

The posts were planted in two rows exactly equidistant from each other, totally encircling the death camp. There were machine gun towers erected in the center of the "no man's land" created by the two rows of concrete posts.

It might have been possible to make it over the first barrier of barbed wire and post; none could dream of making it over the second fence before being riddled with machine gun fire.

German shepherd dogs patrolled the middle ground to make sure the marksmen in the towers knew exactly the location of anyone approaching the fence. Death and torture were art forms for the Nazis.

Little did I know that in the next few days a revelation of truth concerning this fence would explode at Checkpoint Charlie in West Berlin, where I had been invited by the U.S. military to speak in their chapel for five nights concerning the topic of the "Fight for the Family." There are many pressures on a military family that civilians never endure. I accepted the invitation and was delighted with the chapel being packed to the back walls.

The military graciously gave me a guide, a vehicle with a military driver to escort Diana and me wherever we wanted to go. We discovered that West Berlin was a beautiful city with some of the most exciting shopping opportunities Diana had ever discovered on planet Earth.

After I had spoken the five nights at the chapel, I slipped behind what was then called the Iron Curtain to speak on two different occasions. If you can believe it, I was smuggled into East Berlin as an art critic. I have the qualifications to be an art critic like a bumblebee has the potential to be a 747.

As we drove up to Checkpoint Charlie, I was captivated by the barbed-wire fence that separated West Berlin, which looked like heaven on earth compared to the barren and desolate East Berlin, the Utopia of Communism. I could understand why people risked their lives often in a desperate attempt to escape Communist oppression for the paradise of freedom and unlimited abundance in the West.

As we exited the military vehicle to visit the museum at Check Point Charlie, our guide looked at me, pointed at the fence, and asked in disgust with the Almighty, "Pastor Hagee, why did God allow the Communists to build a fence like that around the German people to cage us in like animals?"

In a flash, I saw the fence at Dachau. The fence the Communists had built around the Germans was exactly the same fence as the one at Dachau. The concrete posts were the same height, the same shape, with the arch at the top adorned with razor-sharp wire promising death to anyone who might be foolish enough to attempt escape.

There were the machine gun towers in the middle, equally spaced, with German shepherd dogs patrolling the "no man's land" in the middle. Then it hit me like a ton of bricks, and I answered the guide who was shaken to the core: "God allowed the Communists to build this fence around you, because it is exactly the same fence the Germans built around the Jews in every death camp of the Third Reich. Remember:

exactly what you do to the Jews, God will do to you. God has it the same . . . down to the dog hair!"

AHMADINEJAD'S PAYDAY IS COMING! IRAN'S REJECTION

Unless President Ahmadinejad of Iran is prevented by a military preemptive strike, he will soon have the nuclear power to make his maniacal dreams of a nuclear holocaust a reality. He has threatened on international television and the world press to "wipe Israel off the map." [103]

In a television interview in June 2008, Ahmadinejad said, "Today, the time for the fall of the satanic power of the United States has come and the countdown for annihilation of the emperor of power and wealth has started." [104]

America, it's time to wake up!

We face a clear and present danger from a theocratic dictatorship that has the will and soon will have the nuclear power to destroy us. It's time to shake ourselves out of the stupor of political correctness and embrace reality. The reality is that President Ahmadinejad believes that if he starts WWIII, the Islamic messiah will appear suddenly and mysteriously.

Understand that he doesn't know *who* this messiah is or *where* he is, but he believes the moment that Iran starts this "holy war," which will engulf the entire world in chaos, his messiah will appear. This mysterious messiah will lead the "holy warriors" of radical Islam to a global Sharia, meaning that every nation on the face of the earth will come under Islamic law. Ahmadinejad believes that he has the power and the duty to bring this about.

Remember, history teaches us that those who fail to remember the mistakes of the past are doomed to repeat them. One of the most tragic events of recent history was Hitler's Holocaust against the Jewish people during World War II. There are a number of lessons that we can learn from the Holocaust, but one of the most important is this: when a maniac threatens to kill you, take him at his maniacal word.

When Hitler began his threats to kill the Jewish people, few took him seriously. That was a tragic mistake. Ahmadinejad is the new *Hitler of the Middle East*. He wants a nuclear holocaust. He wants "the Great Satan," which is America, to fall and be in submission to Islam, and he wants to destroy Israel utterly.

Will God permit this madman to attack America with nuclear weapons? I sincerely believe this will happen if Iran is permitted to obtain nuclear weapons. Iran has made a mockery of Western diplomacy and could not care less about America's proposed sanctions. Ahmadinejad and his diplomacy of deception and delay have played England and America like a harp. He wants the bomb at any cost, including a nuclear war in the Middle East.

IRAN IN BIBLE PROPHECY

There are six nations whose exact names are given by the prophet Ezekiel that, at some point in the future, will unify in a massive Islamic army to invade and attempt to destroy Israel.

Who are they?

Will they succeed?

What will be their end?

All of these questions are answered by the prophet Ezekiel. The six nations that will form an Islamic military force "as a cloud to cover the land" will be Persia (Iran), Ethiopia, Libya, Germany, and Turkey—all being led by Russia.

Ezekiel looks into the world of tomorrow and writes: "Persia [Iran], Ethiopia, and Libya are with them, all of them with shield and helmet; Gomer and all its troops; the house of Togarmah *from* the far north and all its troops—many people *are* with you" (Ezekiel 38:5–6 NKJV).

Persia

Persia is modern-day Iran. As this book is being written, Russia and Iran have joined forces to create long-range nuclear missiles that can hit London, Jerusalem, and New York. During the first administration of Israeli Prime Minister Benjamin Netanyahu, Israeli intelligence gave photographic proof to America's intelligence community that Russian scientists were directing and supervising Iran's nuclear weapons programs. There is no doubt a nuclear collision is coming in the near future in the Middle East.

If Israel is forced to attack Iran, it will unify every radical Islamic warrior in the world to wage holy war against the Jewish people and Israel. This could easily launch Ezekiel's war as described in Ezekiel 38–39.

Ethiopia and Libya

Ethiopia and Libya are used in two distinctly different senses in the Old Testament. They were nations in Africa known as Ethiopia and Libya, and their names continued until today. There were also states adjacent to Persia that were known as Ethiopia and Libya.

When Moses fled from Egypt because he had killed the Egyptian, he went into the wilderness, and there he married an Ethiopian. He did not go south into African Ethiopia, but into the Ethiopia of the Arabian Peninsula, where he married an Ethiopian who was a Shemite. Therefore, when Ezekiel speaks of Persia, Ethiopia, and Libya, he is speaking of the Arab states.

When Ezekiel writes concerning Russia in chapter 38, verse 6, he says, "many people are with you." He repeats that concept in verse 9: "You [Russia] will ascend, coming like a storm, covering the land like a cloud, you and all your troops and many peoples with you."

I believe this is a clear suggestion that America's influence with Arab nations will become virtually nonexistent. According to recent polls, President Obama's efforts to charm the Arab nations has produced no benefit whatsoever to the United States and its efforts toward controlling Iran's nuclear ambitions.

However, Russia's influence has dramatically increased and will continue to do so as it joins forces with Iran and other Islamic nations against Israel in the immediate future.

We are watching this courtship as Russia refuses to support any meaningful sanction against Iran in the United Nations. The Russians have also agreed to sell Iran its latest and most sophisticated missile systems, the S-300 missiles, which are similar to the U.S. Patriot missile and capable of shooting down aircraft, cruise missiles, and ballistic missile warheads and ranges over 90 miles at altitudes of about 90,000 feet.

Recently, Russia denied that their freighter, *Arctic Sea,* which was allegedly seized by pirates in the Baltic Sea and purportedly loaded with lumber, was in fact carrying S-300 missiles bound for Iran. Israel has strongly objected to Russia selling the S-300 missiles to Iran. These missiles would protect all of Iran's nuclear sites, making any Israeli Air Force preemptive military attack virtually mission impossible.

On August 10, 2005, BBC News, UK edition, called Russia "Iran's main partner in its effort to develop nuclear power." [105]

What's the payoff for the Arabs? They believe the Islamic fanatical vision of exterminating the Jews can be realized with Russia's help. Absolute control of Jerusalem as the capital for the new Palestinian state will be within their grasp.

However, there's one problem looming on the horizon: God Almighty, whom the Russians defy and radical Islamists denounce, has brought this evil axis of power into Israel to bury it before the eyes of the world. The destruction of Russia and its radical Islamic allies is going to be the most powerful object lesson the world has seen since Pharaoh and his army were drowned in the Red Sea.

Ezekiel writes to the Russian leadership of this Russian-Arab Islamic coalition of nations, saying: "Prepare yourself and be ready, you and all your companies that are gathered about you; and be a guard for them" (Ezekiel 38:7 NKJV).

A better translation of the phrase "be a guard for them" is this: "Be thou a commander unto them." Ezekiel leaves no doubt that Russia is leading the attack on Israel.

In verse 8, Russia makes its move into Israel: "After many days you will be visited. In the latter years [at the end of the age] you will come into the land [Israel] of those brought back from the sword."

Verse 11 reveals the fact that Israel has made a covenant with the false messiah, the new Caesar of the world, who will come out of the European Union and promise peace and safety to Israel. The Bible warns: "For when they say, 'Peace and safety!' then sudden destruction comes upon them" (1 Thessalonians 5:3 NKJV).

In Ezekiel 38:11, Russia is addressing all its allies, suggesting they go into Israel, which is called at that time the "land of unwalled villages." Russia says: "I will go to them that are at rest, that dwell safely" (KJV).

Why is Israel at rest? It is at rest because its leaders are trusting in their peace accord with the European Union to guarantee their safety from Russia and the Arab coalition of nations.

The false messiah will make a seven-year peace treaty with Israel and break it after three and a half years. At that point, the false messiah will set up his image in the city of Jerusalem and demand that the citizens of the world worship him.

WHAT IS AMERICA'S ROLE?

Where is America in this picture? In verse 12, Russia and its allies are going into Israel "to take plunder and to take booty." Russia is going to move militarily against Israel from the north to position themselves geopolitically to have direct access to the rich oil reserves of the Persian Gulf. Russia has to have the oil to make its war machine function and to be reborn as a superpower.

Russia will promise the Islamic nations control of Jerusalem and the Temple Mount. Be reminded that Russia has an ongoing war with the radical Islamists within Russia. They have recently blown up the tracks to an express train killing thirty Russians and injuring almost one hundred people. Russia will benefit greatly by making peace with the radical Islamic force within its own borders to unify with Iran and other Islamists around the world against Israel.

What will be America's response to this brazen act of massive invasion of Israel and the pursuit to control the vast wealth of the world in Persian Gulf oil? Ezekiel answers in verse 13.

"Sheba, Dedan, the merchants of Tarshish," that is, the Western powers, will be upset when Russia invades Israel, but will take no action against this brazen and massive invasion. These nations *"and all their young lions,"*—England's symbol is that of a lion. America is an offspring of England; hence, the "young lions"—will not come to Israel's rescue. They will not send massive military forces to drive Russia and Arabs out of Israel. Instead, the Western world is simply going to make a passive diplomatic response, saying, "Have you gathered your army to take booty, to carry away silver and gold, to take away livestock and goods, to take great plunder?" (Ezekiel 38:13 NKJV).

What a ridiculous response!

It's obvious to the nations of the world what Russia and the radical Islamists are doing, and yet the Western world is doing absolutely nothing to stop them.

Why won't America respond?

Let me venture to say that with the combined factors of America's extended wars in Iraq and Afghanistan and with our overwhelming national debt, America will show no desire to confront Russia, Iran, and the massive military armada they bring together to invade Israel. As Ezekiel says, it will "cover the land" (38:16 NKJV).

Ezekiel makes it clear that America's and Europe's diplomatic inquiry means absolutely nothing to Russia and the radical Islamists. The invasion is on! This invasion is described as follows: "You will come up against My people Israel like a cloud, to cover the land. It will be in the latter days that *I will bring you against My land,* so that the nations may know Me, when I am hallowed in you, O Gog, before their eyes" (Ezekiel 38:16 NKJV).

God makes it clear that He is dragging Russia and its allies into Israel with a hook in their jaw. That hook is oil! (We'll talk more about this in chapter 9.) "I will bring you against my land." When Russia leads Iran and its radical Islamic allies into Israel, the Western superpowers will simply sit on their hands and watch.

Ezekiel portrays Russia as being in complete command. Why? Because the defender of Israel is the God of Abraham, Isaac, and Jacob, and He is dragging the enemies of Israel into Israel for the greatest display of His fury since He drowned Pharaoh and the Egyptian army in the Red Sea.

There is comfort and consolation in Ezekiel's prophetic portrait of the world tomorrow. The message is that God is in total control of what appears to be a hopeless situation for Israel. He has deliberately dragged these anti-Semitic nations into Israel to crush them so that the Jews of Israel and the nations of the world will know that He is the Lord and there is no other. America and Europe will not save Israel . . . (God will!)

Ezekiel reveals a day coming when God's fury explodes against the nations that have tormented his chosen people with relentless wars, suicide bombers, and endless terror. Ezekiel writes a full description of God's anger: ("My fury will show in My face") (Ezekiel 38:18 NKJV).

THE WEAPONS OF WAR

God will destroy Iran and Russia along with this massive Islamic coalition with three weapons of war He has used before in Scripture. These weapons are:

1. A mighty earthquake

2. Every man's sword against his brother

3. Raining from heaven of fire and brimstone

One day soon there will appear on the evening news a battle scene covered by global television with these words:

For in My jealousy and *in the fire of My wrath I have spoken: "Surely in that day there shall be a great earthquake in the land of Israel, so that the fish of the sea, the birds of the heavens, the beast of the field, all creeping things that creep on the earth, and all men who* are *on the face of the earth shall shake at My presence. The mountains shall be thrown down, the steep places shall fall, and every wall shall fall to the ground." I will call for a sword against Gog [Russia] throughout all My mountains," says the Lord GOD. "Every man's sword will be against his brother. And I will bring him to judgment with pestilence and bloodshed; I will rain down on him, on his troops, and on the many people who* are *with him [Arab nations], flooding rain, great hailstones, fire, and brimstone."*

—*Ezekiel 38:19–22 NKJV*

When did God use these weapons of war before? When Moses' leadership was being contested by Korah, Dathan, and Abiram in Numbers 16, God told Moses to get away from the tents of Korah, Dathan, and Abiram because he was about to give Israel an object lesson never to be forgotten in the history of the world—the *first* weapon of war.

Then Moses said, "But if the LORD creates a new thing, and the earth opens its mouth and swallows them up with all that belongs to them, and they [those who are rejecting Moses' leadership] go down alive into the pit, then you will understand that these men have rejected the LORD." Now it came to pass, as he finished speaking all these words, that the ground split apart under them, and the earth opened its mouth and swallowed them up, with their households and all the men with Korah, with all their goods.

—*Numbers 16:30–32 NKJV*

The world is heading toward God's *second* object lesson. Ezekiel makes it clear that God will send an earthquake that will swallow up the enemies of Israel, just as an earthquake swallowed up the enemies of Moses.

God will use the sword of brother against brother as the second weapon of war. When God sent Gideon to destroy the Philistines, Gideon commanded his meager fighting force of three hundred men to sound the trumpets and to break the pitchers. The Philistines turned their swords against each other in massive confusion and slaughtered one another (see Judges 7).

God will bring this battle-tested tactic to wage war against Russia and Iran and their allies when they come against Israel. God will cause confusion to come among them as they turn and fight each other, slaughtering each other in history's greatest demonstration of death by friendly fire.

The *third* weapon in God's arsenal is great hailstones, fire, and brimstone. Two of the most infamous cities that ever existed in history were the cities of Sodom and Gomorrah. Why are they famous? Their fame arises from the fact that they no longer exist. These are the two cities where God poured out fire and brimstone because of their great sin and iniquity, and they were obliterated from the earth.

To this day geologists have sought to discover the location of Sodom and Gomorrah, but God so completely destroyed them they have never been found. Some speculate that they have been buried beneath the Dead Sea, which would explain the rare sulfuric odor and the taste of the water in the Dead Sea.

When Russia and its allies invade Israel, and America and Europe fail to respond, "He who sits in the heavens shall laugh" (Psalms 2:4 NKJV). As He crushes the Russian-Iranian tormentors of the apple of His eye. He will crush them as He crushed Pharaoh, Haman, and Hitler so that Israel and the world "shall know that I am the LORD" (Ezekiel 38:23 NKJV).

The Battle Report

When Iran and Russia, with their allies, march into Israel, they will be expecting to march out in victory. There will be no indication to them of what awaits them. They will have no awareness that they are making that march into Israel because God has put "hooks into (their) jaws," or that He is the one leading their armies to their annihilation.

Yet, in Ezekiel 39, God has revealed the battle report and the outcome of that military confrontation with Israel, telling his prophet what He will do to Iran, Russia, and their allies when they invade Israel in the near future:

And I will turn thee back, and leave but the sixth part of thee, and
will cause thee to come up from the north parts, and will bring thee
upon the mountains of Israel.

—*Ezekiel 39:2 KJV*

God declares He will exterminate all but one sixth of the Iranian-Russian axis of evil that invades Israel. Five out of six warriors in that great army will be killed. That's a death rate of 82 percent within a matter of hours. It's no wonder the world will be shaken with shock and awe.

God continues with His strategy of war by saying:

"Then I will knock the bow out of your left hand, and cause the arrows
to fall out of your right hand. You shall fall upon the mountains of
Israel, you and all your troops and the peoples who are *with you; I will*
give you to birds of prey of every sort and to *the beasts of the field to be*
devoured . . . And I will send fire on Magog [Russia] and on those who
live in security in the coastlands. Then they shall know that I am *the*
LORD."

—*Ezekiel 39:3–4, 6*

The last verse suggests that judgment is coming not only to the invading Russian force but also on the headquarters of that power and upon all who support it or allowed this attack on Israel.

Notice the words: "I will send fire . . . upon those who live in security in the coastlands." The word translated *coastlands* or *isle* in the Hebrew is *'iy.* The word was used by the ancients in the sense of *continents* today. It designated the great gentile civilizations across the seas, which were usually settled most densely along the coastline, just like America.

This fire Ezekiel sees coming to those living securely in the coastlands could be a direct judgment from God by hurricanes and tsunamis, or it could describe a nuclear war via an exchange of nuclear missiles.

Could it be that America, who refuses to defend Israel from the Iranian-Russian invasion, will experience nuclear warfare on our East and West coasts? That's exactly where most of us live today in America.

Why would God allow this?

The Bible gives a clear answer: "I will bless those who bless you, and I will curse him who curses you" (Genesis 12:3 NKJV).

What you do or try to do to Israel, God Almighty will do exactly to you. It's a Bible truth proven repeatedly over the centuries of world history. Remember: those who fail to remember the mistakes of the past are doomed to repeat them.

Ahmadinejad has threatened to wipe Israel off the map. The truth is, Iran and the radical Islamic mob that has tormented Israel for decades will be wiped off the map in one day, according to the word of God as given through his servant Ezekiel.

There is a payday someday for all the enemies of Israel, both small and great. It's coming! Think it can't happen? Think again!

SEVEN

The Criminalization of Christianity

The criminalization of Christianity did not begin with the formation of the ACLU under the leadership of Roger Baldwin, who confessed to being a committed socialist and whose ultimate objective was the promotion of communism.[1]

The criminalization of Christianity began with the Roman Empire and their conspiracy as led by King Herod and Pilate to destroy a Jewish rabbi from Nazareth named Jesus Christ.

The plot of the Roman Empire to destroy the ministry of Jesus was simple and effective: publicly accuse Jesus of things he had never said or done in order to assassinate his character and scatter his followers, wounded by doubt. The concept of slaughter-the-shepherd-and-scatter-the-sheep was not new and is still the modus operandi of some in the liberal media.

Jesus of Nazareth was labeled a heretic, a liar, a drunkard, a demonized madman, and an insurrectionist too dangerous to live.

Before even meeting Jesus, why would Rome fear Him and twelve ordinary disciples who had no wealth, little education, no military experience, and who were virtually unknown?

Rome had Jesus on the "watch list," because He demonstrated the ability to feed five thousand people out of a boy's sack lunch. He had demonstrated the ability to heal the wounded and to raise the dead. He attracted the masses that were ready and willing to follow Him in a revolt to crush the repressive Roman Empire, if He would only give the word. However, He never did, saying, "My kingdom is not of this world."

Add to his government profile that his ministry started in Galilee, which was known as a hotbed for its antigovernment positions, and Jesus had the profile in the Homeland Security Office of the Roman Empire as a right-wing, Bible-believing, hate monger who needed to be on the "watch list," like four hundred thousand Americans are right now in Washington, DC.

He was arrested by Rome in the Garden of Gethsemane, put on trial, falsely accused, and, in a matter of hours, was brutally murdered by the Roman government at the place called Calvary as an insurrectionist too dangerous to live.

Those who present Jesus Christ as a man who was loved by everyone seriously misrepresent the message and ministry of the son of God. If he was loved by everyone, just how did he manage to get himself arrested, thrown into jail, beaten to a bloody pulp, and publicly crucified naked between two known thieves?

The truth is the government hated Jesus because of his massive influence with the public. Jesus left this postscript for those who would follow him through the centuries:

"If the world hates you, you know that it hated Me before it hated you. If you were of the world, the world would love its own. Yet because you are not of the world, but I chose you out of the world, therefore the world hates you.

—John 15:18–19 NKJV

The truth is, the leaders of the New Testament church were in constant trouble with godless governments. Listen to the travelogue of suffering composed by St. Paul who wrote most of the New Testament and was given a guided tour of heaven by God Himself:

In labors more abundant, in stripes above measure, in prisons more frequently, in deaths often. From the Jews five times I received forty stripes minus one. Three times I was beaten with rods; once I was stoned; three times I was shipwrecked; a night and a day have I been in the deep; in journeys often, in perils of water, in perils of robbers,

*in perils of my own countrymen, in perils of the Gentiles, in perils in
the city, in perils in the wilderness, in perils in the sea, in perils among
false brethren; in weariness and toil, in sleeplessness often, in hunger
and thirst, in fastings often, in cold and nakedness—besides the other
things . . . my deep concern for all churches.*

—*2 Corinthians 11:23–28 NKJV*

St. Paul was in jail more than he was out of jail. Much of the New Testament was not written in some secluded seashore cottage with soft sea breezes stimulating the creative energies of the apostle. Much of the New Testament was written in a rat-infested jail cell with blood dripping off his back from the beatings given by sadistic Roman guards. Rome put his body in prison, but they could not capture the fire of his spirit or the passion of his unconquerable soul.

St. Paul writes, "In all these things we are more than conquerors through Him who loved us" (Romans 8:37 NKJV).

The list of Gospel jailbirds runs through the sacred Scripture concluding with John the Revelator on the isle of Patmos, labeled and slandered as an "enemy of the state" because he chose Christ over Caesar.

Martin Niemöller, a devout and passionate German Lutheran pastor trapped in the jaws of the Third Reich, was thrown into prison by Hitler and was executed. Why? Because he dared to say that Germany could not serve two masters. Either Germany would choose to serve Jesus Christ or Adolf Hitler.

The propaganda presses of the Third Reich crucified Niemöller's character and slandered his name; heaven crowned him as a champion of the cross and great was his reward the moment he stepped through gates of splendor into everlasting life.

Question: What would be your response if your pastor were thrown into jail and slandered in the media for preaching the gospel of Jesus Christ from the pulpit of your church?

Would you stand by him or leave the church? Would you be offended by the vicious slander of the media, the cruel office gossip, and the malignant lies told by people on the street who knew nothing of the truth?

Would you, like the Apostle Peter on the night that Christ was arrested by five hundred Roman soldiers from the Antonian Fortress in the Garden of Gethsemane say: "I know not the man!"

Would you be like his disciples who "returned to their nets"? They retreated to their comfort zone rather than face the conflict produced by their convictions. When you are confronted in the future about what you believe based on Bible truth, will you stand up or return to your nets? All men fall; the great ones get back up. You should never complain about what you permit. Your decisions today determine tomorrow's destiny.

As a Bible-believing Christian in America, you need to prepare yourself mentally, emotionally, and spiritually to defend your faith in court in the near future.

Think it can't happen?

Think again!

Get ready for it to happen!

WHEN CHRISTIANITY IS A CRIME

Let me address the title of this chapter, which some may consider to be too harsh: "The Criminalization of Christianity." The word *crime* is defined in Webster's New World Dictionary as "an act committed in violation of a law."

I select the title "The Criminalization of Christianity" because there are laws in place, thanks principally to the ACLU, that when violated, constitute a crime. Understand that it's not a crime according to the teachings of the Bible, but it's a crime in secularized America in the twenty-first century! We are at the point in American history where the laws of men surpass the laws of God Almighty in the courthouse. For instance, it is against the law of the Ten Commandments to commit murder. The U.S. Congress has just passed health care legislation that, in spite of the Presidential Executive Order 13535, does not change the law. As soon as Executive Order 13535 is challenged in a court of law the judge will yield to the law as it existed before the executive order and abortions will be paid for under the health care bill. The presidential executive order is not worth the paper it's written on! The government is taking your dollars and will use them to murder infants in the wombs of their mothers. Abortion is the American holocaust. Forty-three million beautiful babies butchered in America's abortion mills under the banner of "pro-choice."

Roger Baldwin, founder of the ACLU, described himself thusly: "I am for socialism, disarmament, and ultimately for abolishing the state itself as an instrument of violence and compulsion. I seek social ownership of property, the abolition of the propertied class, and sole control by those who produce wealth. Communism is the goal." [2]

"For eight decades, the ACLU has been America's leading censor, waging a largely uncontested war against America's core values, cloaking its war in the name of liberty." [3]

The result of this conflict is that Americans find themselves living in a country that, with each passing day, becomes more foreign to the positions our founders fought and died to preserve.

OUR FOUNDING FATHERS SAID WHAT?

While much has been written in recent years in an effort to deny the fact that America was founded upon the Bible, no efforts of atheist and agnostic secularists can change the facts of history. Anyone who examines the original writings, speeches, or personal correspondence of the Founding Fathers must conclude that their lives and principles were rooted and grounded in the word of God.

For the record, let's examine the statements of some of our Founding Fathers:

George Washington, the father of our nation and the first president of the United States, stated: "It is impossible to rightly govern the world without God and the Bible." [4]

John Quincy Adams, the sixth president, stated: "The first and . . . the only book deserving of universal attention is the Bible. I speak as a man of the world . . . and I say to you 'Search the Scriptures.' " [5]

Andrew Jackson, the seventh president, stated, referring to the Bible: "That book, sir, is the rock on which our Republic rests." [6]

Patrick Henry, governor of Virginia and signer of the Declaration of Independence, stated: "It cannot be emphasized too clearly and too often that this nation was founded, not by religionists, but by Christians; not by religion, but on the gospel of Jesus Christ." [7]

John Hancock, signer of the Declaration of Independence, said: "Principally and first of all, I give and recommend my soul into the hands of God that gave it: and my body I recommend to the earth . . . nothing doubting but at the general resurrection I shall receive the same again by the mercy and power of God." [8]

Henry Knox, Revolutionary War general, stated: "To the supreme head of the universe—to that great and tremendous Jehovah—Who created the universal flame of nature, worlds, and systems in number infinite . . . to this awfully sublime Being do I resign my spirit with unlimited confidence of His mercy and protection." [9]

Charles Carroll, signer of the Declaration of Independence, stated: "Without morals a republic cannot subsist any length of time; they therefore who are decrying the Christian religion, whose morality is so sublime and pure . . . are undermining the solid foundation of morals, the best security for the duration of free governments." [10]

Benjamin Rush, signer of the Declaration of Independence, declared: "My only hope of salvation is in the infinite, transcendent love of God manifested to the world by the death of His Son upon the cross. Nothing but His blood will wash away my sins. I rely exclusively upon it. Come, Lord Jesus! Come quickly!" [11]

John Hancock and John Adams shook the world with one sentence: "We recognize no sovereign but God, and no King but Jesus." [12]

THE ACLU VERSUS CHRISTIANITY

As America drifts further into the abyss of secularism, as liberal federal judges continue to overrule the will of the people in defense of godly moral standards, as the ACLU continues its high-powered and well-funded war against Christianity, the America our Founding Fathers died to birth is on the critical list with infections of political correctness, greed, apathy, immorality, and endless empowerments dragging the republic into an early grave.

The ACLU positions itself as the great defender of freedom. Occasionally they take a case that does exactly that, but the majority of their effort is to control or eliminate the freedom of millions of Americans. The ACLU has an annual budget of $45 million; its staff is stated as being three hundred in addition to sixty full-time attorneys with one thousand volunteer attorneys. This is a legal war machine and Christianity is in its crosshairs.

Bill O'Reilly, author and host of Fox News' *O'Reilly Factor,* states:

"Few Americans realize how radical the ACLU has become and the threat it poses to liberty."[13]

Dr. D. James Kennedy, PhD., founder and president of Coral Ridge Ministries and senior minister of Coral Ridge Presbyterian Church in Ft. Lauderdale, Florida, stated concerning the ACLU: "Perhaps no organization has done more to remove America from its Judeo-Christian moorings than the ACLU—whom I often call the 'Anti-Christian Litigation Union.' "[14]

The ACLU has been against America from the beginning. The objective of the ACLU is to use the judiciary, rather than the electorate, to implement its agenda.

Roger Baldwin's instruction on how to present the ACLU to the general public is expressed thusly, "Do stir away from making the organization look like a Socialist enterprise. Too many people have gotten the idea that it is nine-tenths a Socialist movement. We want to look like patriots in everything we do. We want to get a good lot of flags, talk a good deal about the Constitution and what our forefathers wanted to make of this country, and to show that we are really the folks that stand for the spirit of our institutions."[15]

The ACLU Agenda

As authors Alan Sears and Craig Osten state in their book *The ACLU vs. America:*

- All legal prohibitions on the distribution of obscene material—including *child pornography*—are unconstitutional.

- *Pornographic outlets* can locate wherever they please—whether next to churches or day-care centers or near residential neighborhoods.

- *Tax-funded libraries* should not restrict access of children to pornography on the internet.

- *Parents should have no legal recourse* when it comes to shielding their children from exposure to hard-core pornography.

- *The military* cannot enforce even the most basic codes of conduct—such as discipline of disrespectful behavior toward a superior officer.

- *The military* cannot stop open displays of homosexual behavior within its ranks.

- *Parents cannot limit their children's exposure* to, or participation in, public school classes and assemblies that violate the family's core religious and moral beliefs, except those related to Orthodox Jewish or Christian teachings.

- *Public schools cannot observe recognized religious,* historical, and cultural holidays such as Christmas, Easter, or Hanukkah, despite hundreds of years of American tradition.

- All *legislative, military, and prison chaplaincy* programs should be abolished.

- All criminal and civil laws that prohibit polygamy and *same-sex "marriage"* should be done away with.[16]

The fundamentals of freedom as guaranteed by the Constitution of the United States are being aggressively attacked in an effort to control Christians and Christianity.

Consider the freedom of speech being contested in the case of *Peterson v. Hewlett-Packard Co.,* a Christian worker who exercised his right to free speech in response to a homosexual poster the company had placed near his cubicle. He posted Bible verses to express his beliefs on the matter. He was fired.

Was he in Sweden? Canada? Try Boise, Idaho. The Ninth Circuit Court of Appeals wrote, "An employer need not accommodate an employee's religious beliefs if doing so would result in discrimination against his co-workers or deprive them of contractual or other statutory rights." [17]

Do you, as an American, have the right to practice your religious beliefs in the work place? No, according to the courts in California.

When a lesbian approached two Christian doctors in San Diego County, California, to be artificially inseminated, the doctors refused. Rather than express tolerance toward the doctors' religious convictions and their right not to participate in her plan, she sued them. And a California Appeal Court found that the two doctors were wrong to refuse. Jennifer Pizer, the lesbian's attorney, clarified her legal position on *Hannity & Colmes:* "When the doctor is in her church, she can do religion, but not in the medical office." [18]

Pastors across America are now organizing into the Coalition of Pastors to defend themselves legally in the court of law. Pastors in Pennsylvania are now seeking liability insurance to protect themselves from being prosecuted under the state's new Hate-Speech Law. That's right. They are reacting to the state's recent addition of "sexual orientation" to its hate crime laws. Of particular concern is the expansion of the term *harassment* to include "harassment by communication," which means a person can be convicted on the basis of spoken words alone.[19]

That means that if a pastor stands in his pulpit and reads Leviticus 20:13—"If a man lies with a male as he lies with a woman, both of them have committed an abomination"—he could be sent to jail for harassment by communication, which is considered hate speech by the courts in Pennsylvania.

You may not live in the state of Pennsylvania, but because courts may look to other state's laws for precedent when their state laws are silent, this Pennsylvania law has a real potential to affect you.

Under the banner of diversity, the Sixth Court of Appeals stated: "Adherence of all faiths are equally valid as religions."

That explains why U.S. Army posts have witch chaplains who have equal standing with Christian, Jewish, and Muslim chaplains.[20]

THE THREAT IS SPREADING FASTER
THAN YOU CAN IMAGINE

The following laws are now enforced upon your children and grandchildren who go to public schools. Perhaps it's time for you to consider sending your child to a Christian school where your beliefs are not constantly mocked and your child is not ridiculed and humiliated for what they believe. Consider the following:

Verbal prayer offered in a school is unconstitutional even if that prayer is both voluntary and denominationally neutral. *(Engel v. Vitale, 1962; Abington v. Schempp, 1963; Commissioner of Education v. School Committee of Leyden, 1971)*

- If a student prays over lunch, it is unconstitutional for him to pray out loud. *(Reed v. Van Hoven, 1965)*

- When a student addresses an assembly of his peers, he effectively becomes a government representative; it is therefore unconstitutional for that student to engage in prayer. *(Harris v. Joint School District,* 1994)

- A city council meeting can pray, as long as they don't say the name of Jesus *(Rubin v. City of Burbank,* 1999)

- It is unconstitutional for a classroom library to contain books that deal with Christianity, or for a teacher to be seen with a personal copy of the Bible at school. *(Roberts v. Madigan,* 1990)

- It is unconstitutional for a public cemetery to have a planter in the shape of a cross, for if someone were to view that cross, it could cause "emotional distress" and thus constitute injury "in-fact." *(Warsaw v. Tehachapi,* 1990)[21]

One of the most aggressive attacks on Christian faith came from Samuel Kent, a federal judge who ruled in 1995 that if American students prayed in a public school in the name of Jesus, they would be sentenced to a six-month jail term: "And make no mistake; the court is going to have a United States Marshall in attendance at the graduation. If any student offends this Court, that student will be summarily arrested and will face up to six months incarceration in the Galveston County Jail for contempt of Court. Anyone who thinks I'm kidding about this better think again . . . anyone who violates these orders . . . is going to wish that he or she had died as a child when this Court gets through with it."[22]

If you believe children in public school are being educated on the principles of freedom that made America great, think again! Your children are not being taught what you were taught. Many are being exposed daily to a secular humanist brainwashing from the elementary grades through high school. This is evidenced by the ruling of federal judge Jennifer Coffman, nominated by President Bill Clinton in 1993, who refused to allow a California teacher to show his students the Declaration of Independence because it refers to God.

Judge Jennifer Coffman also ruled that the following documents could not be posted in public schools:

1. The Mayflower Compact, in which the colony's founders invoke "the name of God" and explain that their journey was taken,

among other reasons, "for the glory of God and advancement of the Christian faith"

2. Our national motto of "In God We Trust"

3. Excerpts from our Declaration of Independence

4. The Preamble to the Constitution of the State of Kentucky

5. A page from the Congressional Record of Wednesday, Feb. 2, 1983, vol. 12, no. 8, that declares 1983 as the "Year of the Bible" and lists the Ten Commandments

6. A proclamation by President Ronald Reagan marking 1983 the "Year of the Bible"

7. A proclamation by President Abraham Lincoln designating April 30, 1863, as a National Day of Prayer and Humiliation

8. An excerpt from President Lincoln's "Reply to Loyal Colored People of Baltimore upon Presentation of a Bible," reading, "The Bible is the best gift God has ever given to man."[23]

Pastor Ronnie Floyd, of the First Baptist Church in Springdale, Arkansas, came under fire from the Internal Revenue Service because of his July 4, 2004, sermon, when he told his congregation to "vote God, His Ways, His will, His word."

Barry Lynn, of Americans United for Separation of Church and State, is sending people to churches to videotape sermons for any "irregularities" and report them to the IRS. Lynn is joined by the so-called Mainstream Coalition, which has about a hundred volunteers monitoring churches to see whether pastors are abiding by federal laws governing political activity by nonprofit institutions."[24]

One of the masterstrokes of the ACLU is its quest to mold American law as it desires through judicial activism. The ACLU looks to force international law (at least their selective view of international law) on the American people—with complete disregard for Americans' sovereignty and the U.S. Constitution.

How does this affect you, your family, and your church? Stay tuned!

When I was recently in London, the headlines of *The Daily Telegraph*, on December 19, 2009, blared: "Churches Face Being Sued by Atheists."

As this book is being written, a law is being crafted by Harriet Harmin that will pave the way for churches to face legal action from atheists on a broad array of issues. Asked at a briefing of the religious press whether Michael Foster, the Minister for Equality, thought the Equality Bill going through the House of Lords would lead to legal action between churches and atheists, Mr. Foster replied: "Both need to be lining up their lawyers right now."

The conservative peer Baroness O'Cathain, an evangelical Christian, told the House of Lords this week that "for Christian freedom" the Equality Bill was the "single most damaging bill to come before the House in my eighteen years as a member."

You can be sure the ACLU is watching the precedent being established in England and will be mobilizing its legal juggernaut to bring this law to America. Message? Churches get yourself the best attorney you can find and get ready to defend your faith in the courts. The other option is to become neutered and silenced by the ACLU.

PART THREE

The Beginning of the End

EIGHT

Can You Trust Biblical Prophecy?

Why should you study prophecy?

Prophecy is the history of the future. It is the study of what is to come. Many people in this era of doubt and skepticism feel that a person has to be either mentally unbalanced or a religious fanatic to manifest an interest in Bible prophecy.

The fact is, Bible prophecy can be confirmed by world history, and by confirming the past, we can look intelligently toward the future. Approximately one-fourth of the Bible was prophetic at the time it was written. If God devoted that much space to the subject, it cannot intelligently be ignored.

God introduces himself to mankind as the all-knowing God who knows the "end from the beginning."

> *"I am God, and there is none like Me, Declaring the end from the beginning . . . My counsel shall stand, And I will do My pleasure"*
> *—Isaiah 46: 9–10 NKJV*

Let's begin with a simple prophecy God gave to Abraham in the book of Genesis that can be confirmed by world history. When God determined to destroy Sodom and Gomorrah, he decided to first warn Abraham: "Shall I hide from Abraham what I am doing?" (Genesis 18:17 NKJV).

And while giving Abraham title to the land of Israel, God placed him in a deep sleep and said:

> *"Know certainly that your descendants will be strangers in a land that is not theirs, and will serve them, and they will afflict them four hundred years. And also the nation whom they serve I will judge; afterward, they shall come out with great possessions. Now as for you, you shall go to your fathers in peace; you shall be buried at a good old age. But in the fourth generation they shall return here, for the iniquity of the Amorites is not yet complete . . . On the same day the LORD made a covenant with Abram, saying: "To your descendants I have given this land, from the river of Egypt to the great river, the River Euphrates"*
>
> —*Genesis 15:13–16, 18 NKJV*

God foretold the entire panorama of future events concerning the Jewish people, and every word came true. Prophecy, even a relatively short-term prophecy like the one God gave Abraham, is important!

If you doubt that the word of God is accurate, consider the prophecy concerning a city called Tyre in Ezekiel 26. God forecasted the end of Tyre and that many nations would come against it (see Ezekiel 26:3). He prophesied that Tyre's walls and towers would be broken down (verses 4, 9); the stones, timbers, and debris of the city would be thrown into the sea (verse 12); its location would become a bare rock and a place for fishermen to dry their nets (verses 4–5, 14).

Tyre was no insignificant fishing village. It was a great city of Phoenicia and a prominent world capital for over two thousand years. Yet at the peak of its power, the prophet Ezekiel had the audacity to predict a violent future and ignominious end for the mighty city of Tyre. This downfall would come about because of the city's flagrant wickedness and arrogance, traits personified in its ruler, Ittobal II, who claimed to be God. History proved Ezekiel's words. Many nations did come against Tyre: first the Babylonians, then the Greeks, the Romans, the Muslims, and the Crusaders. After a thirteen-year siege, Nebuchadnezzar of Babylon broke down Tyre's walls and towers and massacred all of its inhabitants, except for those who escaped to an island fortress a half-mile out in the Mediterranean Sea. Centuries after Ezekiel had spoken, Alexander the Great conquered the island fortress of Tyre by building a causeway from Tyre's mainland to the island, using the millions of cubic feet of rubble left from the destroyed city. Thus, Tyre was conquered, just as Ezekiel has prophesied.

In the last chapter of the book of Daniel, there's an interesting prophecy; "Blessed is he who waits, and comes to the one thousand three hundred and thirty-five days" (Daniel 12:12 NKJV).

What's the meaning of this verse?

THE BASICS OF INTERPRETING PROPHECY

First, it's important to remember that prophecy often has both a *primary literal fulfillment*—in this case, of one thousand three hundred thirty-five days, which will come to pass at the end of the age—and a *secondary symbolic fulfillment,* perhaps in this case, years. (Consider Numbers 14:34, "According to the number of days in which you spied out the land, forty days, for each day you shall bear your guilt one year, *namely* forty years, and you shall know My rejection.")

If it is possible for this verse to have a literal year-to-the-day fulfillment, then we have seen this verse come to pass in this century.

Let me explain. Islam began in A.D. 622. Shortly after this time, Jerusalem was taken by Muslims and occupied by them until A.D. 1917. In that year, Jerusalem was released by British General Edmund Henry Allenby, who rode into Jerusalem upon a white horse. About that time, the British government proclaimed that the Jews would be permitted to return to their land. This proclamation, called the Balfour Declaration, was issued exactly 1,335 years later, according to the Islamic system of reckoning time. The coins of the Ottoman empire minted in that year bore the date "1335" on one side and "1917" on the other.

Daniel's prophecy may then mean that after 1,335 years, a time of blessedness would come to the land of Israel. Those who watched and waited would have the opportunity to enjoy great blessing. In 1917, many German Jews returned to Palestine. Perhaps this is the blessing to which Daniel referred.

To illustrate further the pinpoint accuracy of the prophecies found in the Bible, consider the *birth, life,* and *death* of Jesus Christ. There is overwhelming evidence that Bible prophecy is both absolutely accurate and that the Bible is the divinely inspired word of God.

Consider these things:

Jesus would be born of a virgin.

PROPHECY: "Therefore the Lord Himself will give you a sign: Behold, a virgin will be with child and bear a son, and she will call His name Immanuel" (Isaiah 7:14 NASB).

FULFILLMENT: "Now in the sixth month the angel Gabriel was sent by God to a city of Galilee named Nazareth, to a virgin betrothed to a man whose name was Joseph, of the house of David. The virgin's name was Mary . . . Then the angel said to her, 'Do not be afraid, Mary, for you have found favor with God. And behold, you will conceive in your womb and bring forth a Son, and shall call His name JESUS' . . . Then Mary said to the angel, 'How can this be, since I do not know a man [that is I have not had sexual relations with a man]?' And the angel answered and said to her, '*The* Holy Spirit will come upon you, and the power of the Highest will overshadow you; therefore, also, that Holy One who is to be born will be called the Son of God . . . For with God nothing will be impossible.' Then Mary said, 'Behold the maidservant of the Lord! Let it be to me according to your word.' And the angel departed from her" (Luke 1:26–27, 30–31, 34–35, 37–38 NKJV).

Jesus would be the Son of God.

PROPHECY: "I will surely tell of the decree of the LORD: He said to Me, 'You are My Son, Today I have begotten You.' " (Psalm 2:7 NASB). (Psalm 2:7 is a "Royal Psalm," and in it, the Messiah is proclaiming the affirmation of the Father about the sonship of the Messiah.)

FULFILLMENT: "And behold, a voice [God the Father's] out of the heavens said, 'This is My beloved Son, in whom I am well-pleased' " (Matthew 3:17 NASB).

"And the unclean spirits, whenever they saw Him, fell down before Him and cried out, saying, 'You are the Son of God' " (Mark 3:11 NKJV).

Jesus would be of the seed of Abraham.

PROPHECY: "In your [Abraham's] seed all the nations of the earth shall be blessed, because you have obeyed My voice" (Genesis 22:18 NKJV).

"Abraham shall surely become a great and mighty nation, and all the nations of the earth will be blessed in him" (Genesis 18:18 NKJV).

FULFILLMENT: "The book of the genealogy of Jesus Christ, the Son of David, the Son of Abraham" (Matthew 1:1 NKJV).

"The promises were spoken to Abraham and to his seed. The Scripture does not say, 'and to seeds' meaning many people, but 'and to your seed,' meaning one person, who is Christ" (Galatians 3:16 NIV).

Jesus would be a son of Isaac.

PROPHECY: "Then God said [to Abraham], 'Yes, but your wife Sarah will bear you a son, and you will call him Isaac. I will establish my covenant with him as an everlasting covenant for his descendants after him' " (Genesis 17:19 NIV).

FULFILLMENT: "Abraham was the father of Isaac, Isaac the father of Jacob, Jacob the father of Judah and his brothers . . . and Jacob the father of Joseph, the husband of Mary, of whom was born Jesus, who is called Christ" (Matthew 1:2, 16 NIV).

"Jesus . . . the son of Isaac . . ." (Luke 3:23, 34 NIV).

Jesus would be a son of Jacob.

PROPHECY: "I see him, but not now; I behold him, but not near; A star shall come forth from Jacob, A scepter [ruler] shall rise from Israel, And shall crush through the forehead of Moab, And tear down all the sons of Sheth" (Numbers 24:17 NASB).

FULFILLMENT: "Abraham was the father of Isaac, Isaac the father of Jacob, Jacob the father of Judah and his brothers . . . and Jacob the father of Joseph, the husband of Mary, of whom was born Jesus, who is called Christ" (Matthew 1:2, 16 NIV).

"Jesus . . . the son of Jacob . . ." (Luke 3:23, 34 NIV).

Jesus would be from the tribe of Judah.

PROPHECY: "The scepter will not depart from Judah, nor the ruler's staff from between his feet, until he comes to whom it belongs and the obedience of the nations is his" (Genesis 49:10 NIV).

FULFILLMENT: "Judah begot Perez and Zerah by Tamar . . . And Jacob begot Joseph the husband of Mary, of whom was born Jesus who is called Christ" (Matthew 1:3, 16 NKJV).

"Jesus . . . the son of Judah . . ." (Luke 3:23, 33 NIV).

"For it is evident that our Lord arose from Judah" (Hebrews 7:14 NKJV).

Jesus would be of the house of David.

PROPHECY: "For to us a child is born, to us a son is given, and the government will be on his shoulders. And he will be called Wonderful Counselor, Mighty God, Everlasting Father, Prince of Peace. Of the increase of his government and peace there will be no end. He will reign on David's throne and over his kingdom, establishing and upholding it with justice and righteousness from that time on and forever. The zeal of the LORD Almighty will accomplish this" (Isaiah 9:6–7 NIV).

FULFILLMENT: "David the king begot Solomon by her *who had been the wife* of Uriah . . . and Jacob begot Joseph the husband of Mary, of whom was born Jesus who is called Christ" (Matthew 1:6, 16 NKJV).

"Jesus . . . the son of David . . ." (Luke 3:23, 31 NIV).

Jesus descended from the lineage of David, and in his future millennial kingdom, he will uphold the world with righteousness and justice. One day he, as a son of David, will rule from the Temple Mount in Jerusalem, and his kingdom will last forever.

Jesus would be born at Bethlehem.

PROPHECY: "But as for you, Bethlehem Ephrathah, Too little to be among the clans of Judah, From you One will go forth for Me to be ruler in Israel. His goings forth are from long ago, From the days of eternity" (Micah 5:2 NASB).

FULFILLMENT: "Jesus was born in Bethlehem of Judea" (Matthew 2:1 NKJV).

A star would announce the birth of Jesus.

PROPHECY: "I see him, but not now; I behold him, but not near; A star shall come forth from Jacob, A scepter [ruler] shall rise from Israel, And shall crush through the forehead of Moab, And tear down all the sons of Sheth" (Numbers 24:17 NASB).

FULFILLMENT: "Now after Jesus was born in Bethlehem of Judea in the days of Herod the king, Magi from the east came to Jerusalem and asked, 'Where is the one who has been born King of the Jews? For we saw his star in the east and have come to worship Him' " (Matthew 2:1–2 NIV).

Herod would kill the infant children.

PROPHECY: "Thus says the Lord, 'A voice is heard in Ramah, Lamentation and bitter weeping. Rachel is weeping for her children; She refuses to be comforted for her children, Because they are no more' " (Jeremiah 31:15 NASB).

FULFILLMENT: "Then when Herod saw that he had been tricked by the magi, he became very enraged, and sent and slew all the male children who were in Bethlehem and all its vicinity, from two years old and under, according to the time which he had determined from the magi" (Matthew 2:16 NASB).

Wise men came from the east and told Herod that a new king had been born, this one to rule the Jews. Politically, Herod could not afford another uprising in the lands he oversaw for Rome, and the title, King of the Jews, was, at this moment, his. So, not knowing the exact identity of the newborn king, he decreed that all babies two years old and younger should be slaughtered in the desperate hope that by doing so the infant king would be among those killed.

Jesus would be called "Lord."

PROPHECY: "The LORD says to my Lord: 'Sit at My right hand, Until I make Your enemies a footstool for Your feet" (Psalm 110:1 NASB).

FULFILLMENT: "Then Jesus answered and said, while He taught in the temple, 'How *is it* that the scribes say that the Christ is the Son of David? For David himself said by the Holy Spirit: 'The LORD said to my Lord, "Sit at My right hand, till I make Your enemies Your footstool." Therefore David himself calls Him "Lord"; How is He then his Son?' And the common people heard Him gladly" (Mark 12:35–37 NKJV).

The Bible Knowledge Commentary examines David's prophecy: "David heard a heavenly conversation between Lord *(Yahweh)* and David's Lord *(Adonai)*, that is, between God the Father and the Messiah. The verb *says* is . . . a word often used to depict an oracle or a revelation. In this oracle, Yahweh said that David's Lord, the Messiah, is seated at Yahweh's right hand (cf. v. 5) the place of authority, until the consummation of the ages (cf. 2; 8–9). At that time, the Lord will send David's Lord (Jesus), the Messiah, to make his enemies subject to him. A footstool pictures complete subjugation. With his scepter, the Messiah will . . . rule over his enemies." [1]

Jesus shall be called Emmanuel (God with us).

PROPHECY: "Therefore, the Lord Himself will give you a sign: Behold, a virgin will be with child and bear a son and, and, and she will call His name Immanuel" (Isaiah 7:14 NASB).

FULFILLMENT: " 'Behold, the virgin shall be with child, and bear a Son, and they shall call His name Immanuel,' which is translated, 'God with us.' Then Joseph, being aroused from sleep, did as the angel of the Lord commanded him and took to him his wife, and did not know her till she had brought forth her firstborn Son. And he called His name JESUS" (Matthew 1:23–25 NKJV).

Jesus would be a prophet.

PROPHECY: " 'I will raise up a prophet from among their countrymen like you, and I will put My words in his mouth, and he shall speak to them all that I command him' " (Deuteronomy 18:18 NASB).

FULFILLMENT: "And the crowds were saying, 'This is the prophet Jesus, from Nazareth in Galilee' " (Matthew 21:11 NASB).

Jesus would be a priest.

PROPHECY: "The LORD has sworn and will not change His mind, 'You are a priest forever According to the order of Melchizedek' " (Psalm 110:4 NASB).

FULFILLMENT: "Therefore, holy brethren, partakers of a heavenly calling, consider Jesus, the Apostle and High Priest of our confession" (Hebrews 3:1 NASB).

"During the days of Jesus' life on earth, he offered up prayers and petitions with loud cries and tears to the one who could save him from death, and he was heard because of his reverent submission. Although he was a son, he learned obedience from what he suffered and, once made perfect, he became the source of eternal salvation for all who obey him and was designated by God to be high priest in the order of Melchizedek" (Hebrews 5:7–10 NIV).

Jesus would be a judge.

PROPHECY: "For the LORD is our judge, the LORD is our lawgiver, the LORD is our king; it is he who will save us" (Isaiah 33:22 NIV).

FULFILLMENT: "I charge you therefore before God and the Lord Jesus Christ, who will judge the living and the dead at His appearing and His kingdom" (2 Timothy 4:1 NKJV).

God the Father has given the role of judge to Jesus Christ. On one day still to come, every man, woman, and child will stand before Jesus Christ the judge and acknowledge that He is Lord.

Jesus shall be king.

PROPHECY: "Of the increase of his government and peace there will be no end. He will reign on David's throne and over his kingdom, establishing and upholding it with justice and righteousness from that time on and forever. The zeal of the LORD Almighty will accomplish this" (Isaiah 9: 7 NIV).

FULFILLMENT: " 'You are a king, then!' said Pilate. Jesus answered, 'You are right in saying I am a king. In fact, for this reason I was born, and for this I came into the world, to testify to the truth. Everyone on the side of truth listens to me' " (John 18:37 NIV).

Jesus shall be anointed by the Holy Spirit.

PROPHECY: "The Spirit of the LORD will rest on Him, The spirit of wisdom and understanding, The spirit of counsel and strength, The spirit of knowledge and the fear of the LORD" (Isaiah 11:2 NASB).

FULFILLMENT: "After being baptized, Jesus came up immediately from the water; and behold, the heavens were opened, and he saw the Spirit of God descending as a dove and lighting on Him, and behold, a voice out of the heavens said, 'This is My beloved Son, in whom I am well-pleased' " (Matthew 3:16–17 NASB).

Jesus would be preceded by a messenger.

PROPHECY: "A voice is calling, 'Clear the way for the LORD in the wilderness; Make smooth in the desert a highway for our God' " (Isaiah 40:3 NASB).

FULFILLMENT: "In those days John the Baptist came preaching in the wilderness of Judea, and saying, 'Repent, for the kingdom of heaven is at hand!' For this is he who was spoken of by the prophet Isaiah, saying: 'The voice of one crying in the wilderness: "Prepare the way of the LORD; Make His paths straight" ' " (Matthew 3:1–3 NKJV).

Jesus would minister in Galilee.

PROPHECY: "But there will be no more gloom for her who was in anguish; in earlier times He treated the land of Zebulun and the land of Naphtali with contempt, but later on He shall make it glorious, by the way of the sea, on the other side of Jordan, Galilee of the Gentiles" (Isaiah 9:1 NASB).

FULFILLMENT: "Now when Jesus heard that John had been put in prison, He departed to Galilee. And leaving Nazareth, he came and dwelt in Capernaum, which is by the sea, in the regions of Zebulun and Naphtali, that it might be fulfilled which was spoken by Isaiah the prophet, saying: 'The land of Zebulun and the land of Naphtali, By the way of the sea, beyond the Jordan, Galilee of the Gentiles: The people who sat in darkness have seen a great light, And upon those who sat in the region and shadow of death Light has dawned.' From that time Jesus began to preach and say, 'Repent, for the kingdom of heaven is at hand' " (Matthew 4:12–17 NKJV).

The prophecy of Isaiah was fulfilled when Jesus ministered in Capernaum—near the major highway from Egypt to Damascus, called "The Way of the Sea."

Jesus' ministry would include miracles.

PROPHECY: "Then the eyes of the blind will be opened, And the ears of the deaf will be unstopped. Then the lame will leap like a deer, And the tongue of the mute will shout for joy" (Isaiah 35:5–6 NASB).

FULFILLMENT: "Jesus was going through all the cities and villages, teaching in their synagogues and proclaiming the gospel of the kingdom, and healing every kind of disease and every kind of sickness" (Matthew: 9:35 NASB).

Jesus would enter Jerusalem on a donkey.

PROPHECY: "Rejoice greatly, O daughter of Zion! Shout in triumph, O daughter of Jerusalem! Behold, your king is coming to you; He is just and endowed with salvation, Humble, and mounted on a donkey, Even on a colt, the foal of a donkey" (Zechariah 9:9 NASB).

FULFILLMENT: "Now when they drew near Jerusalem, and came to Bethphage, at the Mount of Olives, then Jesus sent two disciples, saying to them, 'Go into the village opposite you, and immediately you will find a donkey tied, and a colt with her. Loose them and bring them to

Me. And if anyone says anything to you, you shall say, "The Lord has need of them," and immediately he will send them.' All this was done that it might be fulfilled which was spoken by the prophet, saying, 'Tell the daughter of Zion, "Behold, your King is coming to you, Lowly, and sitting on a donkey, A colt, a foal of a donkey." ' So the disciples went and did as Jesus commanded them. They brought the donkey and the colt, laid their clothes on them, and set Him on them" (Matthew 21:1–7 NKJV).

The Messiah will be a light to the gentiles.

PROPHECY: " 'I, the LORD, have called You in righteousness, And will hold Your hand; I will keep You and give You as a covenant to the people, As a light to the Gentiles, To open blind eyes, To bring out prisoners from the prison, Those who sit in darkness from the prison house' " (Isaiah 42:6–7 NKJV).

FULFILLMENT: "The people who sat in darkness have seen a great light, And upon those who sat in the region and shadow of death Light has dawned" (Matthew 4:16 NKJV).

"A light [Jesus, the Messiah] to bring revelation to the Gentiles, And the glory of Your people Israel" (Luke 2:32 NKJV).

Jesus would be betrayed for thirty pieces of silver.

PROPHECY: "I said to them, 'If it is good in your sight, give me my wages; but if not, never mind!' So they weighed out thirty shekels of silver as my wages" (Zechariah 11:12 NASB).

FULFILLMENT: "Then one of the twelve, called Judas Iscariot, went to the chief priests and said, 'What are you willing to give me if I deliver Him [Jesus] to you?' And they counted out to him thirty pieces of silver. So from that time he sought opportunity to betray Him" (Matthew 26:14–16 NKJV).

On the evening of the Passover dinner, Judas Iscariot, one of the Jesus' twelve disciples, went to the chief priest and inquired if he might betray Jesus into their hands. As payment for his service, he was given thirty pieces of silver.

The Messiah Jesus would be silent before his accusers.

PROPHECY: "He was oppressed and He was afflicted, yet He did not open His mouth" (Isaiah 53:7 NASB).

FULFILLMENT: "And while He was being accused by the chief priest and elders, He answered nothing" (Matthew 27:12 NKJV).

Throughout the litany of lies and false accusations, Jesus remained silent before his accusers.

Jesus would be scourged and wounded.

PROPHECY: "But He was pierced through for our transgressions. He was crushed for our iniquities; The chastening for our well-being fell upon Him, And by His scourging we are healed" (Isaiah 53:5 NASB).

FULFILLMENT: "Then he released Barabbas to them; and when he had scourged Jesus, he delivered *Him* to be crucified" (Matthew 27:26 NKJV).

Jesus would be smitten and be spit upon.

PROPHECY: "I gave My back to those who struck Me, and My cheeks to those who plucked out the beard; I did not hide My face from shame and spitting" (Isaiah 50:6 NKJV).

FULFILLMENT: "Then they spat in His face and beat Him with their fists; and others slapped Him" (Matthew 26:67 NASB).

Jesus' hands and feet would be pierced.

PROPHECY: "They pierced my hands and my feet" (Psalm 22:16 NASB).

FULFILLMENT: "When they came to the place called the Skull, there they crucified Him" (Luke 23:33 NASB).

It is interesting to note that this psalmist wrote this prophecy over a thousand years before crucifixion was made common by the Romans and the Jews as a form of capital punishment.

Jesus would be put to death alongside transgressors.

PROPHECY: "Because He poured out Himself to death, And was numbered with the transgressors" (Isaiah 53:12 NASB).

FULFILLMENT: "At that time two robbers were crucified with Him, one on the right and one on the left" (Matthew 27:38 NASB).

Jesus' garments would be parted and lots would be cast for them.

PROPHECY: "They divide My garments among them, And for my clothing they cast lots" (Psalm 22:18 NASB).

FULFILLMENT: "Then the soldiers, when they had crucified Jesus, took His garments and made four parts, to each soldier a part, and also the tunic. Now the tunic was without seam, woven from the top in one piece. They said therefore among themselves, 'Let us not tear it, but cast lots for it, whose it shall be,' that the Scripture might be fulfilled which says: 'They divided My garments among them, and for My clothing they cast lots.' Therefore the soldiers did these things" (John 19:23–24 NKJV).

Which did they do? Divide the garments or cast lots? This statement seems almost contradictory until you realize what happened at the cross. They ripped the outer garment, but paused when they picked up the tunic. It was a fine piece of work, all in one piece, and so they decided to cast lots for it.

Jesus would suffer thirst.

PROPHECY: "And for my thirst they gave me vinegar to drink" (Psalm 69:21 NASB).

FULFILLMENT: "After this, Jesus . . . said, 'I thirst!' " (John 19:28 NKJV).

They would offer Jesus gall and vinegar to drink.

PROPHECY: "They also gave me gall for my food, And for my thirst, they gave me vinegar to drink" (Psalm 69:21 NKJV).

FULFILLMENT: "They gave him sour wine mingled with gall to drink. But when He had tasted *it,* He would not drink" (Matthew 27:34 NKJV).

Jesus would utter a forsaken cry at the cross.

PROPHECY: "My God, my God, why have You forsaken me?" (Psalm 22:1 NASB).

FULFILLMENT: "About the ninth hour Jesus cried out with a loud voice, saying, 'Eli, Eli, lama sabachthani?' that is, 'My God, my God, why have You forsaken me?' " (Matthew 27:46 NASB).

None of the bones in Jesus' body would be broken.

PROPHECY: "He guards all his bones; Not one of them is broken" (Psalm 34:20 NKJV).

"And all My bones are out of joint" (Psalm 22:14 NKJV).

FULFILLMENT: "But coming to Jesus, when they saw that He was already dead, they did not break His legs" (John 19:33 NASB).

While hanging on the cross by the hands and feet, it is very likely that all a man's bones would separate from their joints. The Romans used to hasten death by breaking the legs of the crucified criminals, but when they reached Jesus, they saw that He was already dead.

Jesus' side would be pierced.

PROPHECY: "They will look on Me whom they pierced" (Zechariah 12:10 NASB).

FULFILLMENT: "But one of the soldiers pierced His side with a spear" (John 19:34 NASB).

Jesus would be buried in a rich man's tomb.

PROPHECY: "His grave was assigned with wicked men, yet He was with a rich man in His death" (Isaiah 53:9 NASB).

FULFILLMENT: "There came a rich man from Arimathea, named Joseph . . . and asked for the body of Jesus . . . When Joseph had taken the body, he wrapped it in a clean linen cloth, and laid it in his new tomb" (Matthew 27: 57–60 NKJV). In fulfilling these last prophecies, Jesus reflects the supernatural nature of the Messiah.

Jesus would rise from the dead

PROPHECY: "For You will not abandon my soul to Sheol; Nor will You allow Your Holy One to undergo decay" (Psalm 16:10 NASB).

FULFILLMENT: "You seek Jesus of Nazareth, who was crucified. He is risen!" (Mark 16:6 NKJV).

Jesus would ascend into heaven.

PROPHECY: "You have ascended on high" (Psalm 68:18 NASB).

FULFILLMENT: "He [Jesus] was lifted up while they were looking on, and a cloud received Him out of their sight" (Acts 1:9 NASB).

Jesus is seated at the right hand of God.

PROPHECY: "The LORD says to my Lord: 'Sit at My right hand Until I make Your enemies a footstool for Your feet' " (Psalm 110:1 NASB).

FULFILLMENT: "When He had made purification of sins, He sat down at the right hand of the Majesty on high" (Hebrews 1:3 NASB).

In addition to proving beyond all reasonable doubt that Jesus Christ was, in fact, God, these many prophecies and their fulfillment give us reason to study and believe biblical prophecy. How could a mere man control the place or time of His birth? Some skeptics claim that sheer coincidence accounts for these fulfilled prophecies. You might be able to find some men whose lives would agree with a few of the above prophecies, but Jesus Christ is the only person, living or dead, who could have filled all of these many prophecies. And these are only a handful of the Messianic predictions found in Scripture.

We have seen how Jesus fulfilled Scripture related to His first coming as a suffering servant—prepare yourself for what the Bible predicts about the rapture of the church and His second coming, as the terminal generation takes the stage on planet Earth.

NINE

We Are the Terminal Generation

Jesus of Nazareth left the Temple Mount in Jerusalem and climbed the gentle slope of the Mount of Olives, where He sat down on a large stone beneath an ancient olive tree and waited for His disciples to gather around Him. Jesus was a rabbi, and as a master teacher and prophet, He was about to reveal the future of the world to His disciples and the future church in Matthew 24, which I refer to as "the spine of prophecy."

It was in this setting that the disciples asked Jesus three critical questions concerning the future (see Matthew 24:3):

1. When will these things be?

2. What will be the sign of Your coming?

3. What is the sign of the end of the age?

When Scripture tells us that heaven and earth will pass away, you can be sure that this world as we know it will definitely end. There will be a last baby born, a last marriage performed, a last church service, a last kiss, a last song, a last hurrah. This world will not continue forever. The second law of thermodynamics, otherwise known as the Law of Entropy, declares that all organized systems tend to disorder after time. Like all things, the earth, along with this physical universe, will wear out.

When will the world end? The Scriptures are not silent; God tells us when, how, and where the world as we know it will end: Armageddon.

Armageddon is the Hebrew word meaning "The Mountain of Megeddo." The Mountain of Megeddo lies east of Mount Carmel in the northern part of the Israel.

I've stood upon this mountain many times, and from its vantage point I can see a great, extended plain stretching from the Mediterranean Sea eastward across the northern part of Israel.

Napoleon looked at the expanse of Armageddon and described it as the most natural battlefield on the face of the earth, for armies would be able to maneuver easily over its plains. On those plains, the Bible tells us, human blood will flow to the height of a horse's bridle for two hundred miles (see Revelation 14:20). There the false messiah, the Antichrist, will lead the armies of the west to fight the son of God for supremacy of planet Earth. We will discuss the who, when, and why of the Battle of Armageddon in a later chapter.

In this chapter, we will look at ten prophetic signs that clearly indicate that we are the terminal generation and that we are well on our way on the road to Armageddon. If you listen closely, you can hear the hoof beats of the four horsemen of the Apocalypse, racing toward the battle.

1. OIL

There is a very real reason why most prophetic teachings concerning the end time events occur in the Middle East. That reason is oil! This is the first prophetic sign indicating we are part of the terminal generation.

When the prophet Ezekiel revealed to the world thousands of years ago how God Almighty would orchestrate the Russian-Islamic invasion of Israel so graphically described in chapters 38 and 39 . . . he revealed the secret of the future in ten words. The ten words spoken to the invading armies of Israel were: "I will turn you around, put hooks into your jaws" (Ezekiel 38:4).

When the prophet Ezekiel speaks about the invading nations as having "hooks in your jaw," he is referring to oil. Every fisherman knows that once the razor sharp hook has been set into the jaw of the fish, the fish can be dragged without mercy through the waters under the complete control of the fishermen.

God is sovereign!

God is almighty!

God is the fisherman in Ezekiel 38 dragging the Russian-Islamic invasion coalition toward the hills of Israel to crush them, just as he crushed Pharaoh and his Egyptian army in the Red Sea before the eyes of Israel and the nations of the world. And our sovereign God will use the "bait" of oil to drag the Russian-Islamic coalition wherever He wants them to go.

Ezekiel records the future destruction of the Russian-Islamic invasion force with these words:

> *You [the invading armies coming against Israel] will come up against My people Israel like a cloud to cover the land. It will be in the latter days [the end of the age], I will bring you against My land [Israel], so that the nations may know Me, when I am hallowed in you, O Gog, before their eyes.*
>
> —*Ezekiel 38:16*

God Almighty makes it clear: "I will bring you [the Russian-Islamic coalition] against My land [Israel] so that the nations of the world may know Me."

God is warning planet Earth that there is a day of reckoning coming and the death rate will stun the world. God is saying, I am going to crush the nations that have tormented the Jewish people for centuries and millennia. I will avenge the death of every Jewish person in the Holocaust; I will avenge the pogroms of Russia; I will avenge the rockets of Iran (Persia); I will avenge the harvest of death brought by every suicide bomber so that the Gentile nations of the world will know I am the only true God.

God is warning planet Earth that the day of reckoning is coming and the death rate of 84 percent of the invading armies of the Russian-Islamic coalition will stagger the earth. God Almighty, the defender of Israel, has written a Declaration of War through the pen of the prophet Ezekiel in chapters 38 and 39.

God declares in a language that is brutal and direct that he's going to avenge the death of every Jewish person who died or suffered in the Holocaust. He will avenge the death and suffering of the rockets furnished by Iran and launched into Israel by Hamas and Hezbollah in a reign of terror; He will avenge the harvest of death of countless suicide

bombers . . . no one will escape, and His judgment will be complete. All
Israel will rejoice in the supernatural demonstration of Jehovah God's
power and return to the Torah of the God of Abraham, Isaac, and Jacob.

How will God orchestrate this massive drama in which He controls
the nations of the earth with precise movement like pawns on a chessboard? Like a helpless fish being dragged through the water with a hook
in its jaw?

Why will Russia come out of the north and enter into a covenant with
Iran to attack Israel? Oil is the major reason. Oil in the latter part of the
twentieth century became the ultimate weapon of war and remains so
today. Oil is the new gold standard of planet Earth.

The Origin of Oil

What is the source of oil? Begin with the basic concept that God Almighty is the creator of heaven and Earth. As the owner of the earth, He
has the right to do exactly as His sovereign will dictates (see Genesis 1:1
and Psalm 24:1).

The billions of gallons of oil buried deeply in the bosom of the earth
were planted exactly where God intended for them to be to fulfill His
prophetic word millions of years before they were needed. Oil deposits
result from the decomposition of plant and animal life buried ages ago.
That means that forest and abundant vegetation once covered the earth
until destroyed in a vast global cataclysm such as a global flood.

Geophysicist Robert Morgan believes that the earth's richest, deepest,
and largest deposits of petroleum lie under the sands of countries just to
the east of Israel, in the location pinpointed in the Bible as the Garden of
Eden. Eden was a teaming expanse of forest and gardens with rich fertil-
ity unparalleled in human history.[1]

Satan's seduction of Adam and Eve in the Garden of Eden, leading to
its destruction in the genesis of time, may have provided the oil that se-
duces the nations of the world to follow Russia and Iran into the Battle of
Gog and Magog, and ultimately to Armageddon.

Few Americans realize the crucial role of oil in World War II. The
Japanese attack on Pearl Harbor was motivated by the fact that the
United States had cut off oil supplies to Japan. The military leadership
of Japan estimated that Japan had enough oil to operate its machinery
of war (planes, tanks, ships, trucks, etc.) for approximately eighteen

months. Knowing they had little time, the Japanese decided to make a massive and decisive surprise attack on Pearl Harbor on December 7, 1941. It was America's Day of Infamy!

When the Allies invaded Europe during World War II, they immediately began to attack the refineries of the Third Reich. The ability of America to furnish an unlimited supply of oil to the war machine of the Allies turned the tide of battle and the Axis powers were defeated.

America no longer has the ability to sustain an extended war with anyone without the approval of Saudi Arabia and the oil-rich OPEC nations. Consider the following chart on the nations, their oil reserves, and their daily consumption measured in barrels per day. These charts reveal that America's Achilles' heel is indeed foreign oil. Our addiction to foreign oil is a serious threat to our national security.

Oil Reserves by Country[2]

COUNTRY COMPARISON :: OIL - PROVED RESERVES

This entry is the stock of proved reserves of crude oil in barrels (bbl). Proved reserves are those quantities of petroleum which, by analysis of geological and engineering data, can be estimated with a high degree of confidence to be commercially recoverable from a given date forward, from known reservoirs and under current economic conditions.

RANK	COUNTRY	(BBL)	DATE OF INFORMATION
1	Saudi Arabia	266,700,000,000	1 January 2009 est.
2	Canada	178,100,000,000	1 January 2009 est.
3	Iran	136,200,000,000	1 January 2010 est.
4	Iraq	115,000,000,000	1 January 2009 est.
5	Kuwait	101,500,000,000	1 January 2009 est.
6	Venezuela	99,380,000,000	1 January 2009 est.
7	United Arab Emirates	97,800,000,000	1 January 2009 est.
8	Russia	79,000,000,000	1 January 2009 est.
9	Libya	43,660,000,000	1 January 2009 est.
10	Nigeria	36,220,000,000	1 January 2009 est.
11	Kazakhstan	30,000,000,000	1 January 2009 est.
12	United States	21,320,000,000	1 January 2009 est.
13	China	15,550,000,000	1 January 2009 est.
14	Qatar	15,210,000,000	1 January 2009 est.

(NOTE: Observe that twelve of the thirteen top countries in oil reserves are hostile to the United States of America. This is a clear and present danger to our national security.)

Oil Consumption by Country[3]

COUNTRY COMPARISON :: OIL - CONSUMPTION
This entry is the total oil consumed in barrels per day (bbl/day). The discrepancy between the amount of oil produced and/or imported and the amount consumed and/or exported is due to the omission of stock changes, refinery gains, and other complicating factors.

RANK	COUNTRY	(BBL/DAY)	DATE OF INFORMATION
1	United States	19,500,000	2008 est.
2	European Union	14,390,000	2007 est.
3	China	7,999,000	2008 est.
4	Japan	4,785,000	2008 est.
5	Russia	2,800,000	2008 est.
6	India	2,670,000	2009 est.
7	Germany	2,569,000	2008 est.
8	Brazil	2,520,000	2008 est.
9	Saudi Arabia	2,380,000	2008 est.
10	Canada	2,260,000	2008 est.
11	Korea, South	2,175,000	2008 est.
12	Mexico	2,128,000	2008 est.
13	France	1,986,000	2008 est.
14	Iran	1,755,000	2008 est.

The prophet Ezekiel writes in Chapter 38:13: "Sheba, Dedan, the merchant of Tarshish, and all their young lions shall say to you, 'Have you come to take a plunder? Have you gathered your army to take booty to carry away silver and gold, to take away livestock and goods, to take away great plunder?' "

Ezekiel's "young lions" are the offspring of England, whose symbol is a lion; this would be the United States of America as an offspring of England. Ezekiel is describing in this verse the Russian-Islamic coalition coming to invade Israel and all that America will do is send a limp-wristed diplomatic protest. Does that sound familiar?

In short, America does nothing to help Israel after the church has been raptured from the earth. Ezekiel's war of Gog and Magog happens three and a half years after the rapture in the middle of Daniel's seventieth week.

Why does America send a worthless diplomatic protest to Russia and Iran? Why don't they race to defend Israel, our only friend in the Middle East and the only democratic government in that part of the world?

Could it be that the radical Islamic nations—who now control the vast majority of oil in the world and who have a seething hatred for Israel—will order America to stand down, or OPEC will shut off the U.S. supply of oil and cause the struggling American economy to collapse?

Think it can't happen?

Think again!

Do you remember the incident during the Nixon administration in 1973 when Arab nations united to launch an attack on Israel during Yom Kippur? The Arab nations told the United States to back off of its support for Israel.

We did not!

On October 17, 1973, the Arab nations conspired to reduce their oil production to punish nations that supported Israel. They used oil as a weapon of war, and oil is an even greater weapon of war today.

The result of the Arab oil embargo was long gas lines with people fist-fighting each other as they became angry and violent, waiting to get gas at service stations. The price of oil quadrupled and never went down. Billions of dollars were sucked out of America's economy and stacked in the bulging Arab treasuries.

As a sidebar, trillions of America's dollars, which have been exported to OPEC and that flow through your gas tank, are being used to poison the minds of our college and university students today. Saudi Arabia, through a series of foundations, is giving multiplied millions to universities to hire professors who are anti-American and anti-Israel to chair Middle Eastern studies. These professors are generally radical Islamic Wahhabists who poison the minds of our college and university students.

America's refusal to drill for every drop of oil under our control while developing solar, wind, nuclear, clean coal, and natural gas resources is nothing short of national insanity. Our enemies are laughing at our utter stupidity.

America's Addiction to Foreign Oil

America's addiction to foreign oil is our Achilles' heel. OPEC manipulates America to do its bidding like a mule pulling a plow. The global demand for oil has passed 86 million barrels per day and is expected to rise to 98.5 million barrels a day in 2015.[4]

Oil prices have quintupled in the past six years.[5] Notice that the

United States' daily consumption of oil per day is 20,800,000 barrels. That addictive rate of consumption is greater than the next top five nations combined.

The wheels of transportation that make capitalism possible depend on oil, gas, diesel fuel, and high-octane jet fuel. If the wheel stops rolling, America's economy will shatter. The supply line stretches across the world to Saudi Arabia, Iraq, Iran, and the Middle East.

Let's connect the dots: Why will global shortage of oil be a sign that we are living in the terminal generation?

1. First, God created oil and placed it specifically in exact geographic regions, the majority of which is in Islamic nations that now hate both America and Israel.

2. The prophet Ezekiel foretells of a day when six nations will be forced to come to the Middle East by the "hook in the jaw." All of those nations are on center stage of the twenty-first century, breathing out venomous statements against Israel and America.

3. Russia must have oil to become a military superpower again. Ezekiel identifies Russia as the commander of the Russian-Islamic coalition (see Ezekiel 38:7).

   The terms "prepare yourself" and "be a guard for them" better translate as "be a commander of them."

   God makes it clear that Russia will be the leader of the Russian-Iranian Islamic coalition.

   The Russian-Iranian axis of evil has been in full operation for at least two decades. When Iran gets the nuclear bomb, made possible through the assistance of Russian scientists, World War III will happen. It will be the end of the world as we know it, when Iran becomes nuclear—and it could happen any day!

4. For the first time in world history, all the nations mentioned by Ezekiel are in place; America is falling from its position of being a global superpower by our insane addiction to political correctness and commitment to socialism, which only encourages Iran, Russia, and China. We are the terminal generation headed for the iceberg.

2. THE KNOWLEDGE EXPLOSION

The second prophetic sign pointing toward Armageddon is found in Daniel 12:4: "But you, Daniel, shut up the words and seal the book until the time of the end; many shall run to and fro, and knowledge shall increase."

The literal translation of this scripture indicates that during "the time of the end," or the terminal generation, an explosion of knowledge will occur.

Since the Garden of Eden until the twentieth century, there has been no knowledge explosion until the past few years. Until recently, men walked or rode horses—just as King David and Julius Caesar did. In the span of a few years, however, mankind invented the automobile, the jet plane, and the space shuttle. You can fly from New York to Paris in three hours. Just think of all the knowledge involved in developing these marvels of modern technology.

With the press of a button, you can receive faxes in your car, take a message on your sky pager, and explore encyclopedias of vast knowledge small enough to fit in the palm of your hand. You can sit in the quiet of your own home and drown yourself in a sea of information from the internet.

In the past generation, we have put men on the moon and been forced to redefine death. Medical science has the ability to keep a corpse breathing for months on life support. Tiny babies, weighing less than one pound, can survive, and unborn babies can even undergo surgery while within the womb.

However, this knowledge explosion has not produced utopia; rather, it has created a generation of well-informed people who know more about rock stars and desperate housewives than they do about history. Our "enlightened" society seeks freedom and self-expression but is actually enslaved by drugs, materialism, hedonism, sexual perversion, and cultic practices.

We favor death for the innocent and mercy for the guilty. We were taught the benefits of secular humanism and the worship of man's intellect; yet our enlightened, religion-free world is coming unraveled. The foundations of civilization are being destroyed. Why? Because knowledge without God can only produce an intellectual barbarian. Solomon, allegedly the wisest man in the world stated, "The fear of the LORD is the beginning of knowledge" (Proverbs 1:7 NKJV).

Hitler's Nazis threw Jewish children alive into the ovens at Auschwitz. Many of those Nazis were educated men, some had PhDs, but their education was accomplished without the acknowledgment of God. They were educated barbarians. They had brilliant minds, yet they had hearts of stone.

We are the terminal generation, "always learning but never able to come to the knowledge of the truth" (2 Timothy 3:7). This is what happens when a generation seeks truth apart from the knowledge of God. You can't think your way to truth. You can't philosophize your way there. You can't think happy thoughts and find truth. The only way you will ever find eternal, ultimate truth is by seeking and finding the one true God: the God of Abraham, Isaac, and Jacob.

If you reject truth, the only thing left to accept is a lie. America has rejected the truth of God's word. We have rejected God Himself, and all we have left is the secular humanist lie. Jesus said, "You shall know the truth, and the truth shall make you free" (John 8:32).

3. THE MIDDLE EAST PLAGUE: MASSIVE RADIATION BLAST

The third sign we are the terminal generation is the strange and deadly plague mentioned by the prophet Zechariah. My father's generation could not understand this prophetic passage of Scripture until the invention of the atomic bomb:

And this shall be the plague which the Lord will strike all the people who fought against Jerusalem; their flesh shall dissolve while they stand on their feet. Their eyes shall dissolve in their sockets, and their tongue shall dissolve in their mouths. It shall come to pass in that day that a great panic from the Lord will be among them. Everyone will seize the hand of his neighbor, and raise his hand against his neighbor's hand; Judah will fight at Jerusalem. And the wealth of all the surrounding nations shall be gathered together: Gold, silver and apparel in great abundance. Such also shall be the plague on the horse and the mule,

on the camel and on the donkey, and on all the cattle that will be in
those camps. So shall this plague be.

—*Zechariah 14:12–15*

Zechariah had a vision and didn't know how to describe the horror of the vision. He called the gruesome results a plague. The plague which could consume a man's flesh while he was still standing was as much a mystery to my father's generation as it was to Zechariah.

Zechariah's plague could be the logical result of massive radiation. A docudrama about Hiroshima presented a reenactment of the bombing that ended World War II. Watching the program, I saw flesh literally melting off the bones of the victims before the corpses could hit the ground. Suddenly I understood that Zechariah could have been describing nuclear warfare.

Consider this fact: every military weapon ever invented has been used in combat. After we bombed Japan and ended World War II, everyone became aware of the atomic bomb's immense power. An A-bomb can produce a temperature of 150 million degrees Fahrenheit in one-millionth of a second. Under such conditions, a man's tongue can be consumed in his mouth and his eyes can melt in their sockets before his corpse can hit the ground.

But we've come a long way since the A-bomb. A one-megaton nuclear blast is a firecracker compared to the massive H-bomb, creates a great noise (like the one described in 2 Peter 3:10), instantly atomizing everything within a two-mile radius. For the next eight miles, everything instantly catches fire.

The land becomes a raging inferno, a literal hell on Earth. Radiation breaks down at thirty-five miles and the earth is good for nothing for a hundred years. As this book is being written, Iran is trying desperately to produce a nuclear bomb to conquer the entire Middle East.

A U.S. congressman recently sat in my office and told me that many of the nuclear weapons produced by the former Soviet Union have disappeared with the assumption they have been sold to Israel's enemies.

The coming military attack upon Israel will be ferocious and fast. The Bible says, "Let him who is on the housetop not go down to take anything out of his house. And let him who is in the field not go back to get his clothes" (Matthew 24: 17–18 NKJV).

Why? Because the attack will be so sudden, there will be no time.

Israel, of course, knows that she has enemies. Israel currently has the nuclear capacity to turn the sands of Iran into a molten sea of glass if necessary. If you're interested in further reading, I recommend *The Samson Option* by Seymour M. Hersh, which details Israel's nuclear capability.

The Sunday Times of London once printed a story given to them by Mordecai Vanunu. Vanunu reported that Israel had two hundred nuclear bombs in addition to the neutron and H-bomb. After this revelation, Vanunu was immediately arrested by the Mossad and sentenced to eighteen years in prison for the breach of security. His arrest confirmed that he was telling the truth. If he had been lying, the Mossad would never have bothered with him.

Incidentally, we Americans often think that we're somehow protected from a nuclear attack. That's a misguided notion. President Ahmadinejad of Iran has made it very clear that the moment Iran has nuclear capability, those weapons will be shared with radical Islamic terrorists, who will use them on Americans in the major cities of our nation. The persistent and continuing radical Islamic terrorist attacks in America prove they are willing to kill us; when they have nuclear power, they will make 9/11 pale in comparison.

4. THE REBIRTH OF ISRAEL

The fourth prophetic sign that we are the terminal generation is the rebirth of the State of Israel. I remember very clearly the day in May 1948 when I was sitting at our kitchen table with my father, a quiet man with a brilliant mind. I was eight years of age and the evening news on the radio was the major news event of the day. For the benefit of the younger generation, television hadn't been invented.

Dad loved books, and he was a prophecy scholar. He was a man of few words, but when he did speak, what he said was worth hearing.

The radio crackled as the announcer made the shocking statement that brought tears to my father's eyes: "The United Nations has today announced that they have formally recognized the State of Israel."

My father put the book he was holding down on the table and said nothing for a long moment. I knew from the tears in his eyes that he had been profoundly moved. Then he looked me straight in the eye and said,

"We have just heard the most important prophetic message that will ever be delivered until Jesus Christ returns to the earth. This is the greatest miracle of the twentieth century."

I've forgotten many episodes from my youth, but I've never forgotten that night or my father's words. He was right: biblical prophecy states that Israel must experience a rebirth before the coming of Messiah.

The Bible also prophesies that a nation will be born in a day. The prophet Isaiah records these words:

> *"Who has heard such a thing? Who has seen such things? Shall the earth be made to give birth in one day? Or shall a nation be born at once?"*
>
> *—Isaiah 66:8*

The disciples came to Jesus and asked him for the signs of the end of the age:

> *"Tell us," they said, "when will these things be? And what* will *be the sign of Your coming, and of the end of the age?"*
>
> *Jesus responded by saying, "Now learn this parable from the fig tree: When its branch has already become tender and puts forth leaves, you know that summer is near. So you also, when you see all these things, know that it [His coming] is near—at the doors! Assuredly, I say to you, this generation will by no means pass away till all things take place."*
>
> *—Matthew 24:3, 32–34*

In Bible prophecy, Israel is pictured as a fig tree. Jesus says, "As soon as its twigs get tender and its leaves come out," the Diaspora is ending and the Jews of the world are coming home to Israel. Israel is being reborn suddenly! It will be such a dramatic miracle, none can miss it. It happened May 15, 1948. It was one of the most obvious prophetic signs that the terminal generation has arrived.

Jesus said, "This generation will certainly not pass away until all these things have happened." The generation which sees the rebirth of Israel is the terminal generation.

5. EXODUS II

The fifth prophetic sign that we are the terminal generation is Exodus II—that point in history when the Russian Jews would return to Israel in massive numbers.

During the Ronald Reagan administration, the former Soviet Union began to collapse. The door was opened for the Jews trapped behind the Iron Curtain to return to Israel. Because of the generosity of our television partners across the nation and around the world, John Hagee Ministries was able to bring twenty-three thousand Russian Jews home to Israel, by providing $17,317,000 in funding.

This is called Exodus II.

It is recorded in Scripture by the pen of the prophet Jeremiah, who writes:

> *"Therefore, behold, the days are coming," says the Lord, "that they shall no longer say, 'As the Lord lives who brought up the children of Israel from the land of Egypt,' but, 'As the Lord lives who brought up and led the descendants of the house of Israel from the north country [Russia] and from all the countries where I had driven them.' And they shall dwell in their own land."*
>
> *—Jeremiah 23:7–8*

The Jews from the north country (Russia) have returned to Israel by the hundreds of thousands, as have Jewish people from around the globe. We have seen them on national television disembarking from planes in Tel Aviv. We have read it in every form of print media. Today they live in their own land, just as Jeremiah prophesied. Their return to their homeland is another sign that we are the terminal generation.

6. JERUSALEM NO LONGER UNDER GENTILE RULE

The sixth prophetic sign that we are the terminal generation is that Jerusalem is no longer under Gentile control. Jerusalem was under the control of the Gentiles from 70 A.D., when Titus attacked the city and destroyed the Temple, until the Six Day War of 1967. Jesus Christ prophesied that Jerusalem would be "trampled by the Gentiles until the times of the Gentiles are fulfilled" (Luke 21:24). David the psalmist predicted that the Lord would rebuild Zion (Jerusalem) and appear in His glory there (see Psalm 102:16).

That's why David wrote, "Pray for the peace of Jerusalem" (Psalm 122:6). World history proves that when there is peace in Jerusalem, there is peace in the world. When there is war in Jerusalem, there is war in the world. Therefore, to pray for peace in Jerusalem is to pray for peace in the United States of America.

7. WORLDWIDE TELEVISION

The seventh prophetic sign that we are the terminal generation is the invention and development of worldwide television. When my grandfather and my father would discuss the prophetic Scripture, there was a point in the Book of Revelation that no one could understand. How could it be possible that the whole world at one time could see Enoch and Elijah slain in the streets of Jerusalem? How would they see them come back from the dead and ascend into heaven?

The obvious answer is worldwide television functioning by interconnecting satellites. That was not possible in 1950. It is possible today.

John the Revelator tells the story:

And I will give power to my two witnesses [Enoch and Elijah], and they will prophesy one thousand two hundred and sixty days, clothed in sackcloth. [One thousand two hundred sixty days is three and a half years, which is the midpoint of the Tribulation.]

When they finish their testimony, the beast that ascends out of the bottomless pit will make war against them, overcome them, and kill them. And their dead bodies will lie in the street of the great city [Jerusalem] . . . where also our Lord was crucified. Then those from the peoples, tribes, tongues and nations will see their dead bodies three and a half days, and not allow their dead bodies to be put into graves. And those who dwell on the earth will rejoice over them, make merry, and send gifts to one another, because these two prophets tormented those who dwell on the earth. Now after the three and half days the breath of life from God entered them, and they stood on their feet, and great fear fell on those who saw them. And they heard a loud

voice from heaven saying to them, "Come up here." And they ascended
into heaven in a cloud and their enemies saw them.
                                                    —*Revelation 11:3, 7–12*

John states that the whole world will, at the same time, be able to
see the two witnesses in the streets of Jerusalem. My father's generation
could not explain that. How could the whole world see two dead men
lying in the streets of Jerusalem at one time? It was a mystery and considered absolutely impossible!

Then came television, followed by international satellites, the internet,
and wireless communication where you can watch television in the palm
of your hand over an iPhone.

This was not possible in 1900!

This was not possible in 1960!

It is possible today . . . because we are the terminal generation. The
population of the world living during the Tribulation will see the two
witnesses slain in the streets of Jerusalem, will see the Antichrist, will see
their dead bodies ascend into heaven live and in living color on CNN.

8. DAYS OF DECEPTION

The eighth prophetic sign that we are the terminal generation is given by
Jesus to his disciples on the Mount of Olives who warned: "Take heed
that no one deceives you" (Matthew 24:4). Deception is going to be a
cardinal indicator of the terminal generation, and although deception
has always been with us, the coming Antichrist and False Prophet will
elevate deception to an art form.

The Antichrist will come as a man of peace, but he will bring global war
bathing the world in blood.

**Secular humanism will teach that there is no absolute right or ab-
solute wrong.** I wonder what part of "Thou shall not" in the Ten Commandments they don't understand? Secular humanism is deception, for it
holds that man can usurp the role of God.

**Neopagan environmentalism will present Mother Earth as a heal-
ing force** in the world. There is no "Mother Earth." There is only Father

God. If you believe nature can heal you, the next time you get sick, go out and hug a Ponderosa pine and watch the results.

The era of empowerment will convince the nations that debt can be ignored producing rampant and irresponsible spending. The words of Solomon will be forgotten: "The debtor is slave to the lender." Nations will collapse with debt that will pave the way for the introduction of the economic global czar, the Antichrist.

The Bible and its eternal truths will be mocked, and those who believe them will be ridiculed as intellectually inferior.

Bible prophecy declares that deception will be epidemic on the earth in the terminal generation:

> *Everyone will deceive his neighbor, and will not speak the truth; they have taught their tongue to speak lies; they weary themselves to commit iniquity.*
>
> —*Jeremiah 9:5*

But the world will be ready for him, eager and willing to believe anything he says or desires. Why wouldn't it be? For generations, we've been cutting our teeth and weakening our wills with lies from national leaders.

Satanism and teachings of the occult are nothing but deception. The apostate church, which has a form of godliness but denies the power of God, is peddling sheer deception because it has exchanged the truth of God for a lie (see 2 Timothy 3:5 and Romans 1:25). Such churches deliberately ignore the imminent coming of Christ, saying, "Where is the promise of His coming? For since the fathers fell asleep, all things continue as they were from the beginning of creation" (2 Peter 3:4).

You can't find truth in the world's bestsellers! What God wants you to know about the future is written in the word of God. The truth of God's word is the immunization against deception.

9. FAMINES, PESTILENCES, AND EARTHQUAKES

The ninth prophetic sign that we are the terminal generation is given in Matthew 24 that states, "And there will be famines, pestilences and earthquakes in various places" (Matthew 24:7).

America has the ability to feed the world, yet we pay farmers not to grow certain crops lest they glut the market and drive prices down. And every night on television we see footage of starving children with bloated bellies, bulging eyes, and bare ribs. There are many hungry children even in the United States.

Another translation calls these signs "the beginning of birth pains" (NIV). Famine, pestilences, and earthquakes are the pains experienced at the birth of the terminal generation. When a woman begins to feel her first sharp pains, she knows the end of her pregnancy is near. The event she's been waiting and praying for is finally upon her.

The Jewish people know about these birth pangs (pains). Hebrew eschatology, called *acharit ha-yamim,* describes the pre-Messianic era as one of great upheavals and wars, known as "the birth pangs [pains] of the Messiah," and Jewish suffering and exile.

The Talmud describes this era as the "footprints of the Messiah"—a time when arrogance will increase. The government will turn to heresy, and there will be no one to rebuke its wrongdoing. Young people will shame their elders; a person's own family will become his enemies.

Pestilence—incurable disease—is another sign that we have reached the terminal generation. Many years ago, I was preaching about pestilence and a man came up later and said, "Look, Pastor Hagee, I've got a bone to pick with you. You said pestilence is an incurable disease, but medical science has the ability to control every sickness known to man."

I answered that the Bible said things would change. According to Joshua Lederberg, a Nobel laureate from Rockefeller University, many experts were confident in the 1960s that medical science had solved forever the problem of infectious diseases. But today, say the medical experts, disease is on the march, and the human races is not now ready to defend itself against what is really "an unending siege by pestilence."

A few years ago we discovered AIDS, the Ebola virus, and antibiotic-resistant bacteria. None of these will be conquered easily. AIDS alone is a medical black hole that has touched the life of practically every American, and after more than a decade of intense research, many who get it still die.

According to the most recent mortality study conducted by the U.S. Centers for Disease Control and Prevention, AIDS is now the leading cause of death for twenty-five- to forty-four-year-olds and was ranked as the eighth leading cause of death overall for Americans in 1992. Scientists estimate that 1 million Americans—1 in every 250 people—are infected with HIV.

AIDS, Ebola, and killer viruses like swine flu and bird flu are a trumpet blast from the throne of God: *You are the terminal generation!*

In the Bible, God repeatedly used earthquakes to achieve His divine purposes. Revelation 16:18 18–20 records: . . . and there was a great earthquake, such a mighty and great earthquake as had not occurred since men were on the earth . . . Then every island fled away, and the mountains were not found.

God used earthquakes at the crucifixion to split the veil at the Temple from the top to the bottom. It was God's way of saying you no longer need another human being to intercede for you in prayer; you as an individual can walk directly into the presence of God in the Holiest of Holies.

God used an earthquake at the resurrection of Jesus Christ. Not to let Him out, but to let us in. The empty tomb in Jerusalem is the only tourist attraction on Earth where people line up to see nothing.

God used an earthquake to set Paul and Silas free from the jail in Philippi. God will use an earthquake to announce the coming of His son when the islands of the sea disappear and the Mount of Olives splits in half. It will be God's way of saying,

"I am Almighty God; the Antichrist and his armies cannot stop Me. I have returned to the earth as King of kings and Lord of lords to rule and reign forever."

10. AS IN THE DAYS OF NOAH

The tenth prophetic sign that we are the terminal generation is the statement from Jesus to His disciples:

TEN

What's Going to Happen Next?

What is the next earth-shaking event in God's prophetic drama? Some are expecting the Antichrist to suddenly appear and solve the present global economic meltdown. Others are expecting the Great Tribulation—with its earthquakes, famines, wars, and endless tragedies leaving one-third of the earth's population dead.

THE GREAT RAPTURE

The truth is the next prophetic event that will shake the foundations of planet Earth is the rapture of the church. The word *rapture* is the Latin version of a phrase the Bible uses to describe the catching away of all Christians, both dead and alive, on the earth at the appointed time.

The rapture is a global event where every believer on planet Earth will be taken from the earth into heaven in the "twinkling of an eye." Simply stated: billions of people will instantly disappear and not return for seven years!

Think it can't happen?

Think again!

The Ones Who've Gone Before Us

It has already happened and has been recorded in the chronicles of eternal truth for your thoughtful consideration.

The *first* recording of a mortal man being snatched from the earth while alive was the prophet Elijah, who was taken into heaven by a whirlwind and was seen no more (see 2 Kings 2:11). Inasmuch as it is appointed for every man "once to die," Elijah will appear on the earth again during the Tribulation to bring God's message of hope to the world that the Messiah will soon appear on the earth for the second time.

Elijah and Enoch will be killed by the Antichrist on the streets of Jerusalem. Their dead bodies will lie there for the world to see for three days. On the third day, both will stand up and ascend into heaven.

The Revelation states that the whole world will see it and will be stricken with fear! How will they see it? By satellite television! Remember: one of the ten signs of the terminal generation is international television making it possible to see this very event on live television!

The *second* man to leave the earth and go into heaven was Enoch, as recorded in Hebrews 11:5:

> *By faith, Enoch was taken away so that he did not see death . . . and was not found because God had taken him.*

Enoch will join Elijah as messengers of Almighty God during the Tribulation. Jesus Christ made this promise to his disciples just before his crucifixion:

> *In my father's house are many mansions; if it were not so I would have told you. . . .* I will come again and receive you unto Myself; *that where I am [in heaven] there you may be also.*
>
> —*John 14:2–3*

The rapture is the fulfillment of His promise to the disciples and the Church.

The *third* man to leave the earth was the Apostle Paul as recoded in 2 Corinthians 12:2–4, who was in the "third heaven," and then returned to Earth to complete his ministry.

The *fourth* man who went into heaven before his death was the Apostle John, who was called from the Isle of Patmos by Jesus who had the voice of a trumpet that said, "Come up here!" (Revelation 4:1). John ascended into heaven, where he received the Revelation of God, seeing the unspeakable things of horror that would happen on the earth during the rule of the Antichrist during the Tribulation.

Most people are confused about the sequence of past and prophetic events. I refer you to the following chart:

Escape from the Horrors of the Tribulation

The gospel of St. Luke records: "Watch therefore, and pray always that you may be counted worthy to escape those things that are coming upon the earth" (Luke 21:36).

St. Paul records in the book of Hebrews: "How shall we escape if we neglect so great a salvation?" (Hebrews 2:3).

The Rapture is the Great Escape! Escape from what? Escape from the horror of the Great Tribulation that will happen as soon as the church leaves the earth. Walk with me through the pages of Revelation chapters 6, 8, 9, and 16, and let me describe briefly the living hell you will escape by being part of the rapture.

These are but a few of the things that will happen during the Tribulation:

- *One-fourth of mankind will die* (see Revelation 6:8), some because of war, some because of famine, and still others by earthquakes and global disasters. Whether by death that is swift and instant or death that is lingering and excruciating, 25 percent of all people will die. Presently, the world's population is 6.5 billion in 2010. One-fourth of this amount is 1.6 billion, which is more than five times the current population of the United States. Think about it!

- *One-third of all vegetation will be burned up.* All grass, every tree, everything green will be destroyed (see Revelation 8:7).

- *The sun and moon will be darkened,* as nature goes into revolt (see Revelation 8:12).

- *The gates of hell will open and hordes of locusts, the size of horses, will come upon the earth.* These locusts will be allowed to sting men like scorpions, and the pain will last for five months. The Bible says men will beg God to let them die, but they will not die (see Revelation 9:3–6).

- *There will be a worldwide famine,* unlike anything the world has ever seen (see Revelation 18:8).

- *There will be a world war* so bloody that the blood of those killed in battle will flow for two hundred miles up to the bridle of a horse in the valley of Jezreel. This will be the Battle of Armageddon. During the Great Tribulation, one-third of all people on the earth will be killed (see Revelation 14:20).

- *Every person on Earth will be covered with great running, festering boils.* Have you ever had one boil? Imagine being covered with them, not being able to walk, lie down, or sit without pain (see Revelation 16:2–11).

- *The seven seas of the earth will be turned into blood.* Every river, every stream will become as blood. Every basin in your home will run with blood. This plague came upon the Egyptians and drove them to release the Jewish people from captivity. It's the plague that produces mind-numbing thirst from which there is no relief (see Revelation 8:8, 11:6).

- *Mighty men, kings, and men of power will gnaw their tongues in pain* and crawl into caves and beg God to kill them (see Revelation 6:15).

- *The earth will quake so severely that the islands of the sea will disappear.* Puerto Rico and Hawaii will be covered with water. Every building, every wall on earth will crumble. Millions will be trapped beneath the rubble with no one to come to their aid (see Revelation 16:18).

Now I ask you, do you want to escape the coming Tribulation? I do! And I am going to escape. When the archangel blows the trumpet and the dead in Christ rise immediately, those of us who are alive when Jesus the Messiah returns in the clouds of heaven will rise into the air in the twinkling of an eye to trade the coming hell on Earth for the wonder and majesty of heaven. We will meet the real Jesus. He is the Lion of the Tribe of Judah. He is the Lord of Glory. He is the light of the world, the Lamb of God, and the lover of my soul.

The literal, physical appearance of Jesus Christ will come soon. And soon after the church is gone, the Antichrist, the son of Satan, will appear upon the stage of the world to begin his reign of deception and terror.

BIBLE BACKUP FOR THE RAPTURE

The Bible basis for the belief in the rapture is found in the following promises of God. The provisions of God are found in His promises.

> *For the Lord Himself will descend from heaven with a shout, with the voice of an archangel, and with the trumpet of God. And the dead in Christ shall rise first. Then we who are alive and remain shall be caught up together with them in the clouds to meet the Lord in the air. And thus we shall always be with the Lord. Therefore comfort one another with these words.*
> —*1 Thessalonians 4:16–18 NKJV*

> *And then shall appear the sign of the Son of Man in heaven and they [the bride of Christ] shall see the Son of man coming in the clouds of heaven with power and great glory.*
> —*Matthew 24:30 NKJV*

These words were spoken to the disciples as they watched Jesus ascend into heaven:

> *Men of Galilee, why do you stand gazing into the heavens? This same Jesus, who was taken up from you into heaven, will so come in like manner as you have seen him go into heaven.*
> —*Acts 1:11 NKJV*

When Will the Rapture of the Church Happen?

The absolute Bible truth is this: the rapture could happen before you finish reading this page! The preceding chapter gave ten biblically validated signs that had to be fulfilled before the rapture of the church could happen. *All* have been fulfilled! The rapture could happen at any second and as instantly as . . . the twinkling of an eye. St. Paul wrote:

> *Behold I shew you a mystery: We shall not all sleep [in death], but we shall all be changed—in a moment,* in the twinkling of an eye. . .
> —*1 Corinthians 15:51–52*

The twinkling of an eye is a split second. The difference between the twinkling of an eye and the batting of the eye is the time required by the neurological response. For the eye to blink, the neurological message must go to the brain and back forcing the blink of the eye. The twinkling of an eye is the time required for the neurological message to go only to the brain. The batting of the eye takes twice as long as the twinkling of an eye.

Think of it . . . billions of people all over planet Earth will instantly disappear. *Gone!*

The trumpet of God will sound, because in Bible times, trumpets were sounded to announce the appearance of royalty.

Jesus Christ is the Prince of Peace; He is King of all kings and Lord of all lords. The day will soon come when "every knee shall bow and every tongue shall confess that he is Lord to the glory of God the Father."

The shout of the archangel is Christ's shout as He celebrates His absolute victory over the enemy of death. The resurrection morning is Christ's Super Bowl victory over death, hell, and the grave!

Jesus stood at Lazarus' tomb and shouted: "Lazarus, come forth!" and Lazarus awoke from the slumber of death to live again. Jesus shouted to the Apostle John on the Isle of Patmos, "Come up here!" and John instantly was caught up into heaven to receive the contents of the Book of Revelation.

THE DAY OF RECKONING

Very soon, Jesus Christ is going to step out on the balconies of heaven and shout to his church on planet Earth, those who sleep in death, and those that are alive, "Come up here!" Instantly, in the twinkling of an eye, the dead in Christ will rise first, and we who are alive and remain shall be caught up with them in the clouds and so shall we ever be with the Lord. Are you listening for the shout? The rapture is going to happen . . . ready or not!

Instantly all over the earth billions of people will disappear. Wives who have been a living witness to their rebellious husbands will disappear from their arms into heaven while their husbands stand in total shock! They are left behind!

Automobiles will be empty on the freeway, on the streets, and abandoned in tunnels; the motors are running but the drivers are gone to mansions on high.

Homes of believers will be eternally divided in a split second. Sitting at the supper table discussing the crisis on Wall Street, suddenly the children disappear to the marriage supper of the Lamb, while the unbelieving parents are left behind.

Jumbo jets flying at forty thousand feet at 600 miles per hour with three hundred-plus passengers are in for a shock! The captain is a believer; he suddenly disappears from the cockpit, the plane crashes seconds later, and every passenger steps into eternity!

Classrooms in school will suddenly be without teachers and believing students; hospitals will be without dedicated doctors and nurses; parents will be without children; and children will be without parents. The son of God has called His triumphant church to heaven.

Phone circuits will be jammed all over the earth with sobbing people, who always intended to make things right with God who suddenly realize they are lost and left behind.

People will be standing in their front yards looking up toward the heavens, screaming, "O my God" in an effort to relieve the terror that grips their souls.

A global economic crash is guaranteed, as Bible believers who had a strong work ethic leave planet Earth to the maddening designs of social architects who know not the God of Abraham, Isaac, and Jacob! Panic will grip the earth as God's "salt and light" have departed and the son of Satan waits in the wings with his plans to produce a global bloodbath for mankind!

Bold and blaring headlines on the newspapers of every nation on earth will carry the same message:

MILLIONS ARE MISSING:
Christians Have Disappeared from the Earth!

Television networks will have their usual roundtable of masterminds to explain the obvious. Their TV crews will be interviewing shaking, weeping citizens from all nations, describing a plethora of events that have the same ending: they witnessed their Christian friends and family members as they disappeared instantly right before their eyes . . . they're *gone!*

The masterminds sitting around the table will be jabbering about this "right wing, evangelical rapture theory." New Agers will be certain that these masses of people have been taken by an invasion of space ships. Hollywood has been advancing this concept for years.

Churches will be packed with weeping, hysterical people, who state: "The Lord Jesus Christ has come for His church and we are left behind to go through the living hell of the Great Tribulation. Our options are to take the mark of the Beast and lose our souls or be beheaded." The altars will be filled for days, but it's too late now!

Just beyond the clouds, the bride of Christ, the church triumphant, will be gathering around His throne to cast their crowns at His feet. The bride will stand before our bridegroom Jesus and offer Him our dowry, the things we have done in His name. These works do not buy our entrance into heaven, but we offer them in love, as gifts from a loving church to a waiting savior. And for our efforts, we may receive as many as six crowns.

THE CROWNS OF THE BRIDE OF CHRIST

THE CROWN FOR THOSE WHO LOVE HIS APPEARANCE (2 Timothy 4:8): "Finally, there is laid up for me the crown of righteousness, which the Lord, the righteous Judge, will give to me on that Day, and not to me only but also to all who have loved [earnestly longed for] His appearing."

THE CROWN FOR ENDURING TRIALS (James 1:12): "Blessed is the man who endures temptation; for when he has been approved, he will receive the crown of life which the Lord has promised to those who love Him."

THE CROWN FOR THOSE WILLING TO FEED THE FLOCK (1 Peter 5:2–4): "Shepherd the flock of God which is among you, serving as overseers, not by compulsion but willingly, not for dishonest gain but eagerly; nor as being lords over those entrusted to you, but being examples to the flock; and when the Chief Shepherd appears, you will receive the crown of glory that does not fade away."

THE CROWN FOR THOSE WHO ARE FAITHFUL UNTO DEATH (Revelation 2:10): "Do not fear any of those things which you are about to suffer. Indeed, the devil is about to throw some of you in prison, that you may be tested, and you will have tribulation ten days. Be faithful until death, and I will give you the crown of life."

THE CROWN FOR THOSE WHO WIN SOULS (1 Thessalonians 2:19): "For what is our hope, our joy, or crown of rejoicing? Is it not even you in the presence of our Lord Jesus Christ at His coming?"

THE CROWN FOR THOSE WHO MASTER THE OLD NATURE (1 Corinthians 9:24–25): "Do you not know that those who run in a race all run, but one receives the prize? Run in such a way that you may obtain it. And everyone who competes for the prize is temperate in all things. Now they do it to obtain a perishable crown, but we for an imperishable crown."

Once we have received our crowns, we will sit at the wedding feast prepared for the bride of Christ. The church, the body of believers, is the bride without spot or wrinkle, the bride purchased with the blood of Jesus, the Lamb of God who died for us in our place to pay the penalty for our sins.

That dinner will be a glorious celebration, for the bride has been victorious over the powers and principalities of darkness. We, the members of His raptured church, were the salt and light of the earth, the pure in heart, the peacemakers, the ones who endured persecution for the sake of Christ.

If you listen closely, you can almost hear the orchestra of heaven beginning to play the wedding march, "Here comes the bride." Are you ready?

The bride will stand on the Sea of Glass and sing the song of the redeemed: "Thou hast redeemed us from every tribe and from every nation; thou art worthy, O Lord, of worship and praise."

As the celebration of the marriage supper of the lamb begins in heaven, on Earth the Antichrist, the Son of Perdition, meaning the "chief son of Satan," is about to be introduced as the "Man of Peace" who will begin his reign of hope for the future with a "Seven-Year Peace Accord" with the State of Israel. It will be a day of deception and the beginning of the end!

WHAT DIFFERENCE DOES IT MAKE?

I have been a minister of the Gospel for more than fifty years. When faced with the reality of the rapture, people often ask the question: "What difference does it make whether I believe in the rapture or not?"

The answer comes from the source of all truth: the word of God, which states, "To those who eagerly *wait for Him* He will appear a second time."

The point is simply this: if you're not looking for Him to make His appearance, you're not going with Him when He comes. The Bible says:

Watch therefore, and pray always that you may be counted worthy to escape all those things that will come to pass and stand before the Son of Man.

—Luke 21:36

But the end of all things is at hand; therefore be serious and watchful in your prayers.

—1 Peter 4:7

In the parable of the five wise and the five foolish virgins, Jesus urges us to be ready for the appearance of the bridegroom (see Matthew 25:1–13). The point is simply this: if you want to go with Him, you must be watching for Him.

THE FACES OF SKEPTICISM

"Well, I simply don't believe Jesus Christ is ever coming back, and I think this rapture thing is a scare tactic," says the skeptic.

My response? "Good for you! The very fact you doubt His coming is proof positive He is coming." The Bible states in 2 Peter 3:3–4:

Knowing this first, that there shall come in the last days scoffers, walking after their own lusts, and saying, 'Where is the promise of his coming?'

The scoffer, the agnostic, and the atheist are nothing more than cheer-leaders for the doctrine of the rapture.

Those who attack the doctrine of the rapture are usually those who teach that the Bible is not to be taken literally. Some honor the word of God in their hearts but, nonetheless, insist that what is important is the spiritual meaning of Bible passages, which often transcends (and some-times conflicts with) the literal words themselves.

If you abandon the plain meaning of the biblical text, how do you have any way of evaluating what the "spiritual meaning" really is? And thus, they face the possibility of giving Scripture a "private interpreta-tion," which is explicitly warned against:

And so we have the prophetic word confirmed, which you do well to heed as a light that shines in a dark place, until the day dawns and the morning star rises in your hearts; knowing this first, that no prophecy of Scripture is of private interpretation, for prophecy never came by the will of man, but holy men of God spoke as they were moved by the Holy Spirit.

—2 Peter 1:19–21

Still others who have no regard for the word of God insist that what-ever meaning the Scriptures have is allegorical at best. But if the Bible is only a collection of fables and allegories, it's a myth and not fit for hu-man consumption—let alone consideration.

THE BIBLE IS *LITERAL*

Why would God bother to give us a collection of allegories? There is no answer for this because He gave us no such book. The Bible I revere is a literal book from cover to cover, meant to be understood and acted on, not deciphered and dismissed. This is just like God, who, as Augustine somewhere said, "Caught orators by fishermen—not fishermen by orators." Consider the following:

- Jesus was literally born of a virgin named Mary.

- He was literally born in Bethlehem.

- He literally healed people.

- He literally died on the cross.

- He literally died between two thieves.

- He literally was buried in a borrowed grave.

- He literally rose from the dead on the third day and ascended into heaven before His twelve disciples.

If those things are *literally* true, why shouldn't He *literally* come back to Earth with power and great glory? Why shouldn't the Bible be literally true when it says that ". . . every knee should bow . . . and that every tongue should confess that Jesus Christ is Lord, to the glory of God the Father" (Philippians 2:10–11)?

Why shouldn't I literally rise to meet Him in the air, as will every believer who looks for His glorious appearing?

Why shouldn't I literally walk on streets of gold? Why shouldn't I literally wear a crown of life? Why shouldn't I literally live forever and forever? Why shouldn't there be a new Jerusalem? Why shouldn't those who are looking for Him literally walk through heaven's gates shouting, "Glory!"?

Critics of the rapture doctrine are quick to point out that the word *rapture* does not appear in the Bible. That's absolutely true. The Bible does not contain the term *trinity* either, but repeatedly it refers to the "threeness" of God being God the Father, the Son, and the Holy Spirit.

> *Go therefore and make disciples of all the nations, baptizing them in the name of the Father and of the Son and of the Holy Spirit.*
>
> —*Matthew 28:19*

> *But the Helper, the Holy Spirit, whom the Father will send in My name, He will teach you all things, and bring to your remembrance all things that I said to you.*
>
> —*John 14:26*

> *The grace of the Lord Jesus Christ, and the love of God, and the communion of the Holy Spirit be with you all. Amen.*
>
> —*2 Corinthians 13:14*

Though the term *trinity* isn't in the Bible, the truth of God's three-in-one nature is. The same is true with the truth of the rapture: the *term* itself isn't in Scripture, but the *truth* most certainly is.

Other critics of the rapture say, "The rapture teaching is nothing but escapism. You people are trying to escape from the real world." Right now, I'm living in the real world, and if I wanted to escape it, I could think of no better way than working in waiting for the coming of the Lord Jesus Christ. I am thrilled that Jesus is my lord and savior, that heaven is my home, and that I'm not going to walk through the living hell of the Tribulation. If that's escapism, so be it!

Let's face it. Everyone wants to escape from something. Environmentalists want to escape from pollution. The people in peace movements want to escape from war. The people who believe in global warming want to escape carbon emissions into the atmosphere. The Bible teaches us to prepare for our escape:

> *"Watch therefore, and pray always that you may be counted worth to escape all these things that will come to pass, and to stand before the Son of Man."*
>
> —*Luke 21:36*

Those who do not stand before the Son of Man in righteousness will stand before the Son of Perdition, who is the chief son of Satan, who is better known in Scripture as the Antichrist. He's coming in the near future to form the Fourth Reich and rule the world with a fist of iron.

Think it can't happen?

Think again!

PART FOUR

The Final Days

ELEVEN

The Fourth Reich:
The Coming Antichrist

The unspeakable horrors of the Third Reich under the demonic leadership of Adolf Hitler produced the darkest page in the history of the twentieth century.

Out of demonized minds of the Nazi monsters came the nightmare of the Final Solution fathered by Adolf Eichmann, which led to the systematic slaughter of 6 million Jews, two-thirds of the Jewish population in Europe, and the death of 50 million people.

After the guns of World War II fell silent, after Berlin was pulverized by Allied artillery, after the Third Reich—which Hitler predicted would endure for one thousand years—was a wasteland of rubble,150,000 Nazis were charged with war crimes.

Thirty thousand Nazis were tried and fewer were convicted. Where did the 120,000 Nazis vanish to on planet Earth? How did they escape? Who helped them escape and find places of refuge beyond the reach of justice?

Two of the most famous Nazi criminals—Joseph Mengele, the Doctor of Death, and Martin Bormann—escaped and were never brought to trial. How could such monsters avoid and evade the judicial and intelligence systems of every government on the face of the earth?

The Simon Wiesenthal Organization investigated a secret organization labeled ODESSA, an acronym meaning, in German, the "Organisation Der Ehemaligen SS Angehörigen," which translates in English as the Organization of Former Members of the SS.

"But as the days of Noah were so also will the coming of the Son of Man be. For as in the days before the flood, they were eating and drinking, marrying and giving in marriage, until the day that Noah entered the Ark, and did not know until the flood came and took them all away, so also will the coming of the Son of Man be."
                                                    —Matthew 24:37–39

It is true that "no man knows the day nor the hour" that Jesus is returning to the earth. This is a statement of a twenty-four-hour period. Jesus' illustration of Noah is an entirely different prophetic matter.

Here's why!

God told Noah that a great calamity was coming on the earth, and his mission was to build an Ark for the salvation of all who would get on board. It took Noah one hundred twenty years to build the Ark. After the Ark was built, God helped him gather the animals two-by-two placing them on the Ark. Then Noah and his family of eight were the only ones who believed the message of coming doom. Those eight got on the Ark and God shut the door.

When you are Noah on the Ark with your family and the animals with God having just shut the door, you know the only thing left is the flood. The next thing you're listening for is rain. It came and the fountains of the deep were opened and the world and all that were in it drowned in the flood.

Prophetically, we are exactly in the position of Noah on the Ark, hence the words by Jesus, "As it was in the days of Noah . . ." The message has been preached; those who believe are getting on board with Jesus Christ. We are patiently waiting for the sound of the trumpet and the rapture of the church.

The Bible says, "When you see these signs, lift up your heads and rejoice." *The ten prophetic signs have been fulfilled* . . . rejoice, the King is coming. *We are the terminal generation.*

The mystery of how these tens of thousands of Nazis will forever escape detection will remain a secret known only to God Almighty. He will call all men to a day of judgment and will make every secret thing exposed.

According to the prophet Daniel, who was given a vision from God of the end of days, history will repeat itself at some point in the future with a Fourth Reich. This repeat of the future will not cover Europe alone, but will blanket the earth.

It will come to power much like Hitler came to power: on the wings of an economic crisis.

The prophet Daniel states that the leader of the coming Fourth Reich "will cause craft to prosper" (Daniel 8:25). Daniel also writes:

> *He shall have power over the treasures of gold and silver, and over all the precious things of Egypt; also the Libyans and Ethiopians shall follow at his heels.*
>
> *—Daniel 11:43*

John the Revelator records concerning the Antichrist's determination to control absolutely every financial transaction on planet Earth with the words:

> *He [the Antichrist] causes all, both small and great, rich and poor, free and slave, to receive a mark on their right hand or on their foreheads, and that no one may buy or sell except one who has the mark or the name of the beast, or the number of his name. Here is wisdom. Let him who has understanding calculate the number of the beast, for it is the number of a man; his number is 666.*
>
> *—Revelation 13:16–18*

SEVEN REASONS FOR THE MARK

There are seven reasons that the Antichrist will place a mark on those he controls.

1. The mark is open rebellion against the law of God, which states: "You shall not make any cuttings . . . nor tattoo any marks on you: I am the Lord" (Leviticus 19:28).

Your body is the temple of the Holy Spirit and when you decorate it with graffiti, it angers the Lord!

2. *The mark extends favors to those who support the One World Government,* such as food, medicine, and the right to buy and sell (see Revelation 13:16).

3. *The mark identifies and eliminates all opposition to the One World Government.*

4. *The mark tracks and controls all commerce.*

5. *The mark forces people to stop worshipping God.* When you take the mark of the beast, you lose your soul. The Book of Revelation records:

> *If anyone worships the beast and his image, and receives his mark on his forehead or on his hand, he himself shall also drink of the wine of the wrath of God, which is poured out full strength into the cup of His indignation. He shall be tormented with fire and brimstone in the presence of the Holy angels and in the presence of the Lamb of God.*
> —*Revelation 14:9–10*

The point is this: the moment you take the mark of the beast, you no longer look to God Almighty as your source and savior; you are officially recognizing the Antichrist as your provider.

6. *The mark forces people to worship the Antichrist.* When you take the mark of the beast, the only one left to worship is the Antichrist. When you reject truth, all that's left is a lie. Your first step away from light is your first step toward the kingdom of darkness.

7. *The mark permanently ties people to the kingdom of the Antichrist* with absolute control of their lives and their souls.

If you miss the rapture of the Church, you have two alternatives. One is to be beheaded for your refusal to reject Jesus Christ as savior. The other is to receive the mark of the beast and lose your soul for all eternity.

I believe the coming global economic czar, the Antichrist, is now standing in the wings of history, waiting for the economies of the world, now deeply in debt, to crash! He will step onto the stage of world history much like Hitler, as the economic messiah. World rulers will applaud his coming; they will demand his coronation as the new Caesar of the world. You will read this phrase in the print media in the near future: "A global leader for a global problem." Watch for it!

COMPARING HOW HITLER AND THE ANTICHRIST CAME TO POWER

Let's compare the process by which Adolf Hitler came to power and the process by which the prophet Daniel says the Antichrist will soon come to power.

1. Adolf Hitler came to power through the economic crisis created by the Versailles Treaty. This treaty was the womb of World War II. History proves that poorly written treaties are the breeding ground for the next war.

The Treaty of Versailles placed the German people in financial crisis and demanded payment of reparations created by World War I to England and America. This enormous debt, created by the treaty, led to hyperinflation in Germany where the ink on the German mark was more valuable than the money.

Inflation became so severe that people walked into stores with a handful of money to buy a single loaf of bread. Wealthy Germans drove their Mercedes into the countryside and traded them for sacks of potatoes.

Into this chaos came Adolf Hitler and the Nazis. Hitler pledged to revive the German economy by rebuilding the national infrastructure and building a car for the common people. Thus the autobahns were born, as the Volkswagen means "car of the people." Hitler endeared himself to the German people by defying America and England in refusing to repay the onerous war debt required by the Treaty of Versailles. His defiance made him an instant hero to the disheartened German people.

In like manner, the coming Antichrist, leader of the Fourth Reich, will come to the world stage to resolve an economic crisis—not for one nation, but for the nations of the world. Excessive global debt will cause a global economic meltdown accelerated by the rapture of the church when billions of people suddenly disappear.

The leaders of the world will call for and even demand that there be a global economic czar to save the world from an economic catastrophe. That man, like Hitler, will come out of Europe and will be the Antichrist.

2. Hitler made his debut upon the stage of the world with hypnotic charm, charisma, and arrogance. Men cheered his speeches with thunderous applause and mesmerized women wept and some even fainted in extreme ecstasy.

The prophet Daniel presents the coming Antichrist, leader of the coming global Fourth Reich, to be extremely arrogant and demonically anointed as an orator.

> *. . . shall do according to his own will: he shall exalt and magnify*
> *himself above every god, . . . for he will exalt himself above them all.*
> *—Daniel 11:36–37*

Revelation 13:5–6 states:

> *And he [the Antichrist] was given a mouth speaking great things*
> *and blasphemies . . . then he opened his mouth in blasphemy against*
> *God, to blaspheme His name, His tabernacle, and those who dwell in*
> *heaven.*
> *—Psalms 24:1*

The Antichrist will have the arrogance to challenge the right of God Almighty to rule the very earth He created and to which He has complete ownership.

3. Adolf Hitler and the SS were absolutely committed to and controlled by the powers of the occult. The book *The Twisted Cross* reveals historical evidence demonstrating the demonic mind-set and practices of the leaders of the Third Reich. The SS were Hells Angels in long black leather coats!

Just so, the prophet Daniel states that the coming Antichrist, leader of the Fourth Reich, will "understand dark sentences" (Daniel 8:23).

In Scripture, there are two kingdoms: the kingdom of light and the kingdom of darkness. Satan is referred to as the Prince of Darkness. The word *prince* means one who has authority in a specific kingdom. Hence, Satan and his chief son, the Antichrist, have authority in the kingdom of darkness ruled by the occult. When the church, which is God's salt and light, is taken from the world, the Prince of Darkness will be in absolute control of planet Earth.

Simply stated, the coming Antichrist will be anointed by Satan himself to rule the world with demonic deception, total economic control, and brutality that numbs the mind. The Bible says, "His power shall be mighty, but not by his own power" (Daniel 8:24).

The Antichrist will rule the world with the full authority and anointing of Satan himself. Satan and his legions are coming!

Even a casual observer will be aware of the cultic explosion now taking place in Western civilization. The Harry Potter book series is nothing less than Witchcraft 101 and is the most celebrated publication in the history of literature other than the Bible. Children in every country have been exposed to blood curses, witches, and the occult in a positive light. Satan is preparing the youth of the world for the appearance of his messiah, the Antichrist, to rule the world with demonic power!

Cultic movies magnify the demonic power of hell's legions. Books and magazines exalting the power of witchcraft have a large and enthusiastic audience in the Western world.

4. As Hitler came out of Europe, so will the Antichrist come out of the revived Roman Empire. The Antichrist will come from the European Union or a country or confederation that was once part of the Roman Empire. The Roman Empire stretched from Ireland to Egypt and included Turkey, Iran, and Iraq.

In Daniel's vision, the "little horn" sprouted among the other ten, which we know are ten divisions of the final world government, as confirmed by Daniel's vision of the ten toes of Nebuchadnezzar's image (see Daniel 2:31–35 and 7:8). In his rise to power, the Antichrist will weave his hypnotic spell, first over one nation in the ten-kingdom federation, then over all ten. He will conquer three of the ten nations and then take control over all of them. He will then turn his ravenous eye toward the apple of God's eye: Israel. His masterwork of deception will be the Seven-

Year Peace Accord, which Israel will accept (see Daniel 9:27 and Revelation 17:17).

I believe that in the future, global, political, and economic power will shift from America back to Europe. In the final analysis, Israel's salvation will not come from America or Europe; it will come from heaven by the awesome power of the God of Abraham, Isaac, and Jacob.

5. As Hitler did, the Antichrist will come as a man of peace. When England's Prime Minister, Chamberlain, went to Hitler seeking peace for England as the Nazi war machine crushed Poland and France, Hitler gave Chamberlain a written document pledging peace between Germany and England. Chamberlain flew back to England in triumph, joyously disembarked from his plane waving the document Hitler had given proclaiming "peace in our times." But it was a farce, a colossal deception. Hitler never intended to keep the peace; he did exactly what the prophet Daniel said the Antichrist would do in the future:

> *He will destroy wondrously with peace.*
>
> *—Daniel 8:25*

> *Then shall he confirm a covenant [Peace Treaty], with many for one week [seven years]; but in the middle of the week [three and half years after the treaty is signed], he will bring an end to sacrifice an offering.*
>
> *—Daniel 9:27*

The Antichrist will guarantee peace for Israel and the Middle East and sign a seven-year peace treaty but will break the treaty in three and a half years, according to the prophet Daniel.

If you've ever been to Israel, you'll note that their history of betrayal and persecution makes its people extremely cautious about trusting anyone with their safety other than themselves. In fact, this history is part of the great need for the Jewish people to have their own homeland. They can trust their government because their government is truly their own. You can even say that the nation of Israel is an incarnation of their desire as expressed in the solemn utterance "Never again."

Never again a pogrom; never again a persecution; never again an exile; never again a holocaust. So just imagine what it would take for them to entrust their security to another. This gives you an idea both of the coming change of attitude in Israel and of the incredible power of the Antichrist to deceive.

In the months ahead, it is a distinct possibility that Iran will go nuclear and a person out of the European Union will have the political power and presence to guarantee Israel's security. The Jewish people could be granted the right to rebuild the Temple on the Temple Mount and to initiate daily sacrifices as inducement. We know this because the Antichrist will stop the daily sacrifices and offerings at the midpoint of the Tribulation, and sacrifices have to have been started again in order for the Antichrist to stop them. Another clue that the Temple will be rebuilt is that the Antichrist will take over the Temple, an event that occurs at the midpoint of the Tribulation:

> *He will [the Antichrist] oppose and exalt himself over everything that is called God or is worshipped, so that he sets himself up in God's Temple, proclaiming himself to be God.*
> —*2 Thessalonians 2:4*

Again, a temple must have been built in order for the Antichrist to seize and defile it, as he will.

The rebuilding of the Temple constitutes an enormous political and religious problem, for the place the Bible decrees for the location of the Temple is currently occupied by the Dome of the Rock.

The Dome of the Rock is located on the Temple Mount, or Mount Moriah, the third holiest place in the world for Muslims.

If you doubt that the Jewish people would ever attempt something so spectacular, you need to know that some Jewish people are already planning for it, working to make all the necessary preparations for the construction and operation of the third Temple (the first being Solomon's temple and the second being Herod's temple). One of the organizations working toward this end is called the Temple Foundation. I have personally seen their work, and they have created authentic Temple vessels and priestly garments according to biblical specifications.

This is an ongoing process, and to date, over sixty sacred objects have been re-created from gold, silver, and copper. These vessels are not models or replicas, but they are actually made according to all the complicated requirements of biblical law. If the Holy Temple were to be rebuilt immediately, the divine service could be resumed utilizing these vessels.

Only the destruction of the great mosques in Mecca and Medina could have a more explosive effect on Muslims. And no greater blow could be inflicted on the Muslims than Israel to be given the privilege of building the third Temple on the Dome of the Rock. But even as international forces guarantee the security of Israel in their decision to rebuild the Temple, the Islamic nations will prepare for war. The "King of the North" will lead them toward Israel in the Battle of Ezekiel 38–39.

6. As Hitler was a man committed to the force of military power, so will the Antichrist be committed to military power. Revelation 6:2 describes the vision of John on Patmos as the Antichrist rides out on the stage on World History.

> *And I looked, and behold, a white horse and he who sat on it* had a bow; *and a crown was given to him, and he went out conquering and to conquer.*

John again describes the beast saying:

> *Now the beast which I saw was like a leopard, his feet were like the feet of a bear, and his mouth like the mouth of a lion. The dragon* [Satan] gave him his power, *his throne, and great authority.*
>
> —*Revelation 13:2*

Daniel reports:

> *But in his estate, he shall honor the God of forces.*
>
> —*Daniel 11:38*

7. As Hitler had a hatred for the Jewish people, so will the Antichrist determine to destroy the Jewish people. God will prevent it by the Jewish people fleeing to Petra, where God will supernaturally provide for them for three and half years, just as He provided for the children of Israel in the wilderness, following Moses from Egypt to the promised land.

With Satan and his angels cast down to Earth to join forces with the

Antichrist and the False Prophet, the powers of hell will be unfurled on the earth as never before in human history. The Prince of Darkness will attack everything that reminds him of the God of heaven. He will attack both Christians and Jews.

Satan will target the beloved of God, because attacking them is the only way he can retaliate against God. Unable to prevail against God militarily, Satan will seek revenge against Him by targeting the righteous. The Antichrist will be motivated by revenge against the Jewish people who attempted to snuff out his life. All of this will happen at about the same time that the image of the Antichrist is erected in the Temple. God's warning to the seed of Abraham in that day is clear and urgent. Jesus said,

> *Therefore when you see the "abomination of desolation," spoken of by Daniel the prophet, standing in the Holy place [whoever reads, let him understand], then let those who are in Judea flee to the mountains. Let him who is on the housetop not go down to take anything out of his house. And let him who is in the field not go back to get his clothes. But woe to those who are pregnant and to those who are nursing babies in those days! . . . and unless those days were shortened, no flesh would be saved; but for the elect's sake [the Jewish people] those days will be shortened.*
>
> *—Matthew 24:15–22*

God will prepare a special place of refuge for the Jewish people in the desert. Those who follow the words of Jesus and flee to the desert will be supernaturally cared for by the hand of God throughout the last three and a half years of the Tribulation (see Revelation 12:6).

The desert area of divine protection is identified as Edom, Moab, and Ammon—modern-day Jordan (see Daniel 11:41). Undoubtedly, the place of refuge will be Petra. I have been there, and it is the most massive natural fortress in that part of the world. It is here that the Jewish people will receive the same supernatural care the children of Israel received as they journeyed from Egypt to the promised land. Manna from heaven for food and water from a rock, if necessary, will meet their every need. Israel and the Jewish people will survive and prosper in the Tribulation.

8. Just as Hitler was subject to an assassination attempt, so will the Antichrist be wounded in the head and recover miraculously, emulating the death and resurrection of Jesus Christ. People around the world will worship him as God! John the Revelator gives a full and graphic description of the assassination attempt.

> *And I saw one of his heads as it had been mortally wounded and his deadly wound was healed. And all the world marveled and followed the beast. So they worshipped the dragon [Satan] who gave authority to the beast, saying, "Who is like the beast? Who is able to make war with him?"*
>
> *—Revelation 13:3–4*

When the Antichrist seizes the Temple and ends the daily sacrifices, he will enrage the Jewish people.

The location of the Temple is still the same . . . smack in the middle on the third most holy spot in Islam. The Antichrist's actions will enrage the Jewish people, sparking white-hot fury in the very core of their being by the most appalling insults to the true God and the Temple, which is set apart to the holiness of His name. They will be motivated by two outraging factors:

1. They will already be disgusted by the Antichrist's failure to honor his Seven-Year Treaty to come to their aide when Russia and the Islamic coalition invaded them.

2. Israel's heart will already be softening toward the Most High God because of His miraculous intervention to defeat the Russian-Iranian Islamic coalition. Now motivated by a combination of fury and zeal, a lone assassin will attempt to assassinate the Antichrist . . . and he will succeed.

To Hell and Back

With the Antichrist lulled into a sense of complacency by both his arrogance and the ease of his victories, his security breaks down. An assassin will exploit the opportunity and strike a lethal blow to the head of the

Antichrist, a wound so grievous that those attending to him believe he is dead (see Revelation 13:3).

I believe that upon his death, the Antichrist will descend directly into hell. I believe this is at least part of the reason why the Antichrist is depicted in the Book of Revelation as being he who ascends from the Abyss to prevaricate and plunder.

Just as Satan took Jesus up into a mountain, showing Him all the kingdoms of the world and offering them as a reward, I believe that Satan may take the Antichrist into the depths of hell and offer him the kingdoms of the world.

While Jesus refused to bow to Satan, the Antichrist will gladly bow to Satan and worship him. In return for this worship, Satan reanimates the Antichrist, infusing him to the very core of his being with demonic rage and ruthlessness. John makes it clear,

> *The dragon [Satan] gave him his power, his throne, and great authority.*
>
> —*Revelation 13:2*

The Antichrist will capture the imagination and confidence of the world through his miraculous recovery. To the satanically blinded world of the Tribulation, the Antichrist's healing will look exactly like the death and resurrection of Jesus Christ . . . except in this instance, they will see it happen with their own eyes on CNN.

9. As statues of Hitler were planted throughout the Third Reich, so will the Antichrist set up a statue of himself in the city of Jerusalem and demand that the nations of the world worship him. John the Revelator says of the Antichrist,

> *All who dwell on the earth will worship him, whose names have not been written in the Book of Life of the Lamb slain from the foundation of the world.*
>
> —*Revelation 13:8*

It is difficult to imagine a world filled with Satan worshippers, but that's exactly what will happen when the church, the salt and light of God, leave planet Earth. The Antichrist is Satan's son . . . and the world is worshipping him openly and enthusiastically.

The Antichrist will introduce idolatrous worship inside the Holy Temple on the Temple Mount and set himself up as God:

> *Then shall he confirm a covenant [Peace Treaty], with many for one week [seven years]; but in the middle of the week [three and half years after the treaty is signed], he will bring an end to sacrifice an offering. And on the wing of abominations shall be one who makes desolate, Even until the consummation, which is determined, Is poured out on the desolate."*
>
> *—Daniel 9:27 NKJV*

> *He will oppose and exalt himself over everything that is called God or is worshipped, so that he sets himself up in God's temple, proclaiming himself to be God.*
>
> *—2 Thessalonians 2:4 NIV*

10. As Hitler's reign of terror lasted seven years, from Kristallnacht on November 10, 1938, until 1945, so will the Antichrist have complete domination of the earth for seven years.

This world domination of the Antichrist begins with the signing of the Seven-Year Peace Accord with Israel and lasts until the second coming of Jesus Christ, which will be exactly two thousand five hundred twenty days later. A prophetic year is three hundred sixty days in duration. This number times seven gives you the exact date of the second coming of the son of God.

11. As Hitler captured France, Poland, and Czechoslovakia, just so will the coming Antichrist conquer three nations and then establish ten groups of nations as he becomes the new Caesar of the world.

The prophet Daniel teaches that the Antichrist will come up among the ten horns (nations) and uproot three of them (see Daniel 7:7–8, 23–25). The Antichrist will take over the power of three nations—either through seduction or assassination—and the other seven nations will surrender to him quickly. He is then the head of the world government. He is the world's new Caesar!

The New World Order

Our world has been moving to a New World Order for centuries. The United Nations now wants a world constitution, a world currency, a world income tax, a world military power, and a world global ethic, which is another way of saying a One World Religion.

Think it can't happen?

Think again!

Here is a concept of how the ten regions of the New World Order might appear.

Region 1: The United States and Canada

Region 2: The European Union

Region 3: Japan

Region 4: Australia, New Zealand, South Africa, and the Pacific Islands

Region 5: Eastern Europe

Region 6: Latin America: Mexico, Central America, and South America

Region 7: North Africa and the Middle East

Region 8: Central Africa

Region 9: South and Southeast Asia

Region 10: Central Asia[1]

Never in world history has one government completely ruled the world, but the Antichrist will "devour the whole earth" (Daniel 7:23). He will rule over them by their consent and with absolute and total authority (see Daniel 11:36). His personality will be marked by great intelligence, persuasiveness, subtlety, deception, and pomposity. Daniel says his mouth "speaks pompous words" (Daniel 7:8), and he is a "master of intrigue" (Daniel 8:23 NIV). He will be the world's most prominent, powerful, and popular personality in the beginning of his deceptive reign.

There's nothing new about a new world order. Satan has been scheming to institute one ever since Nimrod proposed to build a mighty tower on the plains of Shinar. The purpose of what we know as the Tower of Babel was to defy God's authority on Earth—to cast God out of the earth and institute the government of man. The Bible records the first New World Order thusly:

> *Now the whole earth had one language and one speech. And it came to pass, as they journeyed from the east, that they found a plain in the land of Shinar and they dwelt there . . . And they said, "Come, let us build ourselves a city, and a tower whose top is in the heavens; let us make a name for ourselves, lest we be scattered abroad over the face of the whole earth."*
>
> *—Genesis 11:1–2, 4*

God Almighty endured the arrogance of man for a limited time, then He scattered them across the earth.

After World War I, "the war to end all wars," President Woodrow Wilson crafted the League of Nations to uphold peace through a One World Government. Adolf Hitler told the German people he would bring "a new order" to Europe. He did, dragging Europe into the bowels of a living hell and turning the streets crimson with rivers of human blood.

The Communists of the former Soviet Union pledged to institute a new world order and erected an atheistic empire that has now collapsed like a house of cards. Now the United Nations wants to establish a new world order!

What does that mean? Brock Chisolm, former director of the United Nations World Health Organization, said, "To achieve world government, it is necessary to remove from the minds of men their individualism, loyalties to their families, national patriotism, and religion."

12. Hitler and his Third Reich were destroyed by the righteous might of the U.S. military and their allies. Just so will the coming Antichrist be destroyed "without hand." John the Revelator describes the end of the Antichrist and the False Prophet in Revelation 19:20–21 saying:

> *Then the beast was captured, and with him the False Prophet who worked signs in his presence, by which he deceived those who received*

the mark of the beast and those who worshipped his image. These two were cast alive into the lake of fire burning with brimstone. And the rest were killed with the sword which proceeded from the mouth of him who sat on the horse.

This means that the Antichrist and the False Prophet will be destroyed, not by men and military power, but by the mighty right hand of God's own son, who will crush them as the enemies of righteousness and of the Jewish people.

It's ironic that Hitler ordered his body to be burned with fire as a forerunner of Satan's son, who will receive exactly the same treatment in the future by the hand of God.

HIS NAME EQUALS 666

John the Revelator writes,

Here is wisdom. Let him who has understanding calculate the number of the beast, for it is the number of a man; his number is 666.
—Revelation 13:18

The Antichrist's number of 666 represents the satanic trinity: Satan, the Antichrist, and the False Prophet, who will lead the worldwide cult that worships the son of Satan. The number 666 could also be a reference to the worldwide idolatry attempted by Nebuchadnezzar when he erected a statue of himself and commanded all the world to worship it or face death (see Daniel 3). You might say that 666 was stamped upon the very image of Nebuchadnezzar, since the image was sixty cubits high and six cubits wide.

In Revelation 13 the focal point is the rise of the man, the Antichrist, and 666 is said to be "the number of a man." In light of this emphasis, there is another explanation of the cryptic number "666." Certainly some of John's readers were familiar with the method of calculating a name by the use of numbers, a practice known to the Jews as Gematria (or Gimetria). The Greeks also practiced it, but not as seriously as the Jewish people did.

The transition from number to letter or from letter to number was possible because most ancient languages did not have independent symbols for numbers as we do. Rather, the letters of the alphabet were also used to designate numbers in the way that Roman numerals use letters to designate numbers. It was a simple matter for members of the early church to convert a number into a name or a name into a number.

In Revelation 13:18, John made it possible for the world to positively identify the Antichrist. This cryptic puzzle is not intended to point a finger at some unknown person. It is, however, intended to confirm to the world someone already suspected as being the Antichrist. And in the idolatry of the end time, "the number of a man" is fully developed and the result is 666.

This information about how to identify the Antichrist is of no practical value to the church, since we will be watching from the balconies of heaven by the time he is revealed. But for those of you who are reading this book after the church has been taken in the rapture, and for those of you who come to trust Christ during the Tribulation, you will have the ability to confirm which personality rising out of a European Federation is the devil incarnate, the son of Satan.

Do you think a society that produced Adolf Hitler could never come to America? Do you realize that we have already begun walking down that road?

Hitler returned Christmas and Easter into pagan holidays.[2] Presently, in America, the word "Christmas" is now being referred to as a "midwinter celebration." Children in school are criticized for using the word "Christmas" and are required to use a secular word in its place.

Hitler's Third Reich hung signs the length and breadth of the land saying, "Jews unwelcomed."[3] In his book, *The Case for Israel*, celebrated attorney Alan Dershowitz demonstrates how that some of America's foremost universities are openly anti-Semitic and refuse to allow pro-Israel speakers to address the students at their campuses.

Nazi Propaganda Minister Joseph Goebbels said, "Someday Europe will perish of the Jewish disease."[4] The Jewish people were people of faith, whom the demonized Hitler hated.

In 1996, evolutionist Richard Dawkins was named Humanist of the Year. In his acceptance speech, he compared the threat of AIDS and "mad cow disease" to the threat posed by faith. According to Dawkins, faith is "one of the world's great evils, comparable to the small pox virus but harder to eradicate."

America is now in an all-out culture war for the soul of this nation. There will be a winner and a loser. To the winner go our children, our grandchildren, and the fate of the nation.

During the Third Reich, crosses of Christ in the German class-rooms were replaced with pictures of Hitler.[5] In America, no Christian crosses are allowed in public schools. Christian symbols are now considered off limits. CNSNews.com, on April 15, 2009, reported that the White House requested that Georgetown University cover its monogram "IHS"—symbolizing the name of Jesus Christ—because it was inscribed on a pediment on the stage where President Obama spoke at the university.

How dramatically different from President George Washington, father of our nation, who said, "It is impossible to rightly govern the world without God and the Bible."[6]

Abraham Lincoln, who is recognized by historians as the greatest president in the history of the United States said, speaking of the Bible, "All the Good Savior gave to the world was communicated through this Bible."[7]

Listen to these words from two of our Founding Fathers who had no shame in the proclamation of their faith: "We recognize no Sovereign but God and no king but Jesus."[8] These are the words of John Hancock and John Adams.

Pity! The good savior's name is covered up at Georgetown University to prevent unbelievers from being offended. The Bible says, "But whoever denies me before men, him I will also deny you before my Father who is in heaven."—(Matthew 10:33).

In the Third Reich, block wardens who monitored their neighbors, waiters who reported on their patrons, workers who made note of employer violations, and children who reported on their parents were a reality.[9] "Thought police" in West Virginia and elsewhere have been trained to do the very same things—listen in and report any speech "violations" to law enforcement officials.

Samuel Kent, a federal judge, ruled in 1995 that if American students prayed in the name of Jesus, they would be sentenced to a six-month jail term. Now you can take Jesus' name in vain. You can soak his cross in urine for your art project as practice for when you are funded by the National Endowment for the Arts. But you had better not pray, or you're going to jail.

Samuel Kent is not from China or the former Soviet Union. He is from the United States of America. He is just trying to make America resemble the former Soviet Union.[10]

TWELVE

Armageddon: The Final Battle for Planet Earth

Armageddon is the mother of all battles that will determine who rules and reigns on planet Earth. It is not one battle; it is a desperate three-and-a-half-year campaign by the King of the North (Russia), the King of the South (Islamic nations), the King of the East (China), and the King of the West (led by the Antichrist and the European Union).

In the final battle, John the Revelator describes scenes of absolute horror that stagger the human mind. So many will be slaughtered in this final fight that human blood will flow for two hundred miles up to the horses' bridles. Unbelievable!

> So the angel thrust his sickle into the earth and gathered the vine of the earth, and threw it into the great wine press of the wrath of God. And the winepress was trampled outside the city, the blood came out of the winepress, up to the horses' bridles, for one thousand six hundred furlongs.
>
> —*Revelation 14:19–20*

One thousand six hundred furlongs is two hundred miles.

Armageddon is the great finale of the Prince of Darkness to rule and reign planet Earth. This battle between good and evil, light and darkness, began with the war in the heavenlies before the Book of Genesis was ever written.

This supernatural war was brought to Earth in the Garden of Eden.

Adam and Eve fell to the seductive powers of the serpent and the forces of evil. They were driven out of the garden by angels with flaming swords to live under the curse God spoke into existence all the days of their lives.

God Almighty then sought for Himself a special people who would serve Him only, who would turn from evil, who would bring the Torah of God to mankind, who would bear the torch of truth for generations to come. He chose Abraham who, in time, produced the Jewish people.

God gave Abraham and his seed a royal land grant called the promised land by an everlasting covenant (see Genesis 17:7–8) that remains in effect until this day. Out of Abraham's loins came the nation of Israel, the apple of God's eye, and the target of the legions of the Prince of Darkness. The battle of light verses darkness that started in the Garden of Eden continued to rage.

The history of Israel in the Old Testament is the history of Satan's agenda to wipe the chosen people off the face of the earth. The Jewish people would produce the patriarchs: Abraham, Isaac, and Jacob. The Jewish people produced the prophets and the first family of Christianity: Mary, Joseph, and Jesus. The Jewish people produced the twelve disciples, the Apostle Paul, and, of utmost importance in world history, the word of God. God's promise to Abraham was kept: "And in you all the families of the earth shall be blessed" (Genesis 12:3).

Coming out of Egypt, the Jewish people were attacked by the Amalekites, whose objective was extermination. The seed of Abraham during the reign of the Persian Empire was threatened with the first holocaust plot through the evil mind of Haman. God spared the chosen people through the courage of a Jewish beauty named Esther and the fasting and prayer of the nation of Israel.

In the time of Christ, the iron fist of the Roman Empire ruled the Jewish people. In 70 A.D., Titus attacked the city of Jerusalem, destroyed Herod's temple, and, according to the historian Josephus, killed approximately 1 million Jews. Seventy thousand Jewish men were taken as slaves back to Rome to build the coliseum, where Christians would later be fed to the lions for Rome's amusement. Other Jews would be sold into slavery throughout the Mediterranean basin, beginning what history calls the Diaspora: the dispersal of the Jews.

Sixty years later, in 130 A.D., Rome sent Hadrian to slaughter once again the Jews of Jerusalem. Within three hundred years of the death of

Jesus Christ, who taught the foundational truth of "Love thy neighbor as thyself," people who called themselves Christians were killing Jews in the name of God. Then came the Crusaders who slaughtered tens of thousands of Jewish people, because they refused to convert to Christianity.

Following the Crusades came the Spanish Inquisition, the brutality of which, under the banner of the cross of Christ, would make you sick to your stomach.

Following the Spanish Inquisition came the living hell and horror of Adolf Hitler and the Holocaust in the twentieth century. The evil seed of anti-Semitism produced a harvest of hatred.

Why?

In my judgment, because the Jewish people from the beginning of time have been the source of divine light, and the Prince of Darkness has fought them relentlessly. Every Christian on earth is indebted to the Jewish people for the monumental sacrifices they have paid from the beginning of time to bring light and truth to "those that sat in darkness" (see Luke 2:32). Jesus said in John 4:22, "Salvation is of the Jews."

What does that mean?

That means if you take away the Jewish contribution to the world, there would be no Christianity. Judaism does not need Christianity to explain its existence; on the other hand, Christianity cannot explain its existence without Judaism.

What does this have to do with the Battle of Armageddon? Armageddon is the final battle between light and darkness and takes place on the exact piece of real estate God gave to Abraham and the Jewish people forever. The Jewish people, who were given the light of truth, are once again being attacked by the disciples of the Prince of Darkness. World history has come full circle; it's ending where it began.

Armageddon is the Hebrew word that means the *mountain of Megeddo,* which lies east of Mount Carmel in the northern part of Israel. This battlefield is a great extended plain stretching from the Mediterranean Sea eastward across the northern part of Israel.

For the first time in world history and for the right motives, the armies of the world are in perfect position to fulfill their prophetic destiny. Russia, the king of the north, has a "hook in their jaw" and God is dragging them along with the Iranian Islamic coalition toward the hills of Israel (see Ezekiel 38:5–6). God is bringing the nations of the world to crush them as grapes of wrath in His winepress. King David writes:

> *Behold, He who keeps Israel Shall neither slumber nor sleep.*
> —*Psalm 121:4.*

After watching the Jews of the Holocaust walk into the gas chambers, after seeing the "apple of His eye" thrown into ovens and their ashes dumped by the tons into the rivers of Europe, after seeing the "land of milk and honey" run red with Jewish blood in five major wars for freedom and endless suicide bombers slaughter the innocent, God stands up and shouts to the nations of the world, ENOUGH! "MY FURY SHALL COME UP IN MY FACE" (see Ezekiel 38:18).

GOD RELEASES HIS WRATH AGAINST ISRAEL'S ENEMIES: ENOUGH IS ENOUGH!

God shatters His longstanding silence.

> *"Surely, in that day there shall be a great earthquake in the land of Israel, so that the fish of the sea, the birds of heaven, the beasts of the field, all creeping things that creep on the earth, and all men who are on the face of the earth shall shake at My presence. The mountains shall be thrown down, the steep places shall fall, and every wall shall fall to the ground. I will call for a sword against Gog throughout all My mountains," says the Lord. "Every man's sword will be against his brother. And I will bring him to judgment with pestilence and bloodshed; I will rain down on him, on his troops, and on the many peoples who are with him, flooding rain, great hailstones, fire and brimstone. Thus will I magnify Myself and sanctify Myself, and I will be known in the eyes of many nations. Then they shall know that I am the Lord."*
> —*Ezekiel 38:19–23*

Here comes the judge of all the earth and He is HOT! God releases His supernatural wrath against Israel's enemies with lethal results.

First, He shakes the earth with a mighty earthquake that will neutralize every tank and every foot soldier instantly. Some will doubtless be buried alive.

Second, God causes mass confusion to come upon every invading army on the hills of Israel. Every man turns his sword against his brother. This is called, in moderation combat, "death by friendly fire."

This is exactly what God did when He commanded Gideon to blow the trumpets and break the pitchers. The Philistines became divinely confused and turned their swords on each other. Gideon won a great military victory without one casualty. God will do it again in defense of Israel.

Third, "fire and brimstone" may refer to Israel's release of nuclear weapons, or could be a repeat of Sodom and Gomorrah. God will blast Israel's enemies into oblivion by raining fire and brimstone from heaven. In either case, the results are equally catastrophic.

Ezekiel's graphic account in chapter 39 makes clear just how thorough and disastrous the defeat of Russia and the Islamic coalition will be.

Ezekiel opens chapter 39 by stating: "I am against thee, O Gog." When what is left of the world living in the Tribulation looks at the millions of bloated bodies in the warm Israeli sun, this statement will go down in history as one of the greatest understatements of all time.

In this passage God does not tell us how many died, He tells us how many are left: only a "sixth part" (Ezekiel 39:2 KJV). That means that the casualty rate for this battle will be 84 percent, unheard of in modern warfare.

The narrative of the aftermath of the war continues. Ezekiel says that the bloated bodies of the enemies of Israel will be a banquet for buzzards. The beast of the field will have a feast unlike anything since dogs ate the body of Jezebel (see Ezekiel 39:5–7, 11–16).

The dead bodies of the invaders will be strewn in the fields in the mountains of Israel, and the burial detail will take seven months and will involve all the people of Israel. Ezekiel hints very strongly that even tourists will be asked to look for stray bodies to mark the spot for burial details. *Hamon-Gog* is a Hebrew word for "the multitude of Gog," which is to become the name of this vast cemetery for the invaders of Israel (see Ezekiel 39:17–20).

But not only is there tremendous carnage, the weapons left by these devastated forces provide fuel for Israel for seven years—in other words, beyond the Tribulation and into the Millennium (see Ezekiel 39:9–10).

GOD MAGNIFIES HIMSELF

For God's Glory

Why does God allow the nations to make war upon Israel? First of all: for the glory of God. Ezekiel makes it very clear that the world will know that the God of Abraham, Isaac, and Jacob is God Almighty.

Ezekiel declares:

> *"Thus I will magnify Myself and sanctify Myself, and I will be known in the eyes of many nations. Then they shall know that I am the Lord."*
>
> —*38:23*

The earth is full of many gods but who is the Almighty God? When the God of Abraham, Isaac, and Jacob finishes mopping up the enemies of Israel on the mountains of Israel (note that Jerusalem and the cities of Israel are saved), there will be no doubt that Jehovah God is the Almighty God.

> *"It will be in the latter days that I will bring you against My land, so that the nations may know Me, when I am hallowed in you, O Gog, before their eyes."*
>
> —*Ezekiel 38:16*

The drama of Ezekiel 38–39 and the crushing defeat of Russia, the king of the north, and the Islamic coalition, the king of the south, is a demonstration of God's power not seen in the defense of Israel since Pharaoh and his army were drowned in the Red Sea. Those nations that are bragging about wiping Israel off the map are only predicting their own future.

The Jewish People Turn to God

A second reason for this great display of God's awesome power is to testify to His beloved Jewish people that He alone is their God. Through their miraculous deliverance, the hearts of the Jewish people will begin to soften toward the God of Abraham, Isaac, and Jacob:

"So the house of Israel shall know that I am the Lord their God from that day forward. The Gentiles shall know that the house of Israel went into captivity for their iniquity; because they were unfaithful to Me, therefore I hid My face from them. I gave them into the hand of their enemies, and they all fell by the sword. According to their uncleanness and according to their transgressions I have dealt with them, and hidden My face from them."

Therefore thus says the Lord God: "now I will bring back the captives of Jacob, and have mercy on the whole house of Israel; and I will be jealous for My holy name—after they have borne their shame, and all their inhabitants in which they were unfaithful to Me, when the dwelt safely in their own land and no one made them afraid. When I have brought them back from the peoples and gathered them out of their enemies' lands, and I am hallowed in them in the sight of many nations, then they shall know that I am the Lord their God, who sent them into captivity among the nations, but also brought them back into their land, and left none of them captive any longer. And I will not hide My face from them anymore; for I shall have poured out My Spirit on the house of Israel," says the Lord God.

—Ezekiel 39:22–29

Note carefully that the Jewish people at this point in time do not recognize Jesus as the Messiah. The Bible is very clear that this will happen at the end of the Tribulation, when the Jewish people . . .

"will look on Me whom they pierced. Yes, they will mourn for Him as one mourns for his only son, and grieve for Him as one grieves for his firstborn."

—Zechariah 12:10

That is the day, the Scripture declares, when "all Israel will be saved" (Romans 11:26).

Because of this colossal battle on the soil of Israel, the Jewish people will abandon their disastrous relationship with the Antichrist and begin turning toward the Most High God.

The question is, where was the Antichrist? Didn't he guarantee peace and safety for Israel in the Seven-Year Peace Treaty? The Jewish people recognize that the Antichrist did not resist the Russian-Islamic coalition, that the Antichrist is another false messiah who is, at this point, wounded in the head and presumed dead.

Upon his miraculous recovery, most of the world will worship him, but as the son of Prince of Darkness, he will turn on the children of Light (the Jewish people) with a vengeance. They will take refuge in Jordan at the natural fortress known as Petra. There they will be divinely protected and provided for by God Himself for three and a half years until the battle is over.

NEWS FROM THE EAST

China, the king of the east, needs the oil of the Persian Gulf, just as did Russia. China will gather an army of two hundred million men and march them down the dry riverbed of the Euphrates River toward Israel. In Revelation 16:12, we read,

> *The sixth angel poured out his vial on the great river Euphrates, and the water thereof was dried up, that the way of the kings of the East might be prepared.*

The Antichrist, who intended to pursue the Jewish people to Petra, stops in his tracks when he hears news from the east that troubles him deeply and forces him to change course instantly.

> *But news from the east . . . shall trouble him; therefore he shall go out with great fury to destroy and annihilate many. And he shall plant the tents of his palace between the seas and the glorious holy mountain; yet he shall come to his end, and no one will help him.*
>
> *—Daniel 11:44–45*

Given these facts, describing the Antichrist as "troubled" is without doubt an understatement. He will fight with the forces of China and those Asian countries that come with them who are called in Scripture the kings of the east, for world supremacy.

The Antichrist has three additional allies of his own that are supremely powerful: Satan; the False Prophet, with his ability to call fire down from heaven; and the image of the Beast, which has the power to destroy those who refuse to obey the Antichrist. This grand finale is the mother of all battles.

The Antichrist is the commander of a large military force in Israel and is across the Mediterranean Sea from his supply bases. Daniel writes that the Antichrist will "plant the tabernacle of his palace between the seas in the glorious holy mountain" (Daniel 11:45).

The glorious holy mountain is Jerusalem. "Between the seas" is obviously between the Dead Sea and the Mediterranean Sea. Here the Antichrist, the leader of the European Union, decides he is going to meet this 200 million-strong marching army by setting himself up in the mountains of Judea where there will be some natural defenses.

To conclude this Armageddon campaign, we turn to Revelation chapter 19, where planet Earth will have another invasion. This invasion is not from the king of the north; it's not from the king of the south; it's not from the king of the east or west . . . it's from the King of kings and Lord of lords. It's from Jesus Christ, the son of David, who has come for the second time to claim His throne on the Temple Mount to begin the Golden Age of Peace that will last for one thousand years.

A STAGGERING DEFEAT

The second coming of Jesus Christ to the battle of Armageddon is one of the towering historical moments in world history. It is also the most staggering defeat that any army has ever suffered. No one can improve on John's majestic description of this event in Revelation 19:

> *I saw heaven open and there before me was a white horse, whose rider is called Faithful and True. With justice, He judges and makes war. His eyes are like blazing fire, and on His head are many crowns. He has a name written on Him that no one knows but himself. He is dressed in a robe dipped in blood, and His name is the Word of God. The armies of heaven were following Him, riding on white horses and dressed in fine linen, white and clean. Out of His mouth comes a sharp sword with which to strike down the nations.*
> *"He will rule them with an iron scepter." He treads the winepress of the fury of the wrath of God Almighty. On His robe and on His*

thigh He has this name written: KING OF KINGS AND LORD OF
LORDS.

 And I saw an angel standing in the sun, who cried in a loud voice
to all the birds flying in midair, "Come, gather together for the great
supper of God, so that you may eat the flesh of kings, generals, and
mighty men, of horses and their riders, and the flesh of all people, free
and slave, small and great."

 Then I saw the beast [the Antichrist] and the kings of the earth
and their armies gathered together to make war against the rider on
the horse and his army [Jesus, His angels, and the saints raptured to
heaven at the very beginning of the Tribulation]. But the beast was
captured, and with him the False Prophet who had performed the
miraculous signs on his behalf. With these signs, he had deluded those
who had received the mark of the beast and worshipped his image. The
two of them were thrown alive into the fiery lake of burning sulfur.
The rest of them were killed with the sword that came out of the mouth
of the rider on the horse, and all the birds gorged themselves on their
flesh.

          —verses 11–21 NIV

Think of it! There are 200 millions soldiers fighting for the kings of
the east led by China. There has to be that many soldiers fighting for the
kings of the west, which would be the European Union and what's left
of America. The battle begins, and the invasion from heaven happens.
There are only two survivors—the beast and the False Prophet who are
thrown into the lake of fire. The hand of God kills every other soldier,
general, king, and mighty man. Their bodies are eaten by buzzards.

ISRAEL PROTECTED

Not only will the armies of the world be defeated, but also the Jewish
people—the object of God's loyal covenant love—will be protected.

 One of the most commonly ignored biblical truths is this: What a nation or an individual does to the nation of Israel is what God repays to
them—life for life and stripe for stripe. God couldn't have been clearer:

 "I will bless those who bless you, and I will curse him who curses
you."—Genesis 12:3

The Antichrist will track down, torment, and attempt to destroy Israel; in return, God will track down, torment, and annihilate him and his forces from the face of the earth. The true Messiah will come, bringing the armies of heaven with Him, and the Antichrist and his forces will be demolished.

Remember, what you do to the Jewish people will be done to you. Two-thirds of the Jews of Europe were killed by Adolf Hitler in the Holocaust while the world was silent. During the Tribulation, one-third of the population of Earth will be destroyed. There is a payday someday!

My friends, if you remember nothing else about this book, please grasp with your mind and your heart this overpowering truth from the word of God: *we are the terminal generation.* We are the ones who need to prepare today for eternity. Like no other generation, we are the ones who cannot take tomorrow for granted. We must not put off until tomorrow spiritual decisions that can be made today.

If you are a believer in Jesus Christ, lift up your head and rejoice, for your redemption is drawing near. Remember the words of Jesus:

> *And this Gospel of the kingdom will be preached in all the world as a witness to all nations, and then the end will come.*
> *—Matthew 24:14*

If you have yet to trust Jesus Christ as savior, the signs of the times should compel you to recognize the urgency of making a decision for Christ. If you listen closely, you can hear the footsteps of Messiah walking through the clouds of heaven. You can hear the thundering hoof beats of the four horsemen of the Apocalypse as they race toward the fields of Armageddon.

If this book outlives my time on Earth, and I honestly believe it will, let me assure you that it is not too late to recognize Jesus Christ as the son of God and your savior. Choose this day whom you will serve. You cannot possess what you will not pursue.

THIRTEEN

The Year 2012: The Beginning of the End?

Is there any truth to the fears associated with the winter solstice of December 21, 2012, and the Mayan calendar that marks it? Is the year 2012 the beginning of the end? What is the truth behind the date 12/21/2012? What do you need to know as the clock counts down?

There are those who see 2012 as doomsday . . . where most of the people on planet Earth are destroyed by some terrible, horrific, global cataclysms. Others believe 2012 is not a death sentence but a warning, perhaps even a message of hope. They believe that the enormous attention being drawn to the date 12/21/2012 will cause people to reevaluate their lives and seek to do good.

New agers believe it will cause the people of the earth to have a new beginning leading to a global spiritual evolution and better treatment of planet Earth, which is now being corrupted by polluting humans.

Hollywood's recent movie, *2012*, featured John Cusack and his movie family as they struggled to escape massive earthquakes, tidal waves, shattered houses, ruptured freeways, exploding gas lines, and Earth's terrified legions running for their lives. It has increased awareness and tension of the movie-going public around the globe.

Even before the *2012* blockbuster movie, fears were circulating over the internet that planet Earth is about to be swamped with global floods, fried by solar flares, wiped out by the exploding sun, and flipped over by a reversal of the north and south magnetic poles—caused by a galactic alignment of the earth and sun with the Dark Rift–center of the Milky Way.

Recently Russia sent astronauts into space to examine an asteroid that had the possibility of hitting the earth. The Russians were not motivated by theology but by reality.

All of this global excitement about the year 2012 began with the Mayan calendar. Their complex calendar systems are linked to sophisticated astronomical observations that conceive of time as circular. Every twenty-five thousand years or so, time would end and start all over again.

Science writer Lawrence E. Joseph, author of *Apocalypse 2012: An Investigation into Civilization's End,* says solar scientists believe the next peak of solar-flare activity is due at the end of 2012 or the beginning of 2013, and that could coincide with a weakening of the earth's magnetic field protecting it from the sun's power.

The result, he says, will be fried electrical grids and a loss of power for months or even years, unless surge protectors are installed on grids around the world.

OTHER CIVILIZATIONS' END-OF-DAYS

The fact of history is that most civilizations had their end-of-days scenarios and prophets. Whether you're talking about the Egyptians, the Greeks, or the Mayans, whether it's Edgar Cayce or Nostradamus, all are talking about a time in history when the world as we know it will come to an end.

Think about this: You have three of four civilizations who never communicated with each other talking about similar events happening in the same way. Could they be right? Or are they all wrong?

Richard Hoagland, writer and scientific researcher, believes the Mayans are right; he sees disaster ahead. Hoagland's theory about what could happen in 2012 is that the earth's rotational axis will reorient, setting off a catastrophic chain of events. Hoagland sees a 30,000-foot wall of water racing around the world from the ocean when the planet tips over. It sweeps over every continent and mountain. And then massive earthquakes obliterate our cities, mountains collapse, and the world's volcanoes all erupt simultaneously. Essentially, humanity would be wiped off the planet.[1]

Patmos island, John listened to the screeching of seagulls overhead and the crashing of the waves that would be an unending symphony for years to come.

Then came the day that John received the revelation of the future that was a lightning bolt that struck without warning. John's wrinkled and aged hands trembled as he scratched out countless Greek letters onto scraps of parchment in his prison cave.

Years later, as an exiled, humiliated old man, squinting by candlelight at his growing manuscript, he bore little resemblance to the youth who once stood with Jesus on the Mount of Transfiguration.

Each day John was herded from his prison cave after a breakfast of gruel. He was chained with his fellow exiles and marched by Roman guards up the steep, winding trail to the rock quarries. The cave where he and his fellow prisoners slept at night was now empty, but his pile of parchment pages was stacked neatly in a secret hollow beneath his straw sleeping mat.

One day those pages would be smuggled off the island. One day Christian volunteers would faithfully copy what John had written and deliver the Revelation of Jesus Christ to the churches of Asia. And from those churches, the Apocalypse of John would spread around the world.

Controversy would grow!

Is the Revelation true? Was it trustworthy?

Twice, at the end of Revelation, John records the voice of God saying, "Write this down, for these words are trustworthy and true" (Revelation 21:5), and again,

> The angel said to me, "these words are trustworthy and true. The Lord, the God of the spirits of the prophets, sent His angel to show His servants the things that must soon take place."
> —Revelation 22:6

This is the Apostle John's prophetic revelation to our generation. It is not based on the Mayan calendar; it is not based on the predictions of Nostradamus or Edgar Cayce; it's based on a personal revelation from God Himself in heaven.

The Apostle John received this revelation when he was instantly transported from Patmos into the presence of God the Father and Jesus Christ in heaven. Jesus, whom John loved; Jesus for whom John had forsaken his fishing nets as a teenager and by whose mother he knelt at the base of the cross as Christ died.

JOHN'S MIRACULOUS TRANSPORTATION AND HIS DIVINE VISION

The Apostle John is about eighty-four years of age, and he is suddenly transported in the Spirit into the throne room of the living God, who is about to reveal to John the future of the world. The Apostle John paints an amazing panoramic view of his vision. Allow me to intersperse my words with his as we get an overview of this prophetic narrative. I was transported into heaven from the Isle of Patmos with the divine command that sounded like a trumpet speaking, saying, "Come up here." I saw the Lord on His throne and there were twenty-four elders: twelve representing the patriarchs of the Old Testament and twelve representing the apostles of the New Testament church. They were clothed in white, had crowns of gold on their heads, and were seated on thrones with Christ. This was the bride of Christ.

I saw the twenty-four elders fall on their faces before the one who sat on the throne and cast their crowns at his feet. And I saw in the right hand of Him who sat on the throne a scroll, written inside and on the back, sealed with seven seals.

The Seven Seals

Jesus, the Lion of the Tribe of Judah, the Root of David, was permitted to open the scroll with seven seals. The seven seals contained the first seven judgments in the Book of Revelation, exposing the horrific events of the Great Tribulation that would happen in the terminal generation.

I saw the Lamb open the *first* seal, as the rider on the white horse rode out on the global stage to conquer and control the world. Everyone in heaven knew this was the Antichrist, the chief son of Satan.

I saw the *second* seal broken, as the rider on the red horse thundered out onto the stage of world history to wage global war that would bathe planet Earth in blood. There was given to him the power to take peace from the earth with a great sword.

Then I saw Jesus break the *third* seal, as the rider on the black horse rode out with a pair of scales, which were used to measure grain. We knew this represented the coming global famine in which each person on the earth would pay his daily wages for a small amount of grain. Just enough to live.

I saw Jesus break the *fourth* seal, as the rider on the pale horse rode out representing the color of rotting flesh or death itself. He was given power to strike one-fourth of the earth's population with war, famine, and pestilence.

I saw the Lamb break the *fifth* seal, which was the cry of the martyrs who are beheaded during the Tribulation because they refused to take the mark of the beast. As I saw Jesus break the *sixth* seal, it revealed the coming calamities that will continuously shake the earth during the seven-year Tribulation.

In the *sixth* seal, I saw the great earthquake, the sun became black, and the moon became like blood. Jesus prophesied cosmic calamities while He was on the Earth saying,

> *Immediately after the Tribulation of those days the sun will be darkened, and the moon will not give its light; the stars will fall from heaven, and the powers of the heavens will be shaken.*
> —*Matthew 24:29*

Then I saw a shocking sight!

From the four corners of the earth, God Almighty called and sealed 144,000 Jewish evangelists from the twelve tribes of Israel to evangelize the world. This is the spiritual awakening of Israel St. Paul described, saying,

> *Though the number of the children of Israel be as the sand of the sea, the remnant will be saved.*
> —*Romans 9:27*

Then the Lamb broke the *seventh* seal, and there was silence in heaven for about thirty minutes. The silence of the bride of Christ was created by the shock and awe of the unspeakable horror of God's wrath that was about to be poured out on the earth during the balance of the Tribulation.

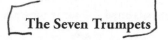

The Seven Trumpets

Then I heard the *first* of seven trumpets, which represent the next seven judgments of the wrath of God to be poured out upon those who had rejected the message of God's son on the earth.

I heard the thunderous blast of the first trumpet and one-third of all the trees and grass on the earth were burned up. I listened and heard the *second* trumpet as a meteor hit the earth and landed in the sea. One-third of the sea turned to blood one-third of all fish died, and one-third of all the ships on the sea were destroyed by the massive tsunami that followed.

I heard the *third* trumpet sound, as God commanded a massive star to fall from the heavens, burning like a torch, falling on one-third of all rivers and springs on the earth. The waters of the earth became as bitter as gall, which was God's judgment for idolatry as recorded by the pen of Moses saying,

> *"So that there may not be among you man or woman or family or tribe, whose heart turns away from the LORD our God, to go and serve the gods of these nations . . . the LORD would not spare him; for then the anger of the LORD and His jealousy would burn against that man, and every curse that is written in this book would settle on him, and the LORD would blot out his name from under heaven."*
> *—Deuteronomy 29:18, 20 NKJV*

When I heard the *fourth* trumpet, I was reminded of the Egyptian plague of darkness God sent just before He delivered the children of Israel from the Egyptians. The sun and the moon and the stars shown with only one-third of their radiance at night. The spirit of despair and depression covered the earth.

As the *fifth* trumpet shattered the silence of the heavens, all of heaven was stunned to see the legions of locusts erupt from the bottomless pit. I saw a star fall from heaven, which was Satan himself. The Master spoke of Satan falling from heaven, and His words were recorded by my friend Luke, who was a gifted physician, saying,

"I saw Satan fall like lightning from heaven."

—Luke 10:18

The prophet Isaiah proclaimed the same message, saying,

"How are you fallen from heaven, O Lucifer, son of the morning! How you are cut down to the ground, you who weakened the nations."

—Isaiah 14:12

The legions of scorpions were the size of horses and were given the power to sting everyone on earth who did not have the seal of God on their forehead. The painful sting of these monster scorpions lasted for five months, and those who were stung sought to die but could not.

The leader of this legion of tormenting scorpions was Apollyon, meaning "the Destroyer." All of heaven watched in awe as men and women all over the earth writhed in agony from the venomous stings of these horrendous scorpions.

Then we heard the *sixth* trumpet blast, as God released four angels who had been *waiting for the hour, the day, the month, and the exact year during the Tribulation to kill one-third of mankind.*

There was an army of 200 million men marching down the river Euphrates to conquer the world. In spite of the sorrow and suffering created by the death of one-third of the earth's population, no one on the earth repented of their murders, their sorceries, their sexual immorality, their thefts, or their ungodly lifestyles.

And then the *seventh* trumpet sounded, as the mighty angel with the little book that was opened in his right hand set his right foot on the sea and his left foot on the land, as he roared like a lion.

When he roared, I heard seven thunders speak to me as clearly as a man speaks. I was about to write down the seven messages of the seven thunders to be recorded in the Book of Revelation, but God forbade me to write them or to reveal their message to the church.

God spoke to me and told me to take the little book from the right hand of the angel, to take it and eat it. As I ate it, it was as sweet as honey in my mouth, but it was bitter in my stomach. The word of God is as sweet as honey in the mouth, but the wrath of God is as bitter as gall, as it falls upon the rebellious and unrepentant.

The Two Witnesses

God the Father then gave me a bamboo-like cane, which was twenty feet in length and which grows in abundance on the banks of the Jordan River.

The angel told me to measure the Temple of God in Jerusalem, the altar, and those who worship there. I was told that the Gentiles would control Jerusalem during the Tribulation for forty-two months and that God's two witnesses, Enoch and Elijah, would have supernatural power to protect themselves from the Antichrist and his One World Government.

Anyone who tried to harm the two witnesses was burned to an ash by the fire that came out of their mouths. The two witnesses also had the power to strike the earth with plagues, to turn the water people drank to blood, to pronounce that no rain should fall from heaven for three and a half years. Their ministry of comfort and consolation to the Jewish people lasted for three and a half years. The specific person the prophet Malachi told the Jewish people to look for in his closing words was Elijah the prophet. Elijah is coming in the near future to bring God's message of hope and deliverance to the Jewish people and to pronounce the soon-coming Messiah.

I saw the Antichrist come up out of the bottomless pit and kill the two witnesses, Enoch and Elijah, in the streets of Jerusalem. People all over the world witnessed the execution of these two witnesses. The nations of the world were so thrilled that these two witnesses sent from God were dead that they gave presents to each other in a global celebration of joy.

Then came the shock!

As the world was celebrating the deaths of Enoch and Elijah, as they observed their dead bodies lying dead in the streets of Jerusalem, the breath of life came into both of them. They stood up on their feet, and terror fell upon the nations of the earth.

Then I heard God the Father give to them the same command He had given me, "Come up here!" And immediately, Enoch and Elijah ascended into heaven, as a massive earthquake struck Jerusalem, killing seven thousand people.

The *seventh* trumpet sounded, and the angels proclaimed with voices of thunder: "The kingdoms of this world have become the kingdom of our Lord and of His Christ, and He shall reign forever and ever." The twenty-four elders fell on their faces and worshipped God.

The Woman and the Dragon

Then I saw the woman, being great with child, clothed with the sun, with the moon under her feet, and on her head a garland of twelve stars.

The woman was the nation of Israel, the child that was born and ascended to God was the Messiah, and the great fiery red dragon with seven heads and ten horns was that old serpent, the Devil, who was ready to devour the child at birth.

The child was caught up into heaven, and the woman, Israel, fled into the wilderness at Petra, where God protected and provided for her for three and a half years, just as He did for the children of Israel in the wilderness for forty years.

The Seven Bowls

In the closing days of the Great Tribulation, I, John, saw the living God pour out seven bowls of wrath upon the earth in rapid succession. These seven bowls of unspeakable suffering were similar to those of the seven trumpets and the plagues God sent to the Egyptians.

The principle difference between the plagues of the seven bowls and the plagues of Egypt was that the plagues of Egypt covered one nation while the plagues of the seven bowls covered the earth.

I, John the Apostle, saw seven angels take the seven bowls of God's wrath and pour them out upon the earth. The _first bowl_ of wrath produced a fowl and loathsome sore on every person on the earth who had taken the mark of the beast.

The _second bowl_ was poured out on the sea, and the waters of the seven seas of the world became as the blood of a dead man; every living thing in the sea died.

The _third bowl_ of God's furious wrath poisoned the rivers and the springs. The _fourth_ bowl produced excessive heat from the sun, until men were scorched and they blasphemed God without repentance.

The _fifth_ angel poured out his bowl "on the throne of the Beast" (16:10), causing darkness and pain so horrendous that men gnawed their tongues in pain, yet they refused to repent.

The *sixth* angel poured out his bowl on the Euphrates River, and its waters were dried up, making it possible for the kings of the east and their marching armies of 200 million men to march down the dry river-bed to the Battle of Armageddon. They would kill one-third of all flesh on the earth.

The *seventh* angel poured out his bowl into the air, and a thunderous voice came from the throne of God saying, "It is done!"

At that moment, the whole earth went into a massive convulsion, created by a mighty earthquake far greater than any in the history of the world. Every nation and city on the face of the earth was shaken into rubble and fell to the ground. Houses, hospitals, government buildings, churches, freeways, and water lines were broken; gas lines erupted with fire; dams holding back mighty reservoirs collapsed, causing catastrophic flooding. The earthquakes caused the seven seas of the world to be covered with monster tsunamis that buried the coastlands of the nations of the world with water. The moaning of the dead and dying could be heard around the world. There was no one to come to their aid, for all nations were destroyed.

So severe was this earthquake that the islands of the sea disappeared; the mountains were shaken to the foundations, as hailstones weighing one hundred pounds each smashed furiously into the earth. God's judgment in the Old Testament for sin was stoning; in His final act of universal judgment, He stoned the earth for its idolatry and rejection of God!

> Then the Lamb that sat on the throne said to me, "These words are faithful and true." . . . Behold, I am coming quickly! Blessed is he who keeps the words of the prophecy of this book. . . . verse 16. I, Jesus, have sent My angel to testify to you these things in the churches. I am the Root and the Offspring of David, the Bright and Morning Star . . . verse 18. For I testify to everyone who hears the words of the prophecy of this book; if anyone adds to these things, God will add to him the plagues that are written in this book; and if anyone takes away from the words of this prophecy, God will take away his part from the Book of Life, from the Holy City, and from the things that are written in this book. "Surely I am coming quickly." Amen. Even so, come, Lord Jesus!
>
> —Revelation 22:6–20

Is the day of doom that John speaks about in Revelation 9:15 the Mayan date of 12/21/12?

Is that two years from now?

Is that next month?

Is that next week?

Is that today?

No one knows for sure; only God!

Are you ready?

Notes

CHAPTER ONE: ANATOMY OF DISASTER!

1 Gary Bauer, American Values, November 18, 2009.
2 FOXNews.com, November 18, 2009, as given during a one-on-one interview with FOX News' Major Garrett and the president.
3 Jeffery Flier, Op-Ed, *Wall Street Journal,* October 18, 2009.
4 Congressional Budget Office, Director's Blog, January 31, 2008, "Technological Change and the Growth of Health Care Spending," http://cboblog.cbo.gov.
5 Amanda Carpenter, *Washington Post,* September 28, 2009.
6 Daily Alert, daily newsletter prepared by The Jerusalem Center for Public Affairs for the Conference of Presidents of Major American-Jewish Organizations. dailyalert@list-dailyalert.org, September 10, 2009.
7 Paul Williams, "American Hirojima," World Net Daily, September 3, 2005.
8 Ibid.
9 Joseph Farah, "Iran Plans to Knock Out U.S. with One Nuclear Bomb," World Net Daily—G2 Bulletin, April 25, 2005.

CHAPTER TWO: IRAN IS READY FOR WAR!

1 "Editorial: Tehran's Nukes," *Washington Times,* May 11, 2009.
2 Rafael Bardaji, "Iran: What We Know That We Know," Daily Alert, September 22, 2009. The writer has served as foreign policy advisor to Prime Minister Aznar of Spain.
3 William J. Broad and David E. Sanger, "Report Says Iran Has Data to Make a Nuclear Bomb," *New York Times,* October 3, 2009.

4 William J. Broad and David E. Sanger, "How Many Other Secret Nuclear Facilities Does Iran Have?" *New York Times,* September 30, 2009.

5 James Blitz, Daniel Dombey and Najmeh Bozorgmehr, "Iran 'Has Secret Nuclear Arms Plan,' " *Financial Times-UK,* September 29, 2009.

6 David E. Sanger and William J. Broad, "Atomic Agency Is Pressed on Iran Records," *New York Times,* August 26, 2009.

7 Matthias Kuntzel, "Ahmadinejad's Demons—A Child of the Revolution Takes Over, *The New Republic,* April 24, 2006.

8 Farhad Khosrokhavar, *Suicide Bombers: Allah's New Martyrs* (London: Pluto Press, 2005), p. 76.

9 Barry Rubin, *Paved with Good Intentions: The American Experience in Iran* (New York: Penguin Books, 1981), p. 303.

10 John Simkin, "Munich Agreement," British Online Encyclopedia. http://www.spartacus.schoolnet.co.ck/2wwmunich.htm (October 4, 2006).

11 BBC on This Day, "1938, " 'Peace for Our Time'—Chamberlain," September 30, 1938, http://news.bbc.co.uk/onthisday/hi/dates/stories/Sep./30/newsid_3115000/3115476.stm, accessed October 4, 2006.

12 Wikipedia.com, s.v. "The Blitz," http://en.wikipedia.org/wiki/London_Blitz (October 3, 2006).

13 Dave Hunt, "A Moment for Truth," http://shalach.org/IslamTruth/IslamTruth.htm and www.thebereancall.org, October 2001.

14 The writer is director of the Vidal Sassoon International Center for the Study of Anti-Semitism at the Hebrew University of Jerusalem and the author of *A Lethal Obsession: Anti-Semitism from Antiquity to the Global Jihad* (New York: Random House, 2010). (Ha'aretz).

15 Fred O. Williams, "Muslim TV Mogul Muzzammil Hassan's Alleged Beheading of Wife, Aasiya Hassan, May Be 'Honor Killing,' " *Buffalo News,* February 17, 2009.

16 FoxNews.com, "Westernized Woman Allegedly Hit by Dad's Car Dies," November 3, 2009.

17 Daniel Pipes, "The Danger Within: Militant Islam in America," *Commentary,* November 2001.

18 Ibid.

19 Support of this family statistic may be found at *All Experts Ency-clopedia,* s.v. "Osama bin Laden," http://experts.about.com/e/o/os/ Osama_bin_Laden.htm (October 3, 2006).

20 See Answers.com, s.v. "Osama bin Laden," http://www.answers .com/topic/osama-bin-laden (October 3, 2006).

21 Quoted on the authority of Ibn'Abbas in *Sahih of al-Bukhari (Part 9)* and attested by numerous Islamic scholars, at Giving and Shar-ing, "Islam," http://www.giveshare.org/islam/index.html (October 3, 2006).

22 Recorded in *Chronicles of the ari, Part 2,* as cited at The Bible Study, "The Apostate Relinquishing the Faith—Part 2," http://www .bibletopics.com/BibleStudy/96a.htm, October 4, 2006.

23 Sheikh Muhammad Bin Abdul Wahhub, "Saudi Arabia—The Ker-nel of Evil," Google Groups, http://groups.google.bg/group/soc .culture.algeria/msg/a00b4921698d4930 (October 4, 2006).

24 Kenneth Timmerman, "Protest Rap Sheet: Saudi Official Should Look to Saudi Clerics Before Blasting Gen. Boykin," October 26, 2003, http://www.kentimmerman.com/2003_10_26jubeir-boykin (October 4, 2006).

25 Gary Bauer, "9/11 Plotters May Walk," American Values, Novem-ber 13, 2009.

26 Ibid.

27 Ibid.

28 Ibid.

29 Joshua Rhett Miller, "New York–Based Muslim's Website Calls for God to 'Kill the Jews,' " October 13, 2009, Fox News.

30 Ibid.

31 Ibid.

32 Ibid.

33 Gary Bauer, "Jihad at Fort Hood," American Values, November 6, 2009.

34 Ibid.

35 Tarek Fatah, "The Significance of Hasan's Attire," *Ottawa Citizen-Canada,* Daily Alert, November 11, 2009.

36 Gary Bauer, "Jihad at Fort Hood," November 6, 2009.

37 Ibid.

38   Ibid.

39   Ibid.

40   Nick Allen, "Fort Hood Gunmen: Infidels Should Have Their Throats Cut," Telegraph-UK, November 8, 2009, www.telegraph.co .uk/news/worldnews/northamerica/usa.

41   Dana Priest, "Fort Hood Suspect Warned of Threats Within the Ranks," *Washington Post,* November 9, 2009.

42   Eric Gorski, "Global Muslim Population Hits 1.57 Billion," AP, October 9, 2009.

43   Ibid.

44   Daymond R. Duck, *The Book of Revelation,* Smart Guide to the Bible Series (Nashville: Nelson Reference, 2006), pp. 151–153.

45   Cal Thomas, "Time for Offense," *Washington Times,* August 14, 2006.

46   Ibid.

CHAPTER THREE: IRAN'S PLAN OF ATTACK

1   Elaine Sciolino, "Showdown at UN? Iran Seems Calm," *New York Times,* March 14, 2006.

2   Dore Gold, *The Rise of Nuclear Iran* (Washington, D.C.: Regnery Publishing, 2009), pp. 11–12.

3   Alireza Jafarzadah, "The Islamic Revolutionary Guards Corps Use Universities for Research to Build the Bombs," Statement to National Press Club, Washington, D.C., March 20, 2006.

4   Therese Delpech, *Iran and the Bomb: The Abdication of International Responsibility* (New York: Columbia University Press, 2003), p. 113.

5   Con Coughlin, "Defiant Iran Begins Nuclear Production for 'Five Bombs,'" *Daily Telegraph,* September 13, 2004.

6   Philip Sherwell, "How We Duped the West, by Iran's Nuclear Negotiator," *Daily Telegraph,* April 3, 2006.

7   Ibid.

8   Michael Rubin, "Diplomacy by Itself Won't Work with Iran," *Investors Business Daily,* February 13, 2009, reproduced by Middle East Forum, February 14, 2009.

9   Dore Gold, "Iran's Nuclear Aspirations Threaten the World," *Los Angeles Times,* August 6, 2009.

10 Ibid.

11 Amir Taheri is the source of this famous Khomeini quote, the veracity of which was contested by Shaul Bakhash and Andrew Sullivan. Taheri has countered saying that the quote can be found in several editions of Khomeini's collected speeches like *Messages and Speeches of Imam Khomeini* (Tehran: Nur Research and Publication Institute, 1981). In subsequent editions, Taheri explains the quotation in question was removed, as Iran tried to mobilize nationalistic sentiment during the Iran-Iraq War. For the details on the debate, see Norman Podhoretz, "A Response to Andrew Sullivan," *Commentary Magazine—Contentions,* November 19, 2007.

12 Barry Rubin, *Paved with Good Intentions, The American Experience and Iran* (New York; Penguin Books, 1981), p. 303.

13 Mehdi Khaliji, *Apocalyptic Politics: On the Rationality of Iranian Policy* (Washington, D.C.: Washington Institute for Near East Policy, 2008), p. 26.

14 "Paper: French FM in Memoir—Ahmadinejad Tells European FMs in 2005 Meeting, 'After the Chaos We Can See the Greatness of Allah,' " he MEMRI Blog, February 2, 2007 (Source: al-Sharq al-Awsat, London, February 2, 2007).

15 Y. Mansdorf and A. Savyon, "Escalation in the Positions of Iranian President Mahmoud Ahmadinejad—A Special Report," MEMRI Inquiry and Analysis Series, No. 389, September 17, 2007.

16 Fox News, "Iran to 'Blow Up the Heart of Israel' If Attacked!" October 10, 2009.

17 Kevin Johnson, "Alleged Terror Threat Seen as 'Most Serious' Since 9/11 Attacks," *USA Today,* September 25–27, 2009.

18 Ibid.

19 Ibid.

20 The above concepts were taken in part from a book review by Joseph Farah, "Muslim Mafia," World Net Daily, January 20, 2010.

CHAPTER FOUR: THE DAY AFTER THE BOMB

1 Joseph Farah, "Iran Plans to Knock Out U.S. with 1 Nuclear Bomb," from Joseph Farah's G2 *Bulletin,* World Net Daily, April 25, 2005.

2 Ibid.

3 Ryan Mauro, "Paul Williams Details 'American Hiroshima,'" *World Net Daily*, September 3, 2005, accessed at http://www .wnDCom/news/article.asp?ARTICLE_ID=46127 on September 30, 2005.

4 Ibid.

5 Andrea Elliott, "Americans Recruited to Join al-Qaeda Linked Somali Terrorist," *Daily Alert*, November 24, 2009.

6 Basic facts of the blast radius, radiation factors, and basic procedures for self-preservation in a nuclear blast are taken in part from "The Day After: Action Following a Nuclear Blast in a U.S. City," *Washington Quarterly*, autumn 2007.

CHAPTER FIVE: DEATH OF THE DOLLAR

1 Craig Karmin, *Biography of the Dollar: How the Mighty Buck Conquered the World and Why It's Under Siege* (New York: Crown Business, 2008), pp. 100–101.

2 Menzie Chinn and Jeffrey Krankel, "Why the Euro Will Rival the Dollar," *International Finance* 11:1 (2008): 50.

3 Karmin, *Biography of the Dollar*, pp. 34, 101.

4 William Greider, *Secrets of the Temple: How the Federal Reserve Runs the Country* (New York: Simon & Schuster, 1987), pp. 254–255; Karmin, *Biography of the Dollar*, pp. 105–108.

5 John Steele Gordon, *Hamilton's Blessing: The Extraordinary Life and Times of Our National Debt* (New York: Walker and Company, 1997), p. 71; James Turk and John Rubino, *The Coming Collapse of the Dollar and How to Profit from It* (New York: Doubleday, 2004), pp. 47–49; Greider, *Secrets of the Temple*, pp. 228, 246–247.

6 Karmin, *Biography of the Dollar*, pp. 110–117; Greider, *Secrets of the Temple*, pp. 282–283; Turk and Rubino, *Coming Collapse of the Dollar*, pp. 53–55.

7 Turk and Rubino, *Coming Collapse of the Dollar*, pp. 56–57.

8 Karmin, *Biography of the Dollar*, pp. 118–119; Greider, *Secrets of the Temple*, 336; Austin Pryor, "A Dollar in Danger Leads Many to Gold," *Sound Mind Investing*, August 2009.

9 Greider, *Secrets of the Temple*, pp. 315–318, 324–325.

10 Karmin, *Biography of the Dollar*, pp. 120–124; Turk and Rubino, *Coming Collapse of the Dollar*, 57; Pryor, "Dollar in Danger."

11 Greider, *Secrets of the Temple,* pp. 335–338; Karmin, *Biography of the Dollar,* pp. 125–127; Turk and Rubino, *Coming Collapse of the Dollar,* 58; Pryor, "Dollar in Danger."

12 Greider, *Secrets of the Temple,* pp. 339–340; Turk and Rubino, *Coming Collapse of the Dollar,* pp. 171–172; Karmin, *Biography of the Dollar,* pp. 129–134; Pryor, "Dollar in Danger."

13 Karmin, *Biography of the Dollar,* pp. 136–139, 144–146.

14 Robert J. Shiller, *The Subprime Solution: How Today's Global Financial Crisis Happened, and What to Do About It* (Princeton: Princeton University Press, 2008).

15 Karmin, *Biography of the Dollar,* pp. 146–147, 253.

16 Nelson D. Schwartz, "In Dollar's Fall, Upside for U.S. Exports," *New York Times,* October 19, 2009.

17 Article I, Section 8.

18 Quoted in Gordon, *Hamilton's Blessing,* p. vii.

19 Gordon, *Hamilton's Blessing,* pp. 61–65.

20 Gordon, *Hamilton's Blessing,* pp. 80–81, 90.

21 Gordon, *Hamilton's Blessing,* pp. 81–102.

22 Greider, *Secrets of the Temple,* pp. 284–285; Gordon, *Hamilton's Blessing,* pp. 103–107.

23 Gordon, *Hamilton's Blessing,* pp. 121–131.

24 Gordon, *Hamilton's Blessing,* pp. 126–127, 132–134.

25 Gordon, *Hamilton's Blessing,* pp. 134–136.

26 Data computed from the Office of Management and Budget, *Budget of the United States Government, Historical Tables.* www.white house.gov/omb/budget/fy2009/his.pdf, table 1.1, pages 21–27.

27 Martin Crutsinger, "Deficit Hits a Record $1.42 Trillion," Associated Press, October 17, 2009.

28 Jonathan Rauch, "The Government in 2008: 40 Years of Stability," *National Journal,* November 7, 2009.

29 Pryor, "Dollar in Danger."

30 U.S. Office of Management and Budget, *Budget of the United States Government, Historical Tables.*

31 David M Smick, *The World Is Curved: Hidden Dangers to the Global Economy* (New York: Portfolio, 2008), pp. 225–226.

32 *The Federal Government's Financial Health: A Citizen's Guide to the 2008 Financial Report of the U.S. Government,* pp. 7–8.

33　"Mountain of Debt," Associated Press, July 4, 2009.

34　Jeb Hensarling and Paul Ryan, "Why No One Expects a Strong Recovery," *New York Times,* November 20, 2009; Robert J. Barro and Charles J. Redlick, "Stimulus Spending Doesn't Work," *Wall Street Journal,* October 1, 2009; Tony Perkins, "Washington Update," Family Research Council, November 19, 2009; Heritage Foundation, "The Pelosi Blueprint for Government-Run Health Care," *Morning Bell,* October 30, 2009.

35　"Are Health Care Reform Cost Estimates Reliable?" Joint Economic Committee, July 31, 2009; Mortimer B. Zuckerman, "The 'Reform' That Ate America," *U.S. News & World Report,* December 2009; John M. Broder, "Climate Deal Likely to Bear Big Price Tag," *New York Times,* December 9, 2009. Original Dirksen quote, using billions instead of trillions of dollars, in Gordon, *Hamilton's Blessing,* p. vii.

36　Mortimer B. Zuckerman, "U.S. No Longer the Great Job Creation Machine," *U.S. News Weekly,* December 4, 2009; James Pethokoukis, "12 Reasons Unemployment Is Going to (at Least) 12 Percent," *Reuters Blogs,* November 11, 2009; Heritage Foundation, "The Road to Recovery Begins with the End of Obamacare," *Morning Bell,* December 3, 2009; George Melloan, "Why 'Stimulus' Will Mean Inflation," *Wall Street Journal,* February 6, 2009.

37　Sara Lepro, "Falling Dollar a Boost for Gold," Associated Press, October 7, 2009.

38　Turk and Rubino, *Coming Collapse of the Dollar,* pp. 29–31.

39　Turk and Rubino, *Coming Collapse of the Dollar,* p. 31.

40　Karmin, *Biography of the Dollar,* pp. 200–205.

41　Karmin, *Biography of the Dollar,* pp. 209–209, 223–225.

42　Joseph E. Stiglitz, "Death Cometh for the Greenback," *The National Interest,* November/December 2009; Karmin, *Biography of the Dollar,* pp. 231–240.

43　David Barboza, "China Urges New Money Reserve to Replace Dollar," *New York Times,* March 24, 2009; Breitbart.com, "Medvedev Sees Single Currency Dream in G8 Coin Gift," July 10, 2009; Malcolm Moore, "China Criticizes Dollar," *Telegraph,* July 10, 2009; Robert Fisk, "The Demise of the Dollar," *The Independent,* October 6, 2009; Jack Healy and Keith Bradsher, "Stocks and

While some predict absolute disaster is coming in December of 2012, others see a rebirth; some others simply believe nothing out of the ordinary will happen.

What do you believe?

Why do you believe it?

What do I believe and why do I believe it?

THE HOUR, MONTH, THE YEAR

So the four angels who had been prepared for the hour and day and month and year, were released to kill a third of mankind.

—*Revelation 9:15*

There is no conceivable evidence that December 21, 2012, will be a day of global disaster, but there is specific evidence that, in the near future, there is a specific day and hour in which one-third of the human race will die in a day.

That prophecy comes from one of the most celebrated seers the world has ever known. The accuracy of his prophecies is absolute and undeniable. He received this detailed and exhaustive revelation of the future of the world while he was a prisoner of the Roman Empire, incarcerated on the Isle of Patmos two thousand years ago.

The Apostle John was taken in chains to the Isle of Patmos as an enemy of the state. What was his crime? He chose Christ over Caesar.

The madness of Caesar worship seized Rome. Caesar believed he was god and demanded that the citizens of Rome recognized him as such. It was a common practice for Roman soldiers to surround a marketplace, line up all the Roman citizens, and demand they burn incense to Caesar, recognizing him as god.

The Apostle John was the pastor of the church at Ephesus and was snared in one of these loyalty-to-Caesar campaigns. When John refused to burn incense and recognize Caesar as god, he was taken immediately as a prisoner, placed on a ship, and sent to Patmos.

Patmos was a rocky island ten miles long and six miles wide packed with criminals who were political enemies of Caesar and Christians who chose Christ as lord over Lord Caesar. As the ship pulled into the port of

Gold Gain as Investors Shun the Dollar," *New York Times,* October 7, 2009; Eamon Javers, "Whodunit?: Sneak Attack on U.S. Dollar," Politico.com, October 8, 2009; Allen Sykora and Matt Whittaker, "Dethroning the Dollar: What If?" *Wall Street Journal,* March 30, 2009; Edmund Conway, "UN Wants New Global Currency to Replace Dollar," *Telegraph,* September 7, 2009; Turk and Rubino, *Coming Collapse of the Dollar,* pp. 195–198.

44 Helene Cooper, Michael Wines, and David E. Sanger, "China's Role as Lender Alters Obama's Visit," *New York Times,* November 15, 2009; Robert Kagan and Dan Blumenthal, " 'Strategic Reassurance' That Isn't," *Washington Post,* November 10, 2009; David M. Smick, *World Is Curved,* pp. 97–102, 115–116.

45 John Maggs, "It's Worse Than You Think," *National Journal,* November 7, 2009; Lawrence Kadish, "Taking the National Debt Seriously," *Wall Street Journal,* October 11, 2009; Paul Kennedy, "The Dollar's Fate," *New York Times,* August 29, 2009; Edmund Conway, "Is This the Death of the Dollar?" *Telegraph,* June 20, 2009; Niall Ferguson, "An Empire at Risk," *Newsweek,* December 7, 2009.

46 Robert L. Heilbroner, *The Worldly Philosophers: The Lives, Times and Ideas of the Great Economic Thinkers,* 5th ed. (New York: Simon & Schuster, 1980), pp. 290–292; Karmin, *Biography of the Dollar,* p. 243; Gordon, *Hamilton's Blessing,* p. 55.

47 John Maynard Keynes, *The Economic Consequences of the Peace* (London: MacMillan and Co., 1920), pp. 220–221.

CHAPTER SIX: THE REJECTION OF ISRAEL

1 The account of the children of Israel was taken from the books of Genesis and Exodus (NKJV).

2 Aish HaTorah, *Discovery* (Jerusalem: Arachim, 1995), p. 79.

3 Carmelo Lisciotto, "The First Nuremberg Trial." Holocaust Education & Archive Research Team. http://www.holocaustresearch project.org/trials/nurnbergtrial.html.

4 Ibid.

5 Ibid.

6 Ibid.

7 "The Nuremberg Laws," Jewish Virtual Library: A division of the

American-Israeli Cooperative Enterprise, 2009, http://www.jewish virtuallibrary.org/jsource/Holocaust/nurlaws.html.

8 Carmelo Lisciotto, "The First Nuremberg Trial," Holocaust Education & Archive Research Team, http://www.holocaustresearch project.org/trials/nurnbergtrial.html.

9 "Nuremberg Trials Project," Harvard Law School Library, http://nuremberg.law.harvard.edu/php/docs_swi.php?DI=1&text=nur_13tr; Scmidt, Dana, Adams. "Army Investigates Suicide of Goering as Mystery Grows," *New York Times,* October 17, 1946.

10 Ibid.

11 Ibid.

12 Schmidt, Dana, Adams, "Goering Note Said to Explain Suicide," *New York Times,* October 19, 1949; Carmelo Lisciotto, "The First Nuremberg Trial," Holocaust Education & Archive Research Team, http://www.holocaustresearchproject.org/trials/nurnberg trial.html.

13 Carmelo Lisciotto, "The First Nuremberg Trial."

14 Ibid.

15 "Last Laugh," *Newsweek,* October 28, 1946.

16 "The 13 Steps," *Newsweek,* October 28, 1946.

17 "Army Investigates Suicide of Goering as Mystery Grows," *New York Times,* October 17, 1946.

18 Ibid.

19 Ibid.

20 Lehmann-Haupt, Christopher, "Books of the Times," *New York Times,* November 4, 1985.

21 Donald E. Wilkes Jr., "The Trial of the Century—And of All Time, Part Two" *Flagpole,* July 17, 2002, http://www.lawsch.uga .edu/academics/profiles/dwilkes_more/his34_trial2.html.

22 Personal interview with Rabbi Scheinberg; and "Ask the Rabbi" *Topic: Haman's Sons, Different Size Letters,* Ohr Shomayach. http://ohr.edu/ask_db/ask_main.php/228/Q5/.

23 Ibid.

24 Ibid.

25 Ibid.

26 Ibid.

27 Aish HaTorah, *Discovery* (Jerusalem: Arachim, 1995), p. 79 (referencing the Zohar—Vayikra 316).

28 Aish HaTorah, *Discovery* (Jerusalem: Arachim, 1995) (referencing the Zohar—Vayikra 316).

29 "Chol HaMoed." National Jewish Outreach Program. http:www .njop.org/html/SukCH.html.

30 Aish HaTorah, *Discovery* (Jerusalem: Arachim, 1995), p. 78.

31 Personal interview with Rabbi Ariyeh Scheinberg.

32 Ibid.

33 E. W. Bullinger, *Number in Scripture: Its Supernatural Design and Spiritual Significance* (London: Eyre & Spottiswoode, 1921), available at http://philologos.org/_eb-nis.

35 Ibid., Genesis 14:4 (NKJV).

36 E. W. Bullinger, *Number in Scripture: Its Supernatural Design and Spiritual Significance* (London: Eyre & Spottiswoode, 1921), available at http://philologos.org/_eb-nis.

37 Aish HaTorah, *Discovery* (Jerusalem: Arachim, 1995), p. 78 (referencing "Mysteries of the Bible" a documentary produced by Multi-Media Entertainment, Inc., and A&E Networks).

38 "The 13 Steps," *Newsweek,* October 28, 1946; Aish HaTorah, *Discovery* (Jerusalem: Arachim, 1995), p. 79.

39 Abraham Sutton, *Pathways to the Torah* (Jerusalem: Arachim, 1987), at 54.40; Melanie Phillips, *Londonistan* (New York: Encounter Books, 2006), p. xx.

41 Ibid., p. 189.

42 Paul Sperry, "The Pentagon Breaks the Islam Taboo," FrontPage Magazine.com, December 14, 2005.

43 Herbert Karliner, (first-person account) "Passenger Stories." The St. Louis Project. http://thestlouisproject.com/p=48.

44 Ibid.

45 Ibid.

46 Ibid.

47 Ibid.

48 *The SS St. Louis Project* (video available at http://thestlouisproject .com).

49 Conrad Black, *Franklin Delano Roosevelt: Champion of Freedom* (New York: Public Affairs, 2003), p. 490.

50 Ibid.

51 Ibid.

52 Ibid.

53 Jennifer Rosenberg, "The Tragedy of the *SS St. Louis,*" 2009, The American-Israeli Cooperative Enterprise, http://jewishvirtual library.org/jsource/Holocaust/stlouis/html (1).

54 Robert N. Rosen, *Saving the Jews: Franklin D. Roosevelt and the Holocaust* (New York: Thunder's Mouth Press, 2006), p. 91.

55 Rosenberg, p. 1.

56 Rosen, p. 91

57 Ibid.

58 Rosenberg, p. 3.

59 Ibid.

60 Ibid, p. 4.

61 Ibid.

62 Rosen, p. 92; Black p. 404.

63 Rosen, p. 92.

64 Ibid.

65 Ibid.

66 Black, p. 493.

67 Rosenberg, p. 1.

68 "The Voyage of the St. Louis," *HERMES,* Columbia Business School, fall 2004, www.4gsb.columbia.edu/hermes/article/70794/The+Voyage+of+the+St-+Louis#.

69 Rosenberg, p. 2.

70 Black, p. 493.

71 Rosenberg, p. 3; Black, p. 493.

72 Ibid.

73 Rosenberg, p. 3.

74 Black, p. 494.

75 Ibid.

76 Rosen, p. 93.

77 Rosenberg, p. 7.

78 Ibid.

79 Ibid.

80 Ibid.

81 Jeff King, "Let Us Weep for Zion," *Charisma.* July 31, 2001, http://charismamag.com/index.php/features2/319-gods-love-for -israel/1271-let-us-weep-for-zion.

82 Black, p. 494.

83   Rosen, p. 95.

84   Ibid.

85   Rosen, p. 94

86   Ibid.

87   Ibid.

88   Black, p. 494.

89   William J. Vanden Huevel, "America and the Holocaust," *American Heritage* July/Aug. 1999, vol. 50, no. 4, http://americanheritage.com/articles/magazine/ah/1999/4/1999_4_34_print.shtml.

90   Black, p. 494.

91   Ibid., p. 3.

92   Vanden, p. 4.

93   "Gustav Schroeder." The Righteous Among The Nations. Yad Vashem   http://www1.yadvashem.org/righteous_new/germany_schroeder_print.html.

94   Black, p. 494.

95   Rosen, p. 103.

96   Rosen, p. 103; Marilyn Henry, "Voyage of the Damned," *Jerusalem Post,* July 20, 1998, http://holocaustforgotten.com/voyageofthedamned.htm.

97   http://www.ushmm.org/museum/exhibit/online/stlouis/search/bot new.htm

98   Black, p. 495.

99   Bernie M. Farber, "Voyage of the SS. *St. Louis:* Journey Toward a Better Future," *Toronto Star,* May 27, 2008, http://www.thestar.com/printarticle/431217.

100 Ibid.

101 Ibid.

102 "Gustav Schroeder." The Righteous Among the Nations Yad Vashem   http://www1.yadvashem.org/righteous_new/germany_schroeder_print.html

103 Aljazeera.net, "Ahmadinejad: Wipe Israel Off Map," October 26, 2005.

104 Kenneth R. Timmerman, "U.S. Intel: Iran Plans Nuclear Strike on U.S., NewsMax.com, July 29, 2008.

105 BBC News Online, "Iran Removes UN's Nuclear Seals," August 10, 2005.

CHAPTER SEVEN: THE CRIMINALIZATION OF CHRISTIANITY

1   Peggy Lamson, *Roger Baldwin, Founder of the American Civil Liberties Union; A Portrait* (Boston: Houghton Mifflin, 1976), p. 192.
2   Ibid., p. 192
3   Alan Sears and Craig Osten, *The ACLU vs. America* (Nashville: Broadman and Holman, 2005), p. 2.
4   *American Patriots Bible,* ed. Dr. Richard Lee (Nashville: Thomas Nelson, 2009), pp. 1–12 .
5   Ibid.
6   Ibid.
7   Ibid.
8   Ibid.
9   Ibid.
10   Ibid.
11   Ibid.
12   Ibid.
13   Sears and Osten, *The ACLU vs. America,* p. 1.
14   Ibid., p. 1
15   Ibid., p. 16
16   Ibid., p. 3
17   Janet L. Folger, *The Criminalization of Christianity* (Portland, OR: Multnomah Publishers, 2005), p. 20.
18   Ibid., p. 23.
19   Ibid., p. 27.
20   Ibid., p. 25.
21   Ibid., pp. 101–103.
22   Ibid., p. 107.
23   Ibid., p. 156.
24   Ibid., p. 162.

CHAPTER EIGHT: CAN YOU TRUST BIBLICAL PROPHECY?

1   John F. Walvoord and Roy B. Zuck, eds., *The Bible Knowledge Commentary New Testament Edition* (Wheaton, IL: Victor Books, 1983), p. 21.

CHAPTER NINE: WE ARE THE TERMINAL GENERATION

1 Robert J. Morgan, *My All in All* (Nashville: B and H Publishing, 2008).

2 CIA World Facebook, accurate as of January 1, 2009.

3 CIA World Facebook, accurate as of January 1, 2009.

4 Fareed Zakaria, "Why We Can't Quit," *Newsweek,* March 24, 2008.

5 Ibid.

CHAPTER ELEVEN: THE FOURTH REICH:
THE COMING ANTICHRIST

1 Damond R. Duck and Larry Richards, *The Book of Revelation* (Nashville, Tenn.: Nelson Books, 2006), p. 186.

2 Janet L. Folger, *The Criminalization of Christianity* (Portland, OR: Multnomah Publishers, 2005), pp. 163–166.

3 Ibid.

4 Ibid.

5 Ibid.

6 Walker P. Whitman, *A Christian History of the American Republic: A Textbook for Secondary Schools* (Boston: Green Leaf Press, 1939, 1948), p. 42.; Henry Halley, *Halley's Bible Handbook* (Grand Rapids, MI: Zondervan, 1927, 1965), p. 18; Gary DeMar, *America's Christian History: The Untold Story* (Atlanta, Ga.: American Vision, Publishers, 1993), p. 58.

7 *The American Patriots Bible,* ed. Dr. Richard Lee (Nashville: Thomas Nelson, 2009).

8 Ibid., pp. 1–1.

9 Janet L. Folger, *The Criminalization of Christianity,* pp. 163–166.

10 Ibid., p. 107.

CHAPTER THIRTEEN: THE YEAR 2012:
THE BEGINNING OF THE END?

1 SyFy TV program *2012—Startling New Secrets,* two-part series, with Mr. Hoagland as one of the investigators.